THE
GRAND
DECEPTION

CORPORATE AMERICA
AND
PERPETUAL WAR

by
MUJAHID KAMRAN

SANG-E-MEEL PUBLICATIONS
25, SHAHRAH-E-PAKISTAN (LOWER MALL) LAHORE.

891.4394 Mujahid kamran
        The Grand Deception : Corporate America
and Perpetual War/ Mujahid Kamran.-Lahore:
Sang-e-Meel Publications, 2013.
        xiv, 316pp.
        Index Included.
        1. History - Columns.
    I. Title.

2013
Published by:
Niaz Ahmad
Sang-e-Meel Publications,
Lahore.

ISBN-10: 969-35-2406-3
ISBN-13: 978-969-35-2406-2

Sang-e-Meel Publications

25 Shahrah-e-Pakistan (Lower Mall), Lahore-54000 PAKISTAN
Phones: 92-423-722-0100 / 92-423-722-8143 Fax: 92-423-724-5101
http://www.sang-e-meel.com e-mail: smp@sang-e-meel.com
PRINTED AT: HAJI HANIF & SONS PRINTERS, LAHORE.

To

the incredibly brave

people of Afghanistan

who have defeated every superpower which
invaded their country and who are keeping up
the proud record despite having been stabbed
in the back by every neighbor and near neighbor

and

to

Michael Ruppert

who represents the dying breed of true Americans
who will suffer and fight for truth to the last

War is peace
Freedom is slavery
Ignorance is strength

George Orwell

During times of universal deceit, telling the truth becomes a revolutionary act.

George Orwell

War against a foreign country only happens when the moneyed classes think they are going to profit from it.

George Orwell

Contents

Preface

This book is a collection of 34 brief articles dealing mainly with global politics with particular reference to the USA. Most of these articles were written in Urdu and appeared as columns in an Urdu newspaper *Waqt* between 27 July 2007 and January 1, 2008. The column carried the title *Pas e Parda* (Behind the Curtain). Subsequently, in 2008, these columns were published in book form with the same title.

The book was surprisingly well received - it got good reviews and sold well. Immediately after publication of the book people began suggesting that I translate it into English. I was lukewarm to the idea but a visit to the US in May 2010 convinced me that the US was no longer the place we all knew it to be. The experience at Logan International airport elicited from me a letter to the US ambassador in Pakistan. The letter remains unanswered and is reproduced in this book. I then sat down and, amid my commitments as Vice Chancellor, carried out the translations.

In this English version of the book, I have generally carried out a faithful translation. However, in view of the somewhat different orientation of English readers, some changes from the original Urdu format have been made. I have added one or more pertinent quotations at the beginning of each chapter. Most of the quotations have been extracted from literature that I possess in my personal library. However, some quotations have been taken, thankfully, from the web site *www.thirdworldtraveler.com*. These quotations were not present in the original columns. Further, I have, in some places, added notes at the end of a chapter, or inserted footnotes. Occasionally some additional detail has been inserted in the text.

Three of the articles in this book were originally published in the English language daily *The Nation*. I have reproduced these as such in the present book. These are "The Truth about Pearl Harbor", "The Darfur Problem", and "Bush Marches Towards Dictatorship". The last article was not present in the Urdu version nor was it published in Urdu. The Urdu versions of the remaining two articles were somewhat different. The final article in the English version "120 Years of US Jihad" has been rewritten and expanded well beyond the original skeletal Urdu column titled "117 Years of US Jihad". All articles in the book have been arranged in chronological order.

The first person to suggest an English translation was Mustapha Kamran. Prof. Mansoor Sarwar also persistently emphasized the need and the usefulness of an English version. I am thankful to both of them, and to several colleagues for the suggestion whose usefulness dawned upon me about two years later. I am also indebted to Mr. Shahid Kamal for his continuous interest in the translation and for valuable advice on the layout of the book. He also carefully proof-read the entire manuscript and uncovered numerous errors. All these errors were corrected. I am however solely responsible for any errors that still might exist. I am indebted to my wife Shazia Qureshi for having gone through most of the translated pieces, and for suggesting valuable changes.

The cover was designed by Mr. Amjad Pervez of the College of Art and Design (CAD) of the University of the Punjab. I am thankful to him for sparing his valuable time and for designing a meaningful cover. He also helped with the overall design and layout of the book and with the actual printing of the book. I am also thankful to Raja Munawar who played a useful role in coordinating the design effort with Mr. Amjad Pervez. Finally I wish to thank Mr. Niaz Ahmad and Mr. Afzal Ahmad of Sang e Meel publications for their interest in the book. The book has been composed in LaTeX.

Mujahid Kamran

August 13, 2010

Note: Although the foreword was written on August 13, 2010, material was incorporated at a few points in the article "120 Years of US Jihad" during the proof-reading stage.

Foreword to the Urdu Edition[1]

This book comprises 33 brief articles pertaining to the real US role in the international arena. With one or two exceptions, these articles were written in the period August to December 2007, and appeared in the daily *Waqt* as a regular column with the title *Pas e Parda*.

There were many questions about 9/11 whose satisfactory answers were extremely difficult to find. However, researchers worldwide, in particular Western researchers, began seeking answers and to get to the bottom of 9/11 immediately after it occurred. Within a few years the picture became quite clear. In order to understand 9/11, it is important to bear in mind that most wars in the world are fought for economic reasons. More often than not, these economic interests are the interests of the wealthy elites of the countries and not the people themselves. However, the wealthy elites in the world stay invisible and control global politics. This reality is assiduously concealed from the people. The domestic and foreign policies of the United States of America are an astonishing illustration of this fact. After going through the book the reader will find ample reasons to believe in this.

Col. Prouty has, in his well known book *The Secret Team,* narrated that upon hearing of the Allied bombing of Rotterdam one night, Churchill uttered the following words:

"Unrestricted submarine warfare, unrestricted

---

[1]The Urdu edition of the book was dedicated to the "honest, magnanimous, powerful and innocent people of America".

xi

air bombing - this is total war." He continued sitting there, gazing at a large map, and then said, "Time and the Ocean and some guiding star and High Cabal have made us what we are."

Prouty further writes that in the dark days of World War II, who could have known better than Churchill of the existence of a "High Cabal". This "High Cabal" is the One World Cabal of today. This "High Cabal" remains ceaselessly active for capturing global resources, and is by and large highly successful in achieving its objectives. At this point in time this cabal is active in destroying the liberties of the people of the US so as to make them its captive and use the capabilities of this remarkable people for perpetual war against mankind. On the outcome of the conflict between this cabal and those sections of the US society who are alive to this danger, will depend the future fate of mankind. Let us hope that mankind will not become a failed species whose existence might one day be uncovered by some other species, just as we have uncovered the existence of dinosaurs.

The Islamic countries possess almost 60 to 70 percent of the global energy resources. Powers that are energy hungry, and are energy addicts, want complete possession of these resources. If the peoples of Islamic countries do not change their attitudes and thought to adopt the correct conduct of everyday life, their further disintegration and further subjugation will become inevitable. If they can overpower the idols of indolence, inactivity and petty personal interests to join the struggle for understanding

Nature and make the creation of Knowledge of Nature an integral and dominant part of their faith, their days will change and the hope for a promising future will become a possibility.

Apart from books cited in the reference list, other references have been taken from reliable web sites. It is noteworthy that the invention of printing has played a fundamental role in the dissemination of knowledge and information. The invention of printing is therefore rightly regarded as one of the most important inventions in human history. In an analogous manner the computer and the internet have made it possible for a very large component of humanity to access such information, while sitting in their homes, that would otherwise require much more time and effort. In this sense the invention of the computer and the internet may be considered inventions of historic significance.

My brief stint as a column writer came to an abrupt end with my appointment as Vice Chancellor, University of the Punjab. Dr. Mujahid Mansoori played a key role in introducing me to the adminstration of Daily *Waqt* and in drawing my attention to the possibility of column writing. Prof. Dr. Shafeeq Jullundari and Prof. Dr. Shaukat Ali also encouraged me to write. I am thankful to all three friends. I am also indebted to Prof. Dr. M. Saleem for his interest in these columns. I am also indebted to my wife Prof. Dr. Najma Najam for her constant and valuable advice while the columns were being written. In fact the title *Pas e Parda* for my columns was suggested by her. I am thankful to Dr. Mansoora Shamim who bought for me, in USA, many of the invaluable books without which it would not have been possible to acquire a deeper comprehension of the internal and external policies of the USA. She also proof-read the manuscript and suggested numerous corrections. I am grateful to her. However, I remain solely responsible for any errors in the book. I want to thank Ali Hassan for typing these pages with great speed.

Mujahid Kamran
July 2008

Chapter 1

The Truth About Pearl Harbor

What would have happened if millions of American and British people, struggling with coupons and lines at the gas stations, had learned that in 1942 Standard Oil of New Jersey [Part of the Rockefeller empire] managers shipped the enemy's fuel through neutral Switzerland and that the enemy was shipping Allied fuel? Suppose that the public had discovered the Chase Bank in Nazi occupied Paris after Pearl Harbor was doing millions of dollars' worth business with the enemy with full knowledge of the Head Office in Manhattan [the Rockefeller family among others]? Or that Ford trucks were being built for the German occupation troops in France with authorization from Dearborn, Michigan? Or that Colonel Sosthenes Behn, the head of the international American telephone conglomerate ITT, flew from New York to Madrid to Berne during the war to help improve Hitler's commu-

1

*nications systems and improve the robot bombs that dev-
astated London? Or that ITT built the Fockewulfs that
dropped bombs on British and American troops? Or that
crucial ball bearings were shipped to Nazi-associated cus-
tomers in Latin America with the collusion of the vice-
chairman of the US War Production Board in partnership with Goering's cousin in Philadelphia when American forces were desperately short of them? Or that such
arrangements were known about in Washington and either sanctioned or deliberately ignored?*

Charles Higham
author of *Trading with The Enemy*

The Japanese attack on Pearl Harbor in 1941 enabled
USA to enter the war in Europe, a war that the White
House wished to enter for strategic reasons but could not,
owing to the opposition of the American public and the
Congress. It may, therefore, be of deep interest to know
as to how it was that the Japanese were able to launch
a "surprise" attack on Hawaii on December 7, 1941. The
question is particularly relevant in the post 9/11 world.

Fortunately, researchers have been able to uncover
the terrible truth behind this attack as a result of the
Freedom of Information Act (FOIA). A "treasure trove"
of documented evidence implicating the then President
Franklin Delano Roosevelt (FDR) and a coterie of confi-
dantes with pre-planned provocation and foreknowledge
of the Japanese attack was uncovered. The documents
were hidden away in naval vaults and were concealed from
nine Congressional inquiries, including the last one held
during Clinton's Presidency in 1995.

FDR was a Democrat. Republicans were immediately suspicious that the authorities knew about the attack but allowed it to happen in order to change the climate of public opinion in favor of entering the war in Europe. But it was only in 2000 that researcher Robert B Stinnett, who himself fought in the Pacific theater during WWII, published a book in which he presented irrefutable documentary evidence confirming these doubts. The book *Day of Deceit: The Truth about FDR and Pearl Harbor* represented seventeen years of persistent effort.

The trail begins with a letter written by the Lt. Commander Arthur H.McCollum, Head of the Far East section of the Office of Naval Intelligence (ONI) to FDR's two most trusted advisers in the White House on October 7, 1940, fourteen months before the Japanese attack. A photograph of this letter, which he uncovered on January 24, 1995, is reproduced in Stinnett's book.

The two advisers were Captains Walter S Anderson, Director ONI at the White House, with direct access to FDR, and Dudley W. Knox a naval strategist and chief of ONI library. After summarizing the strategic dangers that the situation in Europe posed to US interests, the letter suggested an eight-point plan of provoking the Japanese into attacking Pearl Harbor. McCollum had seized upon a treaty between Japan, Germany and Italy, signed only ten days earlier, on September 27, 1940, whereby an attack on any one of the countries would be considered an attack on all three.

The eight-point action plan included an arrangement with the British and the Dutch to use their base facilities in the Pacific, particularly Singapore and Dutch East

indies (Indonesia), giving all possible aid to Chiang Kai
Shek, sending a division of long range heavy cruisers and
two divisions of submarines to the Orient, as well as complete embargo on trade with Japan in collaboration with
the British. The plan also suggested squeezing Japan
by insisting that the Dutch refuse Japanese demands for
economic concessions, particularly oil. The plan also included a proposal for keeping the main strength of the
US Pacific fleet in the vicinity of Hawaii. The aim was to
create a sinister ambiguity that the US was preparing to
attack Japan.

The McCollum letter also stated: *"It is not believed
that in the present state of political opinion the United
States government is capable of declaring war against Japan without more ado."* The letter ended with the following
sentences *"If by these means Japan could be led to commit an overt act of war so much the better. In any case
we should be prepared to accept the threat of war"*.

On October 8, the very next day, FDR held a three-
hour meeting with Admiral Richardson, Commander in
Chief of the US naval fleet. When Admiral Richardson
heard the proposal he was outraged: "Mr. President senior officers of the Navy do not have the trust and confidence of the civilian leadership of this country that is
essential for a successful prosecution of the war in the
Pacific," he said. His refusal to go along with Roosevelt
cost him his career. He was relieved of his command in
February 1941. Richardson also quoted the President as
having said: "Sooner or later the Japanese would commit an overt act against the United States and the nation
would be willing to enter the war". The phrase "overt

4

act" was a reproduction of McCollum's phrase.

Documentary evidence uncovered by Stinnett establishes that each of the eight points suggested by McCollum was acted upon in the subsequent days. The most dangerous provocation was deployment of warships in or close to Japanese territorial waters. FDR himself took charge of these provocations - "pop-up" cruisers as he called them. "I just want them to keep popping up here and there and keep the Japs guessing, I don't mind losing one or two cruisers, but do not take a chance of losing five or six".

Stinnett writes: "From March through July 1941, White House records show that FDR ignored international law and dispatched naval task groups into Japanese waters on three such pop-up cruises." Admiral Kimmel, Admiral Pacific Fleet, objected by saying that this could precipitate war. He did not know that this was precisely FDR's intention.

In a most significant development, US cryptographers were able to decipher two principal Japanese codes - the naval code and the diplomatic code. This happened in the last days of September and early October 1940. The diplomatic code is also known as the Purple code. Stinnett states: "Leading historical publications in the United States have erroneously confused readers by publishing erroneous details on Purple. The truth about Pearl Harbor is found in the naval codes not the diplomatic codes."

There are a very large number of documents that reveal that the US stations in the Pacific region were able to intercept the dominant percentage of secret Japanese diplomatic and naval transmissions once these codes had been broken. There was other intelligence available too. In fact, in January 1941 information about a plan to attack Pearl Harbor was leaked to US intelligence. Stinnett has reproduced this information in his book.

The record shows that once the US and the British Empire began strangulating the Japanese economy through a boycott and through the Dutch, the militants in Japan very quickly gained the upper hand. The diplomats wanted to sort things out diplomatically but in late 1940 and early 1941 Japanese plans for launching a surprise attack on Pearl Harbor were formulated by Admiral Yamamoto.

Stinnett writes that the intercepts and corresponding radio logs of station H in Hawaii, one of the several stations that monitored Japanese signal traffic are

> powerful evidence of American fore-knowledge
> of the attack on Pearl Harbor. Americans
> do not know these records exist - all were
> excluded from the many investigations that
> took place from 1941 to 1946 and the Con-
> gressional probe of 1995.

Stinnett reproduces many messages that unambiguously establish the US foreknowledge of the attack.

There is another cruel side to this deceit. Once Richardson had been removed and Admiral Kimmel installed, Anderson was dispatched to Hawaii as an intelligence gatekeeper. He was well aware of the fact that the US had broken Japanese naval and diplomatic codes but concealed it from Admiral Kimmel, who subsequently paid a heavy price once the attacks had taken place. Kimmel had sensed in February 1941 that he was being excluded from some vital intelligence loop and tried in writing, on at least two occasions, to persuade the establishment to supply him with all vital information. "I can't understand, may never understand why I was denied the information available in Washington", Kimmel wrote sadly after the war.

In November, and during the days of December 1941 leading right up to the attack, the US cryptographers were aware of the impending Japanese attacks. But the key records remained concealed from every inquiry until Stinnett uncovered them. A vital player in this game of concealment was the cryptographer Lt. Commander Joseph J. Rochefort, who withheld vital information from Kimmel and from various Peal Harbor inquiries. Stinnett recovered some of this vital information from Rocherfort's personal effects in possession of his daughter. In his Oral History, Rocherfort told a navy interviewer that the death of a few thousand people was a cheap price to pay for the unification of America.

Although everything had been done by a coterie not only to conceal information from, but also to mislead the Pearl Harbor naval and military command, there still was a possibility that reconnaissance planes, or merchant vessels, would discover the advancing Japanese naval fleet promoting some measures by Kimmel. In order to forestall this possibility a message was sent by FDR to Kimmel on November 28: "*If hostilities cannot be avoided the United States desires that Japan commit the first overt act.*" This was FDR' response to a November 25 alert sent by Admiral Kimmel.

Four days after the attack the cover up began and Rear Admiral Leigh Noyes told a group of subordinates: "Destroy all notes and anything in writing." This was an illegal order because even personal memoranda concerning naval matters cannot be destroyed without approval of the Congress. Fortunately, everything was not, and could not be, destroyed as key information was scattered over different places, including the White House.

The Nation, January 9, 2005

NOTE ADDED

Immediately after the publication of Stinnett's book the US agencies and historians closely connected to them, moved in to confuse the public and to conceal documents that had been opened up under FOIA. It was in 1993 that the US Naval Security Group, which had in its custody what are known as the Crane Files, (these were so named because they were stored in vaults in Crane, Indiana) moved these to a government facility on the College Park campus of the University of Maryland. This was Archive II. However, as Stinnett wrote on December 7, 2003, once *The Day of Deceit* was published (December 7, 1999):

> NSA began withdrawing the pre-Pearl Harbor documents from the Crane Files housed in Archives II. This means that the Government decided to continue 60 years of Pearl Harbor censorship. As of January 2002, over

8

two dozen NSA withdrawal notices have triggered the removal of Pearl Harbor documents from public inspection. The number of pages withdrawn appear to be in hundreds.

Why remove documents a decade after they had been opened to the public? Under the agreement with National Archives, NSA has the right to withdraw documents if their presence in National Archives can lead to defense concerns. What defense concerns could there be sixty years after the events except that the truth must be concealed from the public - otherwise the present phase of US militarism would also be called into question.

One cannot help quoting Professor Peter Dale Scott:

The chronological record of events as reconstructed by archival historians has become increasingly subverted by suppressed or deep history. We now have a chronology for which the public records are either nonexistent or have been falsified.

Chapter 2

US Policies and Money

Osama bin Laden is probably the last witness the United States would like to have interrogated. There is a compelling case to be made that Osama bin Laden has been a well-cultivated, protected, and valued asset of US and British intelligence. It is also possible that he has been used.

Michael Ruppert
author of *Crossing the Rubicon*

If the American people ever allow private banks to control the issue of their money, first by inflation and then by deflation, the banks and corporations that will grow up around them (around the banks), will deprive the people of their property until their children will wake up homeless on the continent their fathers conquered.

Thomas Jefferson

The founding fathers of the United States were not inter-

ested in giving constitutional rights to corporations. In fact, they wanted to regulate corporations very tightly because they had had bad experiences with corporations during colonial times. The crown charter corporations like the East India Company and the Hudson Bay Company had been the rulers of America. So when the constitution was written, corporations were left out of the Constitution. Responsibility for corporate chartering was given to the states. State governance was closer to the people and would enable them to keep an eye on corporations.

Jan Edwards

The US has threatened to attack alleged Al Qaeda bases in Waziristan. President Bush has also expressed his conviction that Osama Bin Laden is hiding in Pakistani territory close to the Afghan border. These claims are based on a one-and-a-half page National Intelligence Estimate (NIE) report that surfaced on July 17, 2007. No proof has been provided in support of the claims made in the said report. The report also claims that Al Qaeda has regained the capability of attacking the Homeland viz. USA and that its members are hiding in FATA (Federally Administered Tribal Areas of Pakistan).

The safe haven of Al Qaeda in the above story was given prominent mention by the *Wall Street Journal* and the *New York Times*. Those who study such matters keenly are aware that US agencies, Wall Street, the World Bank, the IMF, and the media itself are controlled by a very small number of fabulously rich people and are dedicated to the protection of the interests of this elite.

US military presence in this region is a consequence of

the very mysterious 9/11 incident. US economic interests have always had a key position in US foreign policy. However, the US policy makers possess great skill in providing an ideological cover for these interests. The influence of Big Money is not only dominant in US foreign policy but also in its internal affairs. This may be gauged from the following statement attributed to Abraham Lincoln:

> I see in the near future a crisis approaching. It unnerves me and causes me to tremble for the safety of my country. The money power preys upon the nation in times of peace and conspires against it in times of adversity. It is more despotic than a monarchy, more insolent than autocracy, more selfish than bureaucracy. It denounces, as public enemies, all who question its methods or throw light upon its crimes. I have two great enemies, the Southern Army in front of me and the financial institutions at the rear, the latter is my greatest foe. Corporations have been enthroned, and an era of corruption in high places will follow, and the money power of the country will endeavor to prolong its reign by working upon the prejudices of the people until the wealth is aggregated in the hands of a few, and the Republic is destroyed.

Lincoln's remarkable analysis dates from the days of the American Civil War (1861-1865). The trends that he had then identified have now taken deep roots in present day US and appear to have tied the hands of the US people.

Former US Assistant Secretary for Housing and Urban Development Catherine Austin Fitts has been engaged in a heroic battle against the incredible corruption in the US establishment. In the foreword of Michael Ruppert's bestseller on 9/11 (*Crossing the Rubicon*), Miss Fitts writes:

> Indeed, during the 1980s the savings and loans industry were stripped of an estimated $500 billion by syndicates of military, intelligence, and private financial interests. The profits were used to buy up banking, industrial, and media companies and to finance political campaigns. From a position of political, judicial and economic power in the 1990s, the same syndicates then stripped an estimated $6 trillion of investors' value in pump and dump stock market and mortgage market schemes and an estimated $4 trillion of taxpayer money from US federal government.

In an article written in the year 2004, Ms Fitts has described 20 different points that force one to think of the massive scale on which the money of the ordinary people of USA has been plundered. Further there is some connection between this plunder and 9/11. She writes that during the fiscal year 1999-2000 the US Department of Defense showed an expenditure of three trillion dollars for which no documents existed and which were unaudited.

Similarly, prior to 9/11, piles of documentary evidence had been placed before Federal and State leaders in which startling evidence of stealing of $6 trillion from pension funds and stock holdings was presented. The money had been stolen in several ways. She states that as a result of 9/11 most of this evidence has been destroyed. The evidence pertained to investigations against Wall Street firms and members of the Federal Reserve Board. She also states that as a result of the passage of Patriot Act after 9/11, law enforcing agencies were diverted to other tasks instead of investigating such white collar crimes.

In 2002, Kelly Patricia O'Meara, an investigative reporter for the maganzine *Insight* reported that the US Department of Defense was unable to account for an expenditure of $1.1 trillion (i.e., 1100 billion). Some years ago when I brought this to the notice of Imran Khan he promptly asked as to how could it be possible because the Defence budget of the US was around $400 billion annually.

Michael Ruppert has answered this question in his book. He writes:

> A sceptic will say, "How can the Pentagon lose trillions of dollars? Its annual budget is currently only $480 billion(which is larger than all the non-American military spending in the world combined)." The answer is simple. The Pentagon manages the pension funds for two million service people, not counting its civilian employees. It also manages their medical insurance plans. It owns real estate, collects rents and operates concessions and businesses on military bases. And when a multi-year

14

weapons program is approved by Congress all of the earmarked funds go into Pentagon accounts but are disbursed by the year.

In his book Michael Ruppert has produced a table showing the breakup of over $4.6 trillion that was stolen from various sources. He writes "This is taxpayer money. This is retirement money for medical care. This is the wealth of America and it is being stolen." It, therefore appears that the people of the USA who, at this point in human history, constitute mankind's greatest asset, are being controlled by a cunning cabal which intends to utilize the energies and talent of this remarkable nation for capturing the resources and wealth of the entire globe.

Express, July 18, 2007

Chapter 3

Another 9/11?

Almost a year after 9/11 where are we? In the last year the Bush Administration and the financial, economic and oil interests which it serves, have proved their continued ability to move forward into totalitarianism and naked aggression faster than any forces of either domestic or international opposition could organize - either behind them or in front of them. Optimistic and valiant, but inexperienced efforts to fight the juggernaut have started, swirled, eddied and drifted as the Blitzkrieg war "that will not end in our lifetimes" has not even so much as looked sideways. Overwhelming evidence of the regime's crimes in a dozen areas has been brought to surface, and yet each new revelation only spurs the empire to accelerate its long-conceived plans rather than slow down.

Michael Ruppert *No Way Out*

An astonishing measure by the US government was announced in a press release on May 8, 2001, just a few months before 9/11. The press release, issued from the White House, emphasized that the "threat of chemical, biological or nuclear weapons being used against the United States" was "real". It stated that various government agencies carried out various tasks, but in order "to maximize their effectiveness, these efforts need to be seamlessly integrated, harmonious and comprehensive." It announced the establishment of an Office of National Preparedness: "This office will be responsible for implementing the results of those parts of the national effort overseen by Vice President Cheney that deal with consequence management."

It was clear that, as a result of this measure, the responsibility of overall coordination and supervision of all steps carried out to deal with any alleged or real terrorist attack were practically entrusted to Dick Cheney. It is a little known fact that all counter measures and secret activities of the US agencies immediately after 9/11 were directed by Cheney, and not by George Bush. The transfer of powers to Dick Cheney in the wake of 9/11 was part of a secret plan called "Continuity of Government". This plan, sometimes called *Change* of Government by its critics, had been rehearsed clandestinely since 1981.

Six years later, in May 2007, a highly confidential Presidential Order has been issued. This is order number NSPD51/HSPD20. Professor Chossudovsky of Ottawa University, Canada, has the following to say about NSPD51:

While NSPD 51 has the appearances of a domestic national security decision, it is, nonetheless, an integral part of US foreign policy. It belongs to a longstanding military national security agenda. Were NSPD 51 to be invoked, Vice President Dick Cheney, who constitutes the real power behind the Executive, would essentially assume de facto dictatorial powers, circumventing both the US Congress and the Judiciary, while continuing to use President George W. Bush as a proxy figurehead.

For the past several years important personalities of the US establishment have been issuing statements periodically that mention the strong possibility of occurrence of another incident like 9/11. On April 15, 2007, in an interview given to CBS, Dick Cheney stated that the greatest danger was another 9/11 in which a group of terrorists would attack some city with nuclear weapons instead of using air tickets, box-cutters and knives.

Several weeks later, on May 26, 2007, while addressing the Commencement at the West Point Academy, Dick Cheney said:

> We're fighting a war on terror because the enemy attacked us first, and hit us hard.... Al Qaeda's leadership has said they have the right to "kill four million Americans"... For nearly six years now, the United States has been able to defeat their attempts to attack us here at home. Nobody can guarantee that we won't be hit again.

In December 2003, CNN interviewed former Director of

Homeland Security Tom Ridge. According to CNN coverage, Tom Ridge:

> warned of possible strikes more devastating
> than the Al Qaeda airliner attacks of September 11, 2001, on New York and Washington
> and told CNN on Monday that airplanes remain terrorists' weapon of choice. "There is a
> continuous stream of reporting, literally from
> the last two years, that indicates [terrorists']
> preference or desire to use aircraft as a means
> of attack," Ridge said on CNN's "American
> Morning."

It was in the same month (December 2003) that General Tommy Franks, former commander CENTCOM expressed his conviction about another 9/11 attack and stated that the West will have to abandon its democratic system as a consequence. He said:

> a terrorist, massive, casualty-producing event
> [will occur] somewhere in the Western world
> it may be in the United States of America
> that causes our population to question our
> own Constitution and to begin to militarize
> our country in order to avoid a repeat of another mass, casualty-producing event.

General Tommy Franks is an important member of the US establishment and it would be superficial to consider his statement merely an expression of personal opinion. Members of US establishment do not issue sensational statements, certainly not members of military establishment.

A story in the *Guardian* on July 16, 2007 revealed that the thinking of Dick Cheney and his group had begun to dominate White House. They want to attack Syria and Iran. In a recent statement, Michael Chertoff said that he had a "gut-feeling" that the nation faced heightened terrorist threat this summer. On April 23, 2006, the *Washington Post* quoted a responsible officer as having said that another 9/11 would provide both a justification for and opportunity for attacking well known targets. On July 2, 2007 a sensational news appeared on US media. It was alleged that a plan to destroy JFK airport had been uncovered. As usual, no evidence was presented for claims like this. On February 1, 2007, Brzezinski appeared before the Senate Foreign Relations Committee and warned against intrigues taking place in the US establishment. He said:

> If the United States continues to be bogged down in a protracted bloody involvement in Iraq, the final destination on this downhill track is likely to be a head-on conflict with Iran and with much of the world of Islam at large. A plausible scenario for a military collision with Iran involves Iraqi failure to meet the benchmarks; followed by accusations of Iranian responsibility for the failure; then by some provocation in Iraq or a terrorist act in the U.S. blamed on Iran; culminating in a defensive U.S. military action against Iran that

20

plunges a lonely America into a spreading and deepening quagmire eventually ranging across Iraq, Iran, Afghanistan, and Pakistan.

A few days ago the *New York Times* and the *Washington Post* reported that the US wanted the UN General Assembly to declare the Iranian National Guards a terrorist organization. A former CIA analyst told *Time* magazine that such a report could be analyzed in two ways - either these are mere threats, or more seriously, the final steps towards an attack on Iran.

Will the US really attack Iran and Syria? Does the US not face serious difficulties in Iraq and Afghanistan? Is the US economy not in a mess? Are not the people of US fed up with the war? Do the people not desire accountability of Bush and Cheney? Is such an attack possible? The last question was answered by Michael Ruppert two years ago. After arguing that the US was not in a position to attack Iran, Ruppert quoted a Spanish proverb which he translated as "A stupid person is a real possibility!" Any attack by the US on Iran would constitute a realization of the above proverb.

In order to escape the wrath of the people of the US, Bush and Cheney can go to any extent. Only a massive reaction by the US people can stop Cheney and his band from unleashing widespread destruction and ruin. The rulers of the US probably forget that while the US may be the most powerful nation on earth, she too cannot fight the entire world. This lesson will probably be learned through bitter experience.

Waqt, August 9, 2007

NOTE ADDED

Four days after the publication of the above column, the *Oregon Truth Alliance*, a group of watchful citizens of the State of Oregon, displayed the following advisory notice on its website. It shares the same concerns that many people inside the US and abroad shared - a repeat 9/11 with nuclear weapons, to start a global nuclear war with the object of setting up a global empire in the name of the US. The control of such an empire would vest with a handful of the wealthiest families of this planet. It may be added that there is a serious case of missing nukes that disappeared for 36 hours on August 29, 2007. There is a string of deaths that occurred among people connected with this incident. The text of the advisory note is reproduced below.

August 13, 2007 - Portland, Oregon Portland to Host Terrorism Drill "NOBLE RESOLVE 07-2" Aug. 20 to 24 Citizens Warn of Established Pattern for Such Drills to go "live" Contact: Info [at] OregonTruthAlliance dot org
    This is an urgent advisory notice from concerned citizens of Oregon and Washington about an upcoming U.S. Joint Forces Command emergency management exercise known as NOBLE RESOLVE 07-2 that will simulate terrorism or disaster scenarios in the Lower Columbia River Basin between Aug. 20th and Aug 24th, 2007.
NOBLE RESOLVE 07 − 2 was designed and will be directed by U.S. Joint Forces Command (USJFCOM) and

the Department of Homeland Security. We are aware of no public notice concerning this exercise, but preliminary investigation has revealed that Oregon National Guard officials and federal officials will conduct the drill. Details from official sources are minimal.

This advisory is to document our concerns, raise public awareness and urge citizen action based on the following facts:

1. NOBLE RESOLVE is a computer-based simulation of a large-scale emergency situation (e.g. earthquake, hurricane, tsunami, or terrorist attack with nuclear weapon) in order to train for managing all aspects of the emergency response through comprehensive software.

2. Military exercises such as NOBLE RESOLVE 07-2 have a recent history of coinciding with lethal "live" events. This occurred both at the start of Desert Storm in 1990 and on 9/11/01 when five or more major military or security exercises were in progress on the very day of the actual attacks. The same phenomenon occurred with the London Bombings of 7/7/05 during which a drill concerning multiple bomb attacks was being staged on that day.

3. Vice President Cheney, Homeland Security Director Michael Chertoff and former Senator Rick Santorum have all warned of a new 9/11 attack this summer, but are giving no evidence in support. Chertoff based his prediction on a "gut feeling".

4. The May 2007 Presidential Directive NSPD 51 (HSPD20) addressing "continuity of government" in the event of a massive emergency, includes secret "annexes"

which are pertinent additional documents. Some US Congressional Committee on Homeland Security members such as Rep. Peter DeFazio have written to formally request permission to review these secret "annexes" and have twice been denied access by the White House.

5. This particular exercise, NOBLE RESOLVE 07-2, includes one scenario involving an unaccounted for, "loose" ten kiloton nuclear weapon, exactly as Vice President Cheney hinted in recent interviews. Department of Homeland Security chief Michael Chertoff claims he fears the same.

6. The plummeting support for the GOP has triggered comments from its members and analyses of its current political strategy that point to a new 9/11 attack as a contributing factor to GOP political salvation. Moreover, it appears that legends or back stories are being disseminated to support just such an event.

Transparency concerning NOBLE RESOLVE 07 – 2 is vital for the public safety of everyone in the Lower Columbia River Basin. We call on the planners, directors and participants in NOBLE RESOLVE 07 – 2 to be vigilant and to maintain transparency with respect to these military exercises. We also urge citizens and our elected officials to monitor the activities of participants connected with the exercises and alert authorities to any suspicious behavior. These exercises have an established pattern of becoming "live" events. (Please read references below.) We recommend that officials of the Ports of Astoria, Longview, Vancouver and Portland on the Lower Columbia River take extra care in their monitoring and examination of all shipping on the Lower Columbia River while NOBLE RESOLVE 07 − 2 is in progress. Finally, we urge all concerned to voice that concern in letters and calls to elected officials and civil servants requesting full transparency and citizen oversight.

Chapter 4

USA and a Global Empire?

The power of the dollar and the power of the US military had been uniquely intertwined with one commodity, the basis of the world economic growth engine, since before the First World War. That commodity was petroleum, and in its service British, American, German, French, Italian, and other nations called their soldiers to war. As Henry Kissinger once expressed this importance 'control energy and you control the nations.' Oil played a decisive role in the collapse of the Soviet Union. Oil defined American foreign policy in much of the world during the cold war. And oil defines American military actions since the end of the cold war as never before.
      William Engdahl in *A Century of War: Anglo-American Oil Politics and the New World Order*

A hideous ecstasy of fear and vindictiveness, a desire to

kill, to torture, to smash faces in with a sledge hammer, seemed to flow through the whole group of people like an electric current, turning one even against one's will into a grimacing, screaming lunatic. And yet the rage that one felt was an abstract, undirected emotion which could be switched from one object to another like the flame of a blowlamp.

George Orwell 1984

...beginning with Iraq, then Syria, Lebanon, Libya, Iran, Somalia and Sudan. Senior Pentagon official quoted by **Gen. Wesley Clark**

The increasing demand for oil worldwide and the rapid depletion of oil fields are pushing man-kind towards the abyss. Unbridled oil consumption by the US and the deep desire of a handful of fabulously rich families to own all global resources have jeopardized the very existence of the human species. War in the Middle East, US presence in Central Asia, Globalization, New World Order, "terrorism", the mysterious existence of Al Qaeda, propaganda against Islam, and the rapid usurpation of civil liberties and rights of the US public are all aimed at one single objective. On October 6, 2006, Ramsey Clark, 66th Attorney General of USA, stated:

> The policies of the US, since the end of the Cold War are complicated and vast. They involve an intent to dominate and the use of international organizations to advance U.S. economic and geopolitical interests. They also

27

include the conversion of NATO into a sur-
rogate military police force for globalization
and U.S. world economic domination.

The wealthiest families of this planet constitute a secret
brotherhood. Their fabulous wealth is simply staggering.
These families consider themselves superior to, and distinct from, the rest of mankind. For them, mankind exists
to serve them and they regard humanity as their chattels
and slaves. They own governments, defense industry, media, banks and huge corporations with annual budgets
exceeding those of many countries of the third world. An
ordinary human ekes out his existence by sweating and
toiling day and night to make ends meet, but the international financial system erected by these families is such
that the gap between the rich and poor is widening by
the day.

In order to maintain their iron grip on the globe, these
families have set up a network of organizations. Some of
these are secret and others well known. Some of these organizations are edified by the name "think tanks" which
comprise of people on the payroll of these families. The
members of these think tanks are their pet thinkers, belonging to their stable, and spend day and night thinking
up ways to preserve the hold of these families on the
planet. The Council on Foreign Relations (CFR), Trilateral Commission and Bilderberg Group are the most powerful among these think tanks but all members other than
those belonging to the superrich families are paid by the
owners of these group.[1] After the murder of the "rebel"

---

[1]In case someone has any doubts about such a statement,

President John F. Kennedy, there has hardly been a US President who has not served on one or the other of these three groups. The strategy emerging from the deliberations of these think tanks is published in specific journals and, when needed, these are expanded and published in the form of books that receive wide publicity, and also bring financial benefits to these pet authors. *The Clash*

---

it might help to read the following quotes from Professor Peter Dale Scott's comprehensively researched book *The Road to 9/11 - Wealth, Empire, and the Future of America* (University of California. Press, 2007). " ...Bundy's Harvard protege Kissinger was named to be national security adviser after having chaired an important "study group" at the Council on Foreign Relations. As a former assistant to Nelson Rockefeller, Kissinger had been paid by Rockefeller to write a book on limited warfare for the CFR. He had also campaigned hard in Rockefeller's losing campaign for the Presidential nomination in 1968. Thus Rockefeller and the CFR might have been excluded from control of the Republican Party, but not from the Republican White House." (p22).

The following quote from p 38 of the book is also very revealing: "The Kissinger-Rockefeller relationship was complex and certainly intense. As investigative reporter Jim Hougan wrote: "Kissinger, married to a former Rockefeller aide, owner of a Georgetown mansion whose purchase was enabled only by Rockefeller gifts and loans, was always a protege of his patron Nelson R, even when he wasn't directly employed by him"."

On the same page (38) Professor Scott writes: "Nixon's and Kissinger's arrival in the White House in 1969 coincided with David Rockefeller's becoming CEO of Chase Manhattan Bank. The Nixon-Kissinger foreign policy of detente was highly congruous with Rockefeller's push to internationalize Chase Manhattan banking operations. Thus in 1973 Chase Manhattan became the first American bank to open an office in Moscow. A few month's later, thanks to an invitation arranged by Kissinger, Rockefeller became the first U.S. banker to talk with Chinese Communist leaders in Beijing."

of Civilizations is one such book.

Zbigniew Brzezinski is an old and loyal hand of the US establishment. He was the National Security Adviser of President Carter and a member of the CFR. He published a few articles in the journal Foreign Affairs in 1997. These were later expanded into book form and published as the well known book *The Grand Chessboard: American Primacy and its Geostrategic Imperatives*. This book is a blueprint for setting up a global US empire and its contents should be known to everyone. As Ruppert has pointed out this book is sublime in its arrogance. Wherever Brzezinski talks of US dominance, he in fact, means control of the superrich, because the US government serves their purposes. Talking of Europe and Asia, the Eurasian continent as he calls it, he states:

> A power that dominates Eurasia would control two of the world's three most advanced and economically productive regions. A mere glance at the map also suggests that control over Eurasia would almost automatically entail Africa's subordination, rendering the Western Hemisphere and Oceania geopolitically peripheral to the world's central continent. About 75 percent of the world's people live in Eurasia, and most of the world's physical wealth is there as well, both in its enterprises and underneath its soil. Eurasia accounts for 60 percent of the world's GNP and about three-fourths of the world's known energy resources.

Brzezinski also states:

> For America, the chief geopolitical prize is
> Eurasia. For half a millennium, world affairs
> were dominated by Eurasian powers and peo-
> ples who fought with one another for regional
> domination and reached out for global power.
> Now a non-Eurasian power is pre-eminent in
> Eurasia and America's global primacy is di-
> rectly dependent on how long and how effec-
> tively its preponderance on the Eurasian con-
> tinent is sustained.

The above quotes clearly show why the US has come to
Central Asia. It has come here to stay and to give per-
manence to its primacy. It intends to stay here and to
apportion the resources of this region exclusively for itself
(profits will of course go to the super-rich). US "thinkers"
(those working for the wealthy elite) think that the dream
of a global US empire can only be achieved if the US captures Central Asia and its adjoining regions.

What is there for the people of the US in this so-
called "Great Game"? The great and wonderful people
of the US have spent most of their life in an atmosphere of
democratic liberties with individual freedoms being particularly important. The US elite, the traditionally fabulously wealthy families and their appendages, cannot
achieve a global US empire unless a dictatorial system is
set up in the US. Writing about the US of 1997, Brzezinski expresses this opinion in the following words:

> It is also a fact that America is too demo-
> cratic at home to be autocratic abroad. This

limits the use of America's power, especially
its power for military intimidation. Never before has a populist democracy attained international supremacy. But the pursuit of power
is not a goal that commands popular pas-
sion, except in conditions of a sudden threat
or challenge to the public's sense of domestic well-being. The economic self-denial (that
is, defense spending) and human sacrifice (casualties even among professional soldiers) required in the effort are uncongenial to democratic instincts. Democracy is inimical to imperial mobilization.

Will the US succeed in setting up a global empire? Only
time will tell but the final decision about the rise and
fall of powers takes place in the battlefield. The final
outcome of this struggle will be determined in the bat-
tlefields stretching over Central Asia, Afghanistan, Iraq,
Iran and Pakistan. If the people of the US become collectively aware of this state of affairs, mankind will be
spared a bloodbath and destruction that has never before taken place in history. Otherwise, the use of nuclear
weapons in this region by the US cannot be ruled out.

Waqt, September 5, 2007

Chapter 5

Australian Governance?

In the eyes of the public opinion, possessing a "just cause" for waging war is central. A war is said to be Just if it is waged on moral, religious or ethical grounds... The Just War theory upholds war as a "humanitarian" operation. It serves to camouflage the real objectives of the military operation, while providing a moral and principled image to the invaders. In its contemporary version, it calls for military intervention on ethical and moral grounds against "rogue states" and "Islamic terrorists", which are threatening the Homeland.

M.Chossudovsky
Professor of Economics at Ottawa University

On November 9th, Attorney General Ashcroft announced that he was ordering the Justice Department to begin wire-tapping and monitoring attorney-client communications in terrorist cases where the suspect was incarcerated. This was not even discussed in HR 3162. That same day Senator Patrick Leahy (D), Vermont, wrote to Ashcroft. He had many questions to ask about what the Justice Department had been doing by violating the trust of Congress and assuming powers which were not authorized by either law or the Constitution. Leahy even quoted a Supreme Court case (U.S. v. Robel [389U.S.258(1967)]):

"This concept of "national defense" cannot be deemed an end in itself, justifying any exercise of · · · power designed to promote such a goal. Implicit in the term "national defense" is the notion that defending those values and ideas which set this Nation apart · · · It would indeed be ironic if, in the name of national defense, we would sanction the subversion of one of those liberties · · · which makes the defense of the Nation worthwhile."

Leahy asked Ashcroft by what authority had he decided on his own and without judicial review to nullify the Fifth Amendment to the Constitution. He asked for an explanation and some description of the procedural safeguards that Ashcroft would put in place. He asked Ashcroft to appear before the Judiciary committee and to respond in writing by November 13. His answer came a little late. On November 16, Patrick Leahy received an anthrax letter.

Michael Ruppert *The "F" Word* Nov 2001

Dr. Mohammad Haneef, an Indian medical doctor working in Australia, has been deported by the Australian authorities. Dr. Haneef is the most recent victim of the "Global War on Terror". He was deported after the failure of the authorities to punish him on false charges related to "terrorism". He was employed as a Registrar in the Gold Coast Hospital in the state of Queensland. Dr. Haneef was arrested on July 2nd when he was about to board a flight from Brisbane to India. The Australian Federal Police (AFP) arrested him on grounds that his attempt to return to India was "highly suspicious" and "may reflect Haneef's awareness of a conspiracy to plan and prepare acts of terrorism".

The Australian authorities started issuing statements after this arrest. These statements were given sensational coverage in Australian media. In particular, the media owned by fascist media mogul Rupert Murdoch launched a shameful movement by propagating baseless news. Murdoch's media not only maligned Dr. Haneef but also played on fears about the war on terrorism. In fact, a baseless news item, alleging that Dr. Haneef planned to blow up the world's tallest residential building in Gold Coast, was also printed.

In complete disregard of norms of justice, the Australian authorities tried to intimidate Dr. Haneef's lawyers even though they were merely defending their client. The Australian authorities wanted to prevent the public from getting to the bottom of this false case through sheer propaganda, and thus having a pretext for implementing dictatorial laws that had been passed in the name of war against terrorism. The Australian Attorney General Phillip Ruddock stated:

There are certainly some people in the legal profession, particularly those who come out

of the civil liberties groups, who have a view
anything goes, and you see that in the nature
of comments they make.

Such was the state of mind of the Australian authorities that on July 14th Prime Minister John Howard pro-
nounced:

> All of this is a reminder that terrorism is a
> global threat ... you can't pick and choose
> where you fight terrorism. You can't say I will
> fight it over there but I won't fight it here. It
> is also fair to say that the anti-terrorism laws
> that this government has enacted are all to
> their very last clause needed and I have said
> before if we need to strengthen them we will
> strengthen them in the future.

Peter Russo and Stefan Keim, the two lawyers represent-
ing Dr. Haneef, however, countered these tactics through
a thoughtful and courageous strategy. They gave interviews to the media in which they exposed the lies of the
authorities which, according to them, were being deliberately "leaked" to the media. In particular, they released
a transcript of a police interview of Dr. Haneef from
which it became very obvious that the police had been
untruthful. The police had lied to a court in stating that
Haneef had lived with two of his cousins in Britain who
had been arrested in connection with a failed London
bombing. Once this transcript appeared in the press it
also came to light that the police had also lied in stating
that a SIM belonging to Haneef had been found in a Glasgow incident. The British police revealed that the SIM

had been recovered hundreds of miles away, in Liverpool. The entire case against Haneef had been built around this SIM, and now it had turned out to be a false allegation. The Director of Public Prosecution (DPP) had alleged that Haneef had "recklessly" handed over resources to terrorists. Once the lie had been exposed, fear of public reaction unnerved officials. On July 19, Chris Mitchell, editor in chief of the *Australian*, received an anguished call at 6.30 AM from a senior police official "There is all hell breaking loose with the government about this and I need to be able to say it did not come from us···" In a column that appeared on the web on July 28, Mike Head wrote:

> According to media reports, no less than 500 police and lawyers were assigned to the case in an attempt to find or concoct any evidence that could sustain a "terrorist" charge. This massive police-legal taskforce, possibly one of the largest ever assembled in Australia, included 200 Queensland police officers. From day one it was a joint federal-state operation.

The government had planned upon keeping Haneef in its custody indefinitely and thus putting its so called anti-terrorism laws in action. The aim was to influence the public mind in favor of these laws using the Haneef case as a justification. When, on July 16, a magistrate ordered an end to Haneef's solitary confinement, the Australian authorities canceled his visa and continued to keep him in solitary confinement. This petty tactic provoked a severe reaction among the Australian public indicating their high level of integrity - the public was furious at the sordid level to which the Australian government had sunk. The ferocity of the public outcry threw the government off its feet and officials started running for cover. Even Prime Minister Howard retreated and stated that he had no responsibility in the matter which was being dealt by the police! He had completely forgotten the comments he and his ministers had made. The Federal Police Commissioner stated: "Nothing the AFP has done has been done without the advice of the DPP." And the British Police went on record stating that the Australian government was pressurizing the Australian Federal Police!

The intensity of the public outcry can be gauged from the statements of the Law Council of Australia that represents 50,000 Australian lawyers. It attacked the Australian government of "undermining Australia's judicial system" and of "political opportunism". It also attacked the anti-terror laws that permitted "indefinite detention by stealth". The Law Council also attacked the government for canceling Haneef's visa because he had not been proven guilty. It charged the government of "violating the principle that every citizen is innocent until proven guilty." The rising tide of public anger compelled the government to withdraw charges against Dr. Haneef thereby declaring him innocent.

Upon returning to Bangalore, India, Haneef received a hero's welcome. He thanked the people of Australia and the Government of India and the Indian public for their support. The Indian Foreign Minister Pranab Mukherjee has demanded that Dr. Haneef's visa be restored. The administration of the Gold Coast Hospital has offered to keep his job until he returns. The Chief Minister of the Indian State of Karnatka has promised that Haneef will be offered a senior position in some state hospital.

Professor Michel Chossudovsky of Ottawa University wrote in April 2007:

> The "war on terrorism" purports to defend the American Homeland and protect the "civilized world". It is upheld as a "war of religion", a "clash of civilizations", when in fact the main objective of this war is to secure control and corporate ownership of the region's extensive oil wealth, while also imposing under the helm of the IMF and the World Bank (now under the control of Paul Wolfowitz), the privatization of State enterprises and the transfer of countries' economic assets into the hands of foreign capital···
>
> Demonization serves geopolitical and economic objectives. Likewise, the campaign against "Islamic terrorism" (which is covertly supported by US agencies) supports the conquest of oil wealth. The term "Islamo-fascism", serves to degrade the policies, institutions, values and social fabric of Muslim countries, while also upholding the tenets of "Western democracy" and the "free market" as the only alternative for these countries.

It is, therefore, very clear that demonization of Muslims by Western media, which is owned by a handful of corporations, is being carried out to create a psychological environment, where the civilian populations of Western and other nations will accept the large scale massacres and internment of muslim populations without any compunction. This may have been achieved to a greater degree in US than in Australia as is demonstrated by the furious reaction of the Australian public in the Haneef case. The corporate control of Australian media may not be as strong and complete as it is in the US.

Waqt, September 8, 2007

Chapter 6

9/11 - Some Questions

Generally it is impossible to carry out an act of terror on the scenario which was used in the USA yesterday··· As soon as something like that happens here I am reported about that right away and in a minute we are all up.
General Anatoly Kornukov
Commander in Chief of the Russian Air Force (quoted in *Pravda* September 12, 2001)

The most important thing for us is to find Bin Laden. It's our number one priority, and we will not rest until we find him.
George W Bush September 13, 2001

I don't know where he is. I have no idea and I really don't care. It's not that important. It's not our priority.
George W Bush March 13, 2002

Look, if you think any American official is going to tell

41

*you the truth, then you're stupid. Did you hear that? -
stupid.*
Arthur Sylvester, Assistant Secretary of Defense for
Public Affairs 1965.

*In every murder case or felony crime, it is routine to
seal off the crime scene and examine it thoroughly, using
the best scientific methods available. Except 9/11. We
are talking about the biggest mass murder in the history
of the United States. And there was no investigation of
the crime scene. Before the dust even settled, the wreck-
age of the twin towers was cut up and carted away. And
within weeks, Bush ordered the FBI to halt their investigation and devote all their efforts to find out who was
behind the anthrax letters. This alone speaks volumes.*
Dale Allen Pfeiffer *The End of the Age of Oil*

*Why did the White House ram through legal measures
immediately after the attacks that essentially repeal the
Bill of Rights and the Freedom of Information Act?*
John Leonard February 2002

About six years ago, on September 11, 2001, two airline planes struck the World Trade Center (WTC) in the
heart of New York city in front of the cameras of the media. After burning for a while the WTC collapsed in its
own footprints. Another plane was said to have hit the
Pentagon. The US government immediately attributed
this to extremist Muslims - terrorists - acting under the
leadership of Bin Laden. Bin Laden was in Afghanistan
at that time. Using Bin Laden's presence in Afghanistan

as a pretext, the US launched an attack on Afghanistan. After attacking Afghanistan, the US attacked Iraq. The US faces stiff resistance in both countries. Now the US leadership is openly threatening Iran and some informed circles claim that the attack on Iran is likely to take place in the beginning of 2008.

There are numerous questions about 9/11 which have either been left unanswered by the US government, or the answers have holes in them. All these questions have been raised by Western, primarily American, researchers. Was the attack on Afghanistan really due to the 9/11 incident or was the war pre-planned? Has the US government provided any evidence linking 9/11 and Afghanistan? Where are the black boxes of the airliners and what information is contained in them? After 9/11, relatives of Bin Laden were stuck in the US. On whose orders were they allowed to fly on a chartered plane back home while the restrictions on flying civilian aircraft were in force? In his book *Crossing the Rubicon*, Michael Ruppert states that the US Department of Defense gave a 72 million dollar telecommunication contract to the Bin Laden family for the Iraq war. The company owned by the Bin Laden family was named *Iridium Satellite*, and was purchased from *Motorolla* in 1999. It owns 73 satellites. What is the explanation for awarding such a sensitive contract to the Bin Laden family? Before 9/11, the FBI was watching two close relatives of Bin Laden but after 9/11 some unseen hand seems to hand stopped FBI from pursuing these relatives. Who ordered FBI to stop watching these two relatives of Osama?

It is standard practice in USA for the US Air Force

(USAF) planes to quickly reach any planes that had stray-
ed off course. USAF planes belonging to the 121st and
113th fighter squadrons were ready to scramble at the Andrews Airbase at Washington DC. These planes take two
to three minutes to become airborne. Why did the USAF
fighters not take off when it was known that four planes
had been hijacked? All the hijacked planes were visible on the the Federal Aviation Authority (FAA) radar.
Why was no action taken to investigate and fix responsibility for this negligence? Similarly, when Patrick Leahy
of the House Judicial Committee asked Attorney General
Ashcroft as to how could he undermine the Fifth Amendment to the US constitution, Leahy received an envelope
containing anthrax. Only the US army possessed the type
of anthrax received by Leahy. Who sent the anthrax letter to Leahy? What was the motivation behind sending
such a poison laden letter? Were any investigations conducted into this matter? If no, why not? And if yes,
what were the conclusions?

Through his fine investigative journalistic work, Daniel
Hopsicker has been able to establish that the "hijacker"
Mohammad Atta had access to, and had received training at the Maxwell Airbase, Alabama, in the school of
international officers. Who gave access to Atta to the
US military and intelligence facilities and organizations?
Gary North, PhD, has carried out a remarkably detailed
and penetrating study of the passengers lists of all the
four hijacked planes. There is not a single Muslim name
in these lists. How does one explain this?

Michael Ruppert was probably the first one to point
out that between September 1 and 10, 2001, 23,000 British

troops were sailing towards Oman. They were part of an exercise Operation Swift Sword that had been prepared about four years earlier. At the same time, two US aircraft carriers arrived in the Gulf region. Simultaneously, 17,000 NATO troops from Egypt joined these forces in the Gulf. They were part of Operation Bright Star. All these forces were in position *before* 9/11. Was this so because the plan to attack Afghanistan had been prepared four years earlier?

The manner in which the WTC collapsed has given rise to many questions. These questions were raised by experts. For instance, a substantial part of its material was converted to powder. How does one explain this? According to the "official" version the building collapsed because the vertical steel rods, around which the entire structure was erected, were melted by the fire. According to experts, steel melts around 1500 degrees centigrade. Experimental studies with fires in buildings have revealed that the highest temperatures in such fires never exceed 400 degrees centigrade. How does one explain this discrepancy? How could the fire resulting from planes hitting the building on the outside melt, if at all, the steel rods in the center region? According to what has become known, the building had a simple structure - in the middle there were vertical steel rods going right up to the top of the building - the various floors were laid out on steel rods jointed horizontally to the vertical structure just like old records on a record player. If, as claimed, the steel rods did melt, then why did the top half of the rods not bend to one side or the other carrying the upper parts of the building with it? The lower half should then have stayed intact. Why did this not happen? How was it that one of the the tallest buildings in the entire world collapsed symmetrically and perfectly within its footprints? Was it a demolition job?

There is another mystery associated with the collapse of the WTC building. A building which was not hit also collapsed within its own footprints. This building, known as WTC 7, housed offices of the "Internal Revenue Service, the Secret Service, the Securities and Exchange Commission, the Mayor's office of Emergency Management and the CIA's New York Station." How does one explain its collapse? To quote Ruppert: "Nothing makes sense to explain the collapse of this building except by controlled demolition.[1] It is inconceivable that this building was brought down by planes that hit buildings approximately a hundred yards away." Was WTC 7 demolished because it contained records of highly sensitive investigations involving several trillion of money stolen by a tiny elite?

Pictures that came to light showing damage to the Pentagon building do not reveal the kind of impact an airplane would have created - no traces of the impact of the wings is visible, among other things. The hole created in the wall is much smaller than what would have been created by an aeroplane. How does one explain such discrepancies between the claim that the Pentagon was hit by a plane and the physical evidence?

Before 9/11, the stock exchange of the US was in a very bad shape during the months of July, August and the

---

[1]See http://www.wtc7.net/video.shtml.

days of September preceding 9/11. In fact, there was real danger that the economy might crash because the Dow-Jones index had fallen by about 3,000 points. A few days before 9/11, the trends in the sale and purchase of American Airlines shares were distinct from that of all other airlines. During 9/11, it were American Airlines planes that were hijacked - some insider knew of this in advance and, therefore, vast profits were made by unknown individuals. Those who profited from hijacking of American Airline planes have never been brought to light. Why this failure? It would not be difficult to find the names out. In fact, in one publicized case no one came forward to collect his or her profit. According to researches carried out by Tom Flocco and Michael Ruppert, the unusual and highly suspicious sales and purchases of the American Airlines shares just before 9/11 was carried out by Alex Brown investment branch of the Deutsche Bank. Until 1998, this bank was headed by Alex "Buzzy" Krongard. At the time of 9/11, Krongard was the Executive Director of the CIA. Executive Director is the number three position in the CIA and the Executive Director oversees all secret operations. What is the relationship between the insider trading at his former bank and the Executive Director of CIA. Why has the matter of "Profits of Death", to borrow Tom Flocco's phrase, and the title of his article, been suppressed?

Waqt, September 12, 2007

Chapter 7

Mysterious Flight

The US army, navy, air force and marines have all pre-
pared battle plans and spent four years building bases and
training for "Operation Iranian Freedom." Admiral Fal-
lon, the new head of the US Central Command, has in-
herited computerized plans under the name TIRANNT.
New Statesman, 19 February 2007

The broader implications of a US-NATO attack on Iran
are far-reaching. The war and economic crisis are in-
timately related. The war economy is financed by Wall
Street, which stands as the creditor of the US adminis-
tration. The US weapon producers are recipients of the
US Department of Defense multibillion dollar procure-
ment contracts for advanced weapon systems. In turn,
"the battle for oil" in the Middle East and Central Asia
directly serves the interests of the Anglo-American oil gi-
ants. **M. Chossudovsky**, 1 August 2010

It was on September 6, 2007, that a sensational and highly disturbing news item was lifted by media worldwide. On August 30, 2007 a B-52 bomber of the US Air Force carrying 6 nuclear armed cruise missiles, took off from the state of North Dakota and landed in the southern state of Louisiana. It was a three hour nonstop flight and its trajectory ran right through the heart of USA in the north-south direction. North Dakota is located at the Canadian border in the extreme north of USA whereas Louisiana is located on the Gulf of Mexico in the southern extreme of USA. According to news reports, it was only *after* the plane had landed at the Barksdale airport, did the crew discover that the cruise missiles were nuclear armed. According to reliable reports, W80-1 warheads were fitted onto the missiles. These warheads have a strength varying from five to 150 kilotons. The atomic bomb dropped on Hiroshima was a 10 kiloton bomb. Therefore, the cruise missiles were armed with nuclear weapons with a minimum strength of 30 kilotons - the maximum strength would be 900 kilotons, i.e., equivalent of 90 bombs of the strength that destroyed Hiroshima.

It is highly significant that the story first appeared on a US military website and only then did the civilian media pick it up. It is astonishing that such an important news item was placed in the inside pages of such important newspapers as the *Washington Post* and the *New York Times*. The *Washington Post* published it on page 10 while the *New York Times* relegated it to page 16. The publication of this news sent shudders of deep concern worldwide. If the flight had met with an accident, the result would have been horrific destruction. The USAF spokesman stated that at no time during the course of flight was there any threat to public security. The Pentagon spokesman stated that the Chief of the USAF General Michael Forley took immediate notice of the matter and talked to Secretary Defense and then informed President Bush about the matter. The manner of coverage of this astounding event by the American press says something about how it works and how the US people are kept unaware of, or insulated from, reality.

During the Cold War between the US and the Soviet Union, bombers with nuclear payloads used to be in the air at all times of the day and night. In 1968, the USA unilaterally abandoned this policy on account of the accidents which plagued the B-52 bombers. The statement of the USAF spokesman that no danger to the US public existed during the course of the flight was utterly incorrect. If this were the case, then why have such flights been discontinued (for the last 39 years)? It is worth noting that after discontinuing the policy of keeping nuclear armed aircraft airborne in 1968, the US kept such battle ready planes with nuclear payload at the ends of runways so that they could take off at the shortest possible notice. Even this practice was stopped in 1991, after the breakup of the Soviet Union. The Soviet Union kept up the practice of airborne nuclear armed bombers till its break up in 1991. It is only recently, in mid August 2007, that President Putin of Russia has announced resumption of the policy of maintaining nuclear armed aircraft in air after 15 years. The US policy of not having bombers with nuclear payload standing at the ends of runways, while the Soviet Union continued to maintain such bombers in midair round the clock, had only one rationale - public security.

According to informed sources such a mistake, as was committed in this case, could arise if and only if the standard operating procedures (SOPs) are not observed at several steps. A failure to observe SOPs at one or two stages in such a sensitive matter can be digested, but a violation of SOPs at several steps is extremely difficult to accept. In order to placate public doubts a squadron leader, who was in charge of nuclear weapons, was removed from service. Similarly all personnel who dealt with the nuclear weapons in this particular case were forbidden from dealing with these weapons.

In a brief note on the internet, Larry Johnson mentions what he learned from a friend who used to fly B-52 bombers. His friend told him that there are only two circumstances in which nuclear weapons are loaded on planes. Firstly, if you are ready for war, and secondly, if you need to transport nuclear weapons from one location to another. However, if nuclear weapons are to be transported from one location to another, they are placed in the belly of the aircraft and are never attached to the wings. The former B-52 pilot also said that Barksdale airbase is connected to operations in the middle east. The question then arises as to why was it that a plane armed with live nuclear weapons was landed at an airport that is connected with the mideast operations. Is it that the US is trying to send some message to Iran? One may also ask as to who would have the horrific destruction been attributed to in case of mishap? "Terrorists", Muslim extremists, Iran, or someone else?

The orders to place nuclear weapons onto an aircraft must originate at some level in the hierarchy. Bill van Auken has raised an important point in his September 7, 2007 ·article. He states that the navy and the air force is gradually increasing the dual use of cruise missiles. In this dual use, sometimes conventional warheads and sometimes nuclear warheads are fitted onto the cruise missiles. If a mistake is made in this dual use then, by mistake, an enemy may be attacked with a live nuclear armed cruise missile. There is another possibility. It is possible that the orders to attach nuclear warheads to the missiles came from a high level. If this is the case, it is even more disturbing. The leakage of the news through a military website may indicate that someone from within the armed forces is trying to warn the people of USA.

The superrich elite has taken hold of the US, which is increasingly in its grip over the past many decades. Sometimes the people do manage to break their stranglehold but the elite is extremely cunning and operates in great secrecy employing its vast wealth to control USA and the rest of the world. Abraham Lincoln had warned the people against the corporations, and a century later, President Eisenhower also issued a similar warning about the threat of control by a military-industrial complex. The two world wars and the so called war against "terrorism" has given the elite unprecedented, and almost complete control over the lives of US public.

The trajectory of US policy will lead inevitably to global war and horrific loss of human life and property. According to a recent survey, only 7% of the US public approves of the policies of George Bush, while 83% want an end to war. Historically, whenever the US elite wishes to take the US into major war, some incident takes place in which innocent American lives are lost, so that it arouses the indignation and anger of the US public. By attributing the loss of American lives to the "enemy", the leadership has been able to take the US into major wars. Fifty years down the road, when all those responsible for the deception have been consigned to their graves with honors, will the Freedom of Information Act reveal that the "incident" was the result of the planning of US leaders and agencies working in the interests of the superrich elite, which remains anonymous, hidden, ceaselessly active, silent and lethal at all times.

Waqt, September 14, 2007

Chapter 8

Bush and the "Axis of Evil"

It is bad. enough that the Bush family helped raise the money for Thyssen to give Hitler a start in the 1920s, but giving aid and comfort to the enemy in time of war is treason. The Bush bank helped the Thyssens make the Nazi steel that killed Allied soldiers. As bad as financing the Nazi war machine may seem, aiding and abetting the Holocaust was worse. Thyssen's coal mines used Jewish slaves as if they were disposable chemicals. There are six million skeletons in the Thyssen closet, and a myriad of criminal and historical questions to be asked about the Bush family's complicity.

Attorney John Loftus

A few years before 9/11, Dick Cheney had asked the Project of New American Century PNAC, to prepare a document about rebuilding America's military might.

54

The PNAC report clearly states that the disintegration of the Soviet Union has created a window of opportunity for the US to become permanently pre-eminent. The mysterious 9/11 incident has provided US with the pretext to launch a war for control of global energy resources so as to be able to cripple its enemies by denying them oil and at the same time meeting its ever growing and insatiable thirst for oil and gas. In order to hoodwink its own people, and the rest of the world, the US leadership calls it a "War on Terror". Alan Greenspan, former President of the World Bank, has clearly stated in his recently published biography that the war against Iraq is a war for oil. Greenspan was part of the inner circle that took the decision to go to war. In a recently published article, Henry Kissinger has stated that the real reason for attacking Iraq should have been Saddam's ability to disrupt the supply of items that are crucial to the stability of the global economy. Evidently these items are none other than oil and gas.

In order to make the widespread civilian casualties in the wars for oil and gas acceptable to the people of the US in particular, and of the West in general, the undefined terminology of terrorism has been coined. For the very same reason, countries that were expected to resist the US onslaught were dubbed "Axis of Evil" by George Bush. The use of such insulting language about other countries by the President of a nation as great as the United States of America, is highly inappropriate. In fact, in a strangely ironical twist of fate, researchers have uncovered facts about the history of the Bush family that indicate that a substantial part of the fortune of the elders of the Bush family came from black money. Of course, the "free" US media has concealed this ugly and evil reality from the people of the US. You will not find such stories in the mainstream media. You will only find them in little read books published by researchers, or on the wonderful medium of internet. Webster Griffin Tarpley and Anton Chaitkin have written *George Bush: the Unauthorized Biography* in which the dark past of the Bush family has been uncovered. One of the writers to expose the Nazi connection of the Bush family was John Buchanan. Reviewing the book by Tarpley and Chaitkin, John Buchanan has stated:

> The book gave a detailed accounting of the Bush family's long Nazi affiliation, but no mainstream media entity reported on or even investigated the allegations, despite careful documentation by the authors. Major booksellers declined to distribute the book, which was dismissed by Bush supporters as biased and untrue. Its authors struggled even to be reviewed in reputable newspapers.

This tells us how free, and how unbiased present day mainstream US media is!

The aforementioned authors have contributed to the uncovering of the links of the Bush family with the Nazi evil. But John Loftus has taken this connection to its deepest, truest, and most disturbing level, exposing its absolutely evil nature. Very few people are aware that Herbert Prescott Bush, the grand-father of George Bush (43rd US President), and the father of George Herbert

56

Walker Bush (41st President of US) alongwith George Herbert Walker, father-in-law of Prescott Bush, were complicit in the crimes of the German industrialist»banking family, the Thyssens who funded the Nazi party. Their money laundering as well as other business activity as frontmen for the Thyssen interests continued even after the US had entered World War II. When, in October 1942, the US government found out that these gentlemen were trading with the enemy, it took action against companies which were partially or mainly owned by Herbert Prescott Bush and Prescott Bush's father-in-law George Herbert Walker. Strangely enough, the US government did not punish them nor did it let the media know about it on the grounds that it may adversely affect the morale of the public! However, with the passage of time clear cut evidence has been uncovered that establishes beyond doubt that the two gentlemen mentioned above were not only involved in money laundering but also profited from forced labor of Jews and gypsies from Auschwitz. The final discovery in this regard, which completed the vital chain of investigative effort, was made by a former US intelligence official named William Gowen, a long time after his retirement. John Loftus was able to find out the truly evil things from William Gowen to completely solve the puzzle.

August Thyssen was the king of German steel industry. During World War I, he employed 50,000 workers in his factories churning out one million tons of iron and steel annually. He foresaw German defeat and did not want to lose his assets to the victors. He, therefore, carried out a series of manoeuvres. He owned the August

57

Thyssen bank in Berlin. During the course of the war, he married off one of his sons, Heinrich Thyssen, into Hungarian aristocracy and moved him to Hungary where he quietly changed his name to Baron Thyssen Bornemisza de Kaszon. The elder son Fritz Thyssen had studied in the best technical business schools of Europe. Before the end of World War I, August Thyssen opened a bank in neutral Holland, named it Bank voor Handel en Sheepvaart, but kept its ownership secret so that he could launder his money out of Germany. In 1924, a bank named Union Banking Corporation (UBC) was opened by August Thyssen in New York City. The ownership of the UBC was also kept a secret. The real owner was August Thyssen through the Dutch bank that he owned. The general impression was that the UBC was owned by Prescott Bush, his father-in-law George Herbert Walker and Averell Harriman. However, this was not the case. Averell Harriman had founded UBC on behalf of August Thyssen and Bank voor Handel en Sheepvaart. It is to be noted that since 1922 at least, the Thyssen family had been financing Hitler's Nazi party. In fact, the autobiography of Fritz Thyssen was titled *I Paid Hitler*. As John Buchanan wrote about UBC:

> According to government documents, it was in reality a clearing house for a number of Thyssen-controlled enterprises and assets, including as many as a dozen individual businesses. UBC also bought and shipped overseas gold, steel, coal and US Treasury war bonds. The company's activities were admin-

istered for Thyssen by a Netherlands-born, naturalized U.S. citizen named Cornelis Lievense, who served as President of UBC. Roland Harriman was chairman and Prescott Bush a managing director.

When August Thyssen died in 1926, his sons Fritz Thyssen and Heinrich Thyssen took over the industrial-banking empire. Fritz Thyssen and his father had come into contact with Hitler in 1923 and had begun financing him. And while they were connected so deeply with the Nazis, Prescott Bush and his father in law George Herbert Walker were working for them and kept on working with the Thyssens for more than two decades, in fact right up to 1951, the year Fritz Thyssen died in Argentina. Nazis did not trust Fritz Thyssen and knew that his Berlin bank was carrying out transactions with the Dutch bank, Bank voor Handel en Sheepvaart. German auditors suspected that Fritz Thyssen had concealed money to evade taxes. Therefore, during World War II, after capturing Holland in May 1940, the Nazis began looking for the missing Thyssen money in the Dutch bank. However, there was no clue and nobody knew who the owner was. Fritz Thyssen had very cleverly moved the ownership papers back to his Berlin bank and hidden them right under the Nazi nose! All he had to do was to move the papers back to the Dutch bank once the Germans lost the war and the allied powers moved into Berlin in the year 1945, dividing it into two zones.

When the war ended a problem arose. The building of the August Thyssen Bank in Berlin had been de-

stroyed by allied bombing and the papers lay in a safe
under the rubble. To compound problems, the destroyed
building of the bank fell in the Russian zone of occupation. The recovery of these documents is a fascinating
story that also reveals deep interconnections between the
global elite. It was Prince Bernhard who came to the rescue of the Thyssens. He was married to then Princess and
later Queen Juliana. The Russians were informed that
precious crown jewels of the Princess had been stolen by
the Nazis during their Dutch occupation, and placed in
the destroyed bank building. Prince Bernhard, German
by birth, a one time Nazi who later fought the Germans
as a Dutch, headed an intelligence unit that carried out
the operation for recovery of the ownership papers of the
Dutch bank owned by the Fritz and Heinrich Thyssen.[1]
Thus Fritz Thyssen was able to get back his bank and his

---

[1] It is astonishing to note that Prince Bernhard, who was a Nazi
at one time, was married to the lady who became the reigning
Queen of Belgium (she had shares in the Royal Dutch Shell Oil Co
owned by the Rothschild family). It was he who brought back the
ownership papers for Thyseen. He then went on to become, along
with former CIA chief General Walter Bedell Smith, one of the four
founding members of the Bilderberg Group. The German born war
criminal Henry Kissinger was also among the first members of the
Bilderberg Group - he was probably the youngest member of the
Group. The interconnections of the elite are most astonishing in
the sense that Jews and ex-Nazis mingle together. Add to this the
Bush family elders, the Harrimans, John and Allen Foster Dulles
and others. No wonder James Angleton told the author Joseph
Trento that he had become Head of Counterintelligence wing in CIA
by promising Allen Dulles not to subject him and 60 of his closest
friends to polygraph tests. Angleton said: "They were afraid that
their own business dealings with Hitler's pals would come out."

money. The ownership remained a shared secret. How could the husband of the future Queen of Netherlands do this at a time when, under the law, all Nazi assets were to be confiscated. He was himself an ex-Nazi and so was Fritz Thyssen!

The story took a dramatic turn in 1945. A manager working for Thyseen's Dutch bank discovered that the bank was owned by Fritz Thyssen, an ex-Nazi. In 1947, this innocent manager threatened to reveal the real ownership of the bank and was sacked. He knew of the extensive dealings of the bank with the the UBC in New York City and also knew that UBC was also owned by Fritz Thyssen because he owned the Dutch bank. He wanted to talk to Prescott Bush and tell him that the UBC might also be confiscated. The unsuspecting manager traveled to New York. Little did he know who he was dealing with. Two weeks later he was found dead. Similarly, in 1996, a Dutch journalist Eddy Roever traveled to London to interview Baron Thyssen who, incidentally, was the next door neighbor of Mrs Margaret Thatcher at the time. Not surprisingly two days later his body was found. Both deaths involved men with important knowledge, both were healthy, and both deaths were made to look like heart attacks.

The US government had already found out quite a bit about the trading activities of Prescott Bush, his father in law George Herbert Walker, and the Harrimans with the Nazis. However, the real ownership of UBC was revealed only in 1999. The Thyssens owned Silesian Coal and Steel Company located close to Auschwitz. This company employed slave labor - Jews, gypsies and others worked in the industry. The iron and steel produced by this company played a vital role in keeping the Nazi war machine functional during World War II. When in 1951 Fritz Thyssen died, Prescott Bush and his father-in-law received $ 1.5 million each because they had a single share each in the UBC. This amount played a role in enabling Prescott Bush to be elected as senator and in setting up a royalty company. This political step in the wake of, and perhaps on account of, the money received by virtue of services rendered to the enemy industrialist-banker Fritz Thyssen, paved the way for his son to become the 41st and his grandson the 43rd President of the United States of America. That money must have smelt of the sweat and blood of those who toiled and died at Auschwitz.

Since the Nazis were evil and his ancestors not only collaborated with them, but profited immensely from that illegal, immoral and treasonous relationship, Mr. George W Bush, 43rd President of the United States of America, must think twice before calling any one evil.

Waqt, September 25, 2007

Chapter 9

Freedom of US Media?

Many of the ugliest truths about deliberate U.S. abandonment or ordered extermination of POWs are extremely well documented in Monika Jensen Stevenson's 1990 bestseller, Kiss The Boys Goodbye (Dutton). Stevenson, a former Emmy award winning producer for CBS News' 60 Minutes, produced mountains of eyewitness statements, documents, and even admissions from Ronald Reagan and other White House officials as well as from intelligence experts in the Pentagon and the National Security Council showing that: the U.S. knowingly left POWs behind in Southeast Asia in 1973; the U.S. government sabotaged at least a half dozen rescue attempts with high probabilities for success; and that the U.S. government ordered covert operatives to "liquidate" alive POWs if sighted.

On pages 318 − 323, Stevenson described a failed 1981 POW rescue mission involving the perennial "covert source" (and often hard to fathom) Scott Barnes who wrote a book about the mission entitled BOHICA (Bend Over

Here It Comes Again). After passing polygraph and truth serum exams, Barnes recounted how he had been issued atropine (nerve gas antidote) injectors as a prelude to entering areas in Laos where POW camps were known to exist. He also states that, once in the region, he was ordered to "liquidate the merchandise." "Merchandise" was the code word for POWs.

(NOTE: Atropine was issued to U.S. troops in the Persian Gulf war to counter anticipated Sarin attacks by Iraq).

If Barnes' statement was not enough, his return from the mission was immediately followed by the alleged violent suicide of Army chemical warfare and Sarin gas expert General Bobby Robinson. Local police doubted the suicide findings of the military. What's more, Robinson was known to have been involved in moving Sarin supplies into the region at the time... As one source put it "It's much more likely that Robinson could have exposed the use of his Sarin to kill Americans and he had to be killed - especially if he found out what his precious chemical agents were used for."

Michael Ruppert

In the Cold War era, US was considered the torch bearer of democracy and liberty. The impression that the US was a place where freedom of speech and expression existed had an effect on the youth of the world, and attracted them like a magnet. In reality, the issue of freedom of speech and expression, even in Cold War era US, was not so simple. But the new laws that have been speedily passed and enforced in the past decade-and-a-half, along with the dictatorial trends in the US elite, have significantly modified global opinions about the US. Only a few days ago, it was reported that Dan Rather, the well known anchor person of CBS, has been removed from his job. It has also been reported that Dan Rather has sued CBS for damages and filed a 70 million dollar suit in the New York Supreme Court. The real reasons for termination of Dan Rather's job were two-fold. Firstly, he aired a program regarding draft dodging by President Bush during the Vietnam war by using Bush family influence. Secondly, he aired a program on Abu Gharib despite resistance from the CBS administration. This program brought to light globally, a hitherto hidden aspect of the conduct of the US armed forces in their war against Iraq.

This is not the first time a prominent media person has had to lose his job for exposing influential people, or for exposing the criminal conduct of US agencies or forces. There are numerous examples of such influence, wielded by the US elite and the US agencies and armed forces, on US media. One of the most interesting cases is that of CNN producer April Oliver and her colleague Jack Smith who lost their jobs for airing a program "*Operation Tailwind*" in 1998. In this program, it was established that the Studies and Observation Group (SOG) of the CIA had employed Sarin gas to kill those US soldiers who had deserted during the Vietnam war and sought refuge in Laos. As soon as the program was aired, the Chairman Joint Chiefs of Staff of the US Armed Forces, Gen Colin Powell and former Secretary of State Henry Kissinger launched very strong protests and demanded that CNN withdraw the program. As a result of this pressure, the CNN not only dismissed the two producers, it also aired an apology and withdrew the program.[1] It is important to note that CNN regularly uses US military satellites to beam its programs worldwide. Naturally the CNN owners could not afford to ignore pressure from the armed forces as their programs would have gone off the air.

The truth of the matter was that the program was based on real facts and the conclusions arrived at after painstaking work. The mainstream US media did not dare to raise its voice on this incident, and the impression that the story was not factually correct, was allowed to sink in the public mind. However, a remarkable investigative reporter named Michael Ruppert dug into the entire story and put up the results of his investigations on his web newsletter. That is how those who read his article were able to find out the truth of the matter.

The poisonous Sarin gas storage facility in the US was, at that time, under the command and control of General Singlaub. He had commanded the SOG in the period 1966-68. In the wake of the CNN retraction, he filed a suit for defamation and slander against April Oliver as well as the CNN. General Singlaub "also demanded a public apology and exoneration". Admiral Thomas Moorer also

---

[1] I was then a regular viewer of the CNN. I remember watching, in 1998, this gripping program around 6 or 7 AM in Pakistăn. The following day they aired an apology and announced the retraction of the program. I was very surprised but never got to the bottom of it until I read Michael Ruppert several years later. And that too while working in Saudi Arabia!

came out openly in support of General Singlaub. Admiral Moorer was the Chairman of the Joint Chiefs of Staff during the Nixon era. In a court deposition, Admiral Moorer claimed that he had never allowed the use of Sarin gas as Chairman Joint Chiefs of Staff. However, when April Oliver filed a counter suit, a very interesting situation emerged. April Oliver's attorney was able to extract a fundamental admission from Admiral Moorer, viz, the SOG was not controlled by the Pentagon but by the CIA and by Henry Kissinger. This admission was enough to make his claim of not having ordered use of Sarin gas redundant and invalid;it was not his jurisdiction. Most interesting was the revelation that General Singlaub was himself the real, originally confidential, source of the story. By filing a suit against April Oliver, Singlaub had breached that confidentiality. April Oliver had taken detailed notes of her interviews with both Moorer and Singlaub, had shown these notes to Admiral Moorer, and obtained his signatures.

During cross questioning in the court, April Oliver's attorney extracted extremely important admissions from Admiral Moorer. Moorer admitted that he did not dispute the conclusions of CNN that, in 1970, SOG had terminated about 20 defectors. Moorer also admitted that termination of defectors had a "high priority" on all defectors inside Laos. He also confessed that Sarin gas was used and that the missions were successful! Moorer also made the shocking admission that it was a routine option to employ Sarin gas to kill crews of downed pilots if the rescue craft were unable to extract them. This was done to prevent them from falling into "enemy" hands! These staggering admissions in a court of law by a former Chief of the Joint Chiefs of Staff of the US Armed Forces constitute undeniable evidence of war crimes - the use of any poison gas is, under international law, a war crime.

The question then arises what was the real reason that compelled the authorities at the highest level in the CIA, and in the US armed forces, to kill its own soldiers. Michael Ruppert, who routinely communicated with Vietnam veterans and with several Special Forces veterans (his parents worked for the CIA and he himself worked for LAPD until he tried to expose CIA drug trafficking during Iran-Contra scandal), has answered this fundamental question in the following words:

> As Station Chief in Laos Ted Shackley ran the single largest covert operation in CIA's history, a war financed almost in its entirety on the proceeds of heroin. The war fought almost exclusively by Hmong tribesmen and a Laotian rebel Army under the command of General Vang Pao, an opium warlord who derived his entire budget from heroin. Legion are stories of CIA's involvement in drug trafficking to fund that war but one anecdote is telling. Former Air America pilot Bucky Blair, who flew supply missions to CIA's Site 85 in Laos, sitting on a remote mountain top, told me that when he flew in to make his drops he could "see the poppy fields stretching out for miles in all directions". Site 85 was overrun in 1968 and eleven alive Ameri-

cans were captured. Imagine what they might
have told under intense torture of Pathet Lao
or North Vietnamese interrogators and how
could they have been used as a propaganda
against an America already disintegrating under the war? Imagine what they might have
told other POWs they met as they moved
from camp to camp?

So these unfortunate men were murdered faraway from
their country, by an agency of that very country for which
they had come to lay their life, so that CIA secrets pertaining to drug trafficking and money laundering could
be protected. Or else why would CIA keep control of
such an operation? CIA and drug smuggling is another
interesting topic which will be taken up in another column.

What happened in the court? The court took a decision but ordered that the parties will not utter a word
about the decision. This injunction says something about
the US justice system. The fact that April Oliver bought
a six bedroom house and a new car, soon after the decision, indicates that she won the case - she happily stands
by every word of her story.

Waqt, September 29 2007

Chapter 10

The World's Largest Jail?

The US, along with only Somalia, has never ratified the Convention on the Rights of the Child. It stands in violation of the international human rights standards contained in that Charter that prohibit the incarceration of children with adults. According to the report, one third of the youth offenders now serving life without parole in the US entered adult prison when they were still children.
                                            Debra Watson

The penal system is privatized throughout, by degrees. Most prisons contract out food preparation, transportation and maintenance obligations to private corporations. Because incarceration has become such a lucrative venture for business and investors, rational sentencing limits and leniency for nonviolent violations are discouraged...the subjugation of human and social well being to the profit

motive - finds a sharp expression in America's prisons.
Naomi Spencer

*Whether anyone likes it or not, at the end of the blind
alley that is Europe... there is Hitler. At the end of capitalism, which is eager to outlive its day, there is Hitler.
At the end of formal humanism and philosophic renunci-
ation, there is Hitler.*
Aime Cesaire

*Do you begin to see, then, what kind of world we are
creating? It is the exact opposite of the stupid hedonistic
Utopias that the old reformers imagined. A world of fear
and treachery and torment, a world of trampling and being trampled upon, a world which will grow not less but
more merciless as it refines itself. Progress in our world
will be progress toward more pain.*
George Orwell 1984

It was only a few days ago that President George W Bush
lectured the UN and the world on democracy, human
rights, and human liberties. It is a measure of the trans-
formation in the global political climate that nobody took
the words of George W Bush seriously. Almost everyone
now knows that the US employs these slogans as a deception and the real intent is to enslave mankind for a high
cabal. The manner in which Mr. Bush has condemned
the website http://www.moveon.org, and the manner in
which the US Congress has passed a resolution against
this organization is incredible. And thoughtful circles

worldwide have noticed this. US democracy has now become a big question mark in the eyes of the world. It is also very clear that the Bush election "victories" of 2000 and 2004 resulted, if not from outright rigging and fraud, at least from highly questionable tactics. And after the brutality in Iraq and Afghanistan the claim to be a democratic power or a champion of human liberties seems irrelevant and meaningless.

The people of the United States are extremely agitated at this state of affairs. However, US agencies and the military have become so powerful and emboldened by their ever increasing grip on American society, that people have been marginalized - the people are practically helpless. Laws passed in the last two-and-a-half decades; particulary during the last decade or so, have strangulated the voice of the people. The increasing rich-poor divide in US, the plight of the poor who do not have access to the most basic health facilities, the endless plunder by corporations, unbridled profiteering, and the generally criminal and callous conduct of the elite, has generated an inhuman culture. This highly unjust state of affairs has produced serious cracks in US society. However, the US rulers, and the powerful and real elite behind these rulers, are ready to deal with any unrest. They have firmly decided that global war abroad, accompanied by dictatorship at home is the only "solution".

The jails of the US give us a valuable insight into certain aspects of US society. The nation that held aloft the torch of democratic values, human liberties and human dignity, and which by virtue of this impression, was respected worldwide for a long time, has been transformed into a country whose jails are teeming with prisoners. Today the correctional population of USA is over 7 million. These over 7 million Americans are either incarcerated in jails, or are on parole or probation. Of these, 2.2 million are serving time and the sword of being sentenced to prison hangs on the heads of another 4.8 million. The state of a society, in which over 7 million people are serving time or are living in fear of being sent to jail, need not be commented upon. These are not just 7 million or more individuals; these are 7 million families that live in a state of uncertainty and insecurity. Yet another 4.3 million ex-convicts also reside in the US. These numbers are unparalleled in human history. It is important to note that the 2.2 million were serving time at any one time in US jails in 2006. However, there is an even larger number of people who are in and out of jails or in US police stations on small time confinements. A 2007 survey carried out by Pew Charitable Trust puts the total number of people who spend sometime in correctional facilities in a year at over 10 million! This is both astonishing and deeply disturbing.

In 1980, only half a million prisoners were in US jails. The number of 2.2 million prisoners in 2006 represents an increase by a factor of 4.4, i.e., a 440% increase in the US prison population. The US population in this period has increased only by 20%. The above statistics have come from the US Justice Department, Bureau of Justice Statistics. The US population is approximately 5% or so of the global population, but the US prison population is 25% of the global prison population. And the world has 194 countries! The prison population of China stands at

number two position where the prison population is estimated at 1.5 million. One must, however, bear in mind
that the Chinese population is approximately four times
that of the US population. The democratic US has about
740 prisoners per 100,000 of population whereas the corresponding figure for China, not considered a democracy
by Western standards, stands at 118, i.e., less than a factor of over 6 compared to the US. It is important to note
that in the population of 7 million in jails or under probation or on parole in the US, 41% of the adult component
is black and 19% are Hispanics. In the 25-29 year age
group, one out of 9 blacks are in jail. For Hispanics, this
figure is one out of 26 and for the whites, the number is
one out 56. These figures portray a clear cut and deeply
worrying picture of racial discrimination in US society.

The major reason for these disturbing figures lies in
the losses suffered by education and health programs as
a result of widespread plunder and loot by the rich seg-
ments of US society. Also, in the last twenty or twenty-
five years, strict laws punishing minor crimes have been
passed. For instance, many minors and women are incarcerated for possession of drugs. The irony is that there is
undeniable evidence of CIA involvement in drug trafficking. In fact, according to experts, CIA controls the global
drug trade. During Iran-Contra scandal, for instance,
it was established that the CIA was smuggling drugs
into black residential areas of Los Angeles in particular.
Where should the blacks go? Data collected by the Sentencing Project indicates that 14% of the drug users are
black. However among those arrested on drug charges,
37% are blacks, while of those jailed on drug charges 56%

are blacks. These statistics shed damning light on the US justice and law enforcement system. Apart from these statistics, despite instructions from superior courts, minors are incarcerated with adults leading to sexual abuse and violence. In recent years, the number of incarcerated women is on the rise which is another disturbing trend. A very large number of US jails are now administered by private corporations. These corporations are paid on a per inmate basis. Naturally the greater the number of inmates, the greater the profits. Even in those jails that are administered by the government, services such as catering, etc., are contracted out to private firms. At this time corporations are doing a business of $40 billion per annum in US jails. The same corporations have been awarded contracts in Iraq by the Department of Defense. In such circumstances, Mr. Bush's lecture on democracy, human values and liberty becomes meaningless.

Waqt, October 2, 2007

Chapter 11

US Media Ownership

The corporate grip on opinion in the United States is one of the wonders of the Western world. No First World country has ever managed to eliminate so entirely from its media all objectivity - much less dissent. Of course, it is possible for any citizen with time to spare, and a canny eye, to work out what is actually going on, but for the many there is not time, and the network news is the only news even though it may not be news at all but only a series of flashing fictions...

Gore Vidal

Following the same course that virtually every other major industry has in the last two decades, a relentless series of mergers and corporate take-overs has consolidated control of the media into the hands of a few corporate behemoths. The result has been that an increasingly authoritarian agenda has been sold to the American people by a massive, multi-tentacled media machine that has be-

come, for all intents and purposes, a propaganda organ
of the state.

David McGowan

... the issue is whether we want to live in a free society or whether we want to live under what amounts to
a form of self-imposed totalitarianism, with the people
marginalized, directed elsewhere, terrified, screaming patriotic slogans, fearing for their lives, and admiring with
awe the leader who saved them from destruction, while
the educated masses goose-step on command and repeat
the slogans they are supposed to repeat and society de-
teriorates at home. We end up by serving a mercenary
enforcer state, hoping that others are going to pay us to
smash up the world.

Noam Chomsky

The media are a corporate monopoly. They have the same
point of view. The two parties are two factions of the
business party. Most of the population doesn't even bother
voting because it looks meaningless. They're marginalized
and properly distracted. At least that's the goal.

Noam Chomsky

Don't you see that the whole aim of Newspeak is to narrow the range of thought?... Has it ever occurred to you,
Winston, that by the year 2050, at the very latest, not
a single human being will be alive who could understand
such a conversation as we are having now?... The whole
climate of thought will be different. In fact, there will be
no thought, as we understand it now. Orthodoxy means

not thinking - not needing to think. Orthodoxy is uncon-
sciousness.

George Orwell

Although people residing in various parts of the world are aware that the US media paints a distorted pictures of events, they do not know as to why is this so. Similarly, there are innumerable highly unjust and illegal aspects of US foreign policy which become possible on account of the vast power of the media that is employed to influence the thinking of an inherently fair and truthful US public. Then in various movies remarks or dialogues are subtly injected that present certain nations or religions in a negative manner. In order to understand these things it is important to know who controls US media. Is it that there are a large number of media owners in the US belonging to diverse schools of thought? Or is US media owned by a few individuals or a few families? If the media is owned by a few people, then do these people belong to different view points and different shades of thought, religion, and ethnic backgrounds? It is to be borne in mind that the media world of today includes TV channels, newspapers, magazines, movie companies, music recording and selling companies, book publishers, etc.

The biggest media corporation in the US, and in the world, is (see footnote 1 on the next page) Time Warner. It was at the turn of twentieth century that two Jewish brothers set up a movie company, the now famous Warner Brothers that was to emerge as the most powerful film company of the twentieth century. Similarly Time Inc was a publishing company that published, among others, the world famous Time magazine. When internet was invented and became public the largest internet company was AOL with over 35 million subscribers. These three entities merged to form the AOL Time Warner company. However when the authorities started investigations into the accounts of AOL the name of the company was changed to Time Warner. In 2003 this company had a revenue of 39.6 billion dollars.[1] This corporations owns AOL, Time Publishers, CNN, HBO, Cinemax, Warner Music, New Line Cinema, Castlerock Entertainment, Winamp and many other such companies. The CEO and Director of Time Warner was Jewish - his name was Gerald Levin. In view of his conflict with Ted Turner, a Gentile, who lost 85% of his money (about $7 billion) as a result of deliberate tactics of Gerald Levin, the latter was forced to relinquish his position. Ted Turner remained on the board as an outspoken member but not with the same influence and control he once had when he owned CNN and Turner Broadcasting System prior to merger with Time Warner. Turner stepped down as Vice Chairman in 2006.[2]

The second largest US media company is Walt Disney. It belonged at one time to the Gentile Walt Disney family and was founded, in 1923, by two brothers Roy and Walt Disney. Its CEO, till 2005, was Michael Eisner. Eisner is Jewish. According to one writer: "In

---

[1]In 2006 this had risen to $44.224 billion. In 2008 the figure was $46.984 billion, but in 2009 the revenues fell to $25.785 billion, displacing it from the number one position in terms of revenues.

[2]The current CEO of Time Warner is Jeffery L Bewkes.

2003, Roy E. Disney, the son of Disney co-founder Roy
O. Disney and nephew of Walt Disney, resigned from his
positions as Disney vice chairman and chairman of Walt
Disney Feature Animation, accusing Eisner of microman-
agement". Its current CEO Robert Iger is also Jewish. In
2003 this company had a revenue of 27.1 billion US dollars.[3]. Walt Disney TV, Walt Disney Motion Pictures,
Hollywood Pictures, Miramax, Touchstone Pictures, etc
are all components of Walt Disney Co. All these names
are known worldwide in connection with movies. The
ABC network, which has dozens of TV stations, is part of
Walt Disney. The ABC owns 54 radio stations -the number of radio stations on which its programs are broadcast
is however much larger. The sports channel ESPN, A &
E, Lifetime TV and History channel are also part of Walt
Disney Co. The ABC family channel has 84 million view-
ers. The Zionist mouthpiece Rev Pat Robertson utters
his poison against Muslims from this very channel. Walt
Disney also owns over a dozen internet companies.

The third corporation that owns a substantial part
of US media, is named Viacom. Viacom came into existence as a result of an anti-monopoly court decision
directing CBS to separate a part of its cable operations
and syndicated programs. Sumner Redstone owns almost
three fourths of the shares of Viacom Inc. Interestingly
Sumner's original name was Murray Rothstein. It is not
clear as to why he changed his Jewish name. Viacom

---

[3]Since the original lines were written the revenues of Walt Disney have continued to increase. In 2007, 2008 and 2009 the revenues
were, respectively 35.510, 37.843 and 36.149 US dollars so that in
2009 its revenues were more than that of Time Warner.

is probably the largest cable provider worldwide. MTV, Nickelodeon, Show Time, Black Entertainment all belong to Viacom. Viacom owns 39 TV stations and is linked, through its CBS network, to another 200 TV channels. Further it also makes motion pictures because Paramount is also a component of Viacom.

In addition to the three corporations mentioned above, there a few other big media corporations. NBC Universal is the fourth large media corporation. A profile of the corporation on the net states "NBC Universal owns and operates the NBC television network and the NBC Universal Television Stations group, which includes 14 broadcast television stations, all affiliated with NBC. In total the NBC television network has over 230 affiliates. The company also owns a group of cable news and entertainment networks, television production operations, the Universal Pictures motion picture company and the Universal theme parks." Until 2007 its CEO was a Gentile named Bob Wright, who was often associated with Jewish causes. The real power lay with the Jewish Bronfman family. Edgar Bronfman Sr was the President of the World Jewish Congress from 1981-2007. His son Edgar Bronfman Jr bought Vivendi. The current CEO of NBC, Jeff Zucker, is also Jewish. In 2005 the NBC Universal had revenues of $15.7 billion.[4]

Another media Mogul happens to be Rupert Murdoch who has recently purchased Wall Street Journal. Murdoch owns News Corporation. In 2003 News Corporation

---

[4]In 2008 the revenues were almost, $17 billion ($16.969 billion) which fell to $15.7 billion in 2009.

had revenues of 19.2 billion US dollars.[5] NewsCorp was established in Australia in 1979 but it entered US market soon afterwards and 70% of its revenues come from the US market. Apart from Fox News, Fox TV and FX channel, Murdoch owns a number of newspapers worldwide as well as the well known publishing giant Harper and Collins. He also owns Twentieth Century Fox. Murdoch is a great supporter and promoter of the so called War on Terror and employs the entire strength of his own media in this direction.

An article, US Electronic News & Entertainment Control, posted on *rense.com* in 2007, has the following to say

> The big three in television network broadcasting used to be ABC, CBS and NBC. With the consolidation of media empires, these three are no longer independent entities. While they were independent, however, each was controlled by a Jew since its inception: ABC by Leonard Goldensen, NBC first by David Sarnoff and then by his son Robert; and CBS first by William and then by Laurence Tisch. Over several decades these networks were staffed from top to bottom with Jews, and the essential Jewishness of the network television did not change when the networks were absorbed by other Jewish-dominated media corporations.

This is true of other networks as well, particularly in the

---

[5]In 2009 News Corporation had revenues of 30.423 billion US dollars making it the second largest media company in the world.

news divisions.

This dominance of a minority is not just restricted to broadcast networks. The newspapers also present a similar picture. According to one writer (writing in 2007) 80% of US newspapers are owned by large newspaper chains. In 1945 80% of US newspapers were independently owned. The situation is now the reverse. Most of the small number of independent newspapers cannot afford to maintain independent staff for news coverage and have to depend on news agencies. The Associated Press is under Jewish control. Further, these newspapers depend upon the rich Jews for advertisements. In addition the Newhouse family, which is also Jewish, owns many important newspapers. The most important newspapers are either owned by Jews or are controlled by them. Until the *Wall Street Journal,* by far the paper with the largest circulation in US, was bought by Murdoch, it was owned by a Jewish family. However Murdoch has the same policy as his predecessors in regard to US foreign policy matters. The *New York Times* and the *Washington Post* are owned by Jews. In these circumstances the freedom of speech and expression exists in a highly distorted and controlled state in the United Sates of America.

An anonymous writer states in his article on *rense.com*

> The Jewish control of the American mass media is the single most important fact of life, not just in America, but in the whole world today. There is nothing - plague, famine, economic collapse, even nuclear war - more dangerous to the future of our people.

> Jewish media control determines the foreign
> policy of the United States and permits Jew-
> ish interests, rather than American interests,
> to decide questions of war and peace. With-
> out Jewish media control, there would have
> been no Persian Gulf War, for example. There
> would be no NATO massacre of Serb civil-
> ians. There would have been no Iraq War,
> and thousands of lives would have been saved.
> There would have been little, if any, Ameri-
> can support for the Zionist state of Israel, and
> the hatreds, feuds, and terror of the Middle
> East would never have been brought to our
> shores.

For how long will the exploitation of the sweet and kind
people of the US continue? It is important to emphasize
that a substantial number of American Jews do not like
this kind of control. In 2003 John Whitley posted an article on the web with the title "Seven Jewish Americans
Control Most US media". It is a reflection on the changed
state of things in America that the author of an article
from which we have quoted above, has chosen to remain
anonymous - his (or her) article was posted on the web
in September 2007.

Waqt, October 9, 2007

Chapter 12

US and the Genocide of Iraqis

*I spent 33 years in the Marines, most of my time being
a high-class muscle man for big business, for Wall Street
and the bankers. In short I was a racketeer for Capitalism.*
Brig. Gen. Smedley D Butler
in *War is a Racket* (first published in 1935)

*The crimes of the US throughout the world have been
systematic, constant, clinical, remorseless and fully documented...*
Harold Pinter Nobel Laureate

*Because of its power and global interests U.S. leaders have
committed crimes as a matter of course and structural
necessity. A strict application of international law would
... have given every U.S. president of the past 50 years*

Nuremberg treatment.
Edward Herman

After the 9/11 attacks the US government lied to create a war for oil in Iraq telling us that Saddam Hussain had weapons of mass destruction, almost-ready atom bombs, poison gas and deadly germs. We were told that he helped execute the 9/11 attacks. It was all lies, and no one was held accountable for the hundreds of thousands of deaths (murders) in Iraq and Afghanistan since then. Few have tried to hold the government accountable for 2500 Americans who have died needlessly, and those who have, have been remarkably ineffective
Michael Ruppert
By the Light of a Burning Bridge 2006

Big corporations and big billionaires fund 90 percent to 98 percent of the Democratic and Republican Party budgets.
Howard Zinn

Politicians have become corporate prostitutes.
Helen Caldicott MD

Today the US is the preeminent power on the globe. From 1870 onwards at least, the US leadership and society embarked upon a comprehensive program of acquiring scientific and technological knowledge with the objective of become world leaders in the realm of science and technology and becoming a global power. The two world wars gave the US the desired pre-eminence. It is the US preeminence in scientific knowledge and creativity that is the ultimate source of its technological, military and economic dominance. It was in 1951 that a Pakistani writer Inayatullah Khan AlMashriqi had pointed out, that without the creative power of the scientist, the money of the capitalist, and the arms of the laborer, cannot produce much.

At this point in time (2007), the US military is present in at least 132 countries in all continents. Such preeminence has never been bestowed by Nature on any power in history. And dominance does not come without certain qualities of character. Human beings belonging to a dominant nation go about their daily work and activity with one thing in mind - to be the best in the world and to be preeminent on the surface of the earth. The reward of preeminence has been bestowed upon the United States of America on account of its outstanding conduct and perseverance. By observing the democratic and humane principles built into the US constitution, the US society stayed peaceful and united, and an atmosphere prevailed in which every individual could flourish and nurture his or her innate gifts and talents. The principles of the US constitution are a milestone in human history. But alas, today the US leadership has practically said goodbye to these great principles.

The rise and fall of nations is an eye opening clause of the laws of nature. It was only yesterday that the awesome power of the Soviet Union was smashed by a poor nation like the Afghans. Will the US dominance meet a similar fate? Or will Nature provide further opportunity to US to remain pre-eminent? Only time will answer this question. It appears that just as Nature does not create perfect humans it also does not shape perfect nations. Even in the greatest of nations some deficiency, some flaw, some defect is built that slowly erodes its strength and drags it down from the pinnacle of power to the ground. The greatest weakness of the United States is complete control of a handful of corporations, owned by a few superrich families, over its national life. As David Korten has written in his famed *The Post Corporate World*:

> The corporation is not a person and it does not live. It is a lifeless bundle of legally protected financial rights and relationships brilliantly designed to serve money and its imperatives. It is money, not blood, that flows in its veins. The corporation has neither soul nor conscience.

The greedy and heartless corporate owners are continually exploiting and subjugating mankind. With extraordinary cunning and ruthlessness, they have captured the US and having practically controlled the US people, are now trying to use them to capture the globe. With the exception of 1891, there has not been a single year in which US forces have not been used abroad for the cause of corporate profit. Today the corporations completely control the US government and the government will go to any extent to defend corporate interest. As William Shirer has put it

> You don't need a totalitarian dictatorship like Hitler's to get by with murder...you can do it

in a democracy as long as the Congress and the people Congress is supposed to represent don't give a damn.

For many decades the US government has been controlled and run by people who, according to highly reliable and reputed researchers, are murderers and criminals. According to these writers Nixon, Kissinger, Rumsfeld and many others are all lairs and their hands are red with blood. Kissinger for instance is not only responsible for many deaths in Vietnam and Latin America, he is also, according to researchers, responsible for the murder of those American soldiers who absconded during the Vietnam war and took refuge in Laos. It was Kissinger who controlled the Studies and Observations Group - SOG. - that killed these unfortunate men by using Sarin nerve gas.

The Iraq war too is based on a lie. It was about a year ago, in October 2006, when a highly reputed journal *Lancet* revealed that over 650,000 Iraqis had lost their lives in the current war. The US administration, and its stooges in the media, had dismissed these figures with great contempt. They had forgotten that reputed research journals do not publish papers easily - due refereeing is carried out by foremost experts before a paper is accepted for publication. Even at that time thoughtful people, aware of the facts, had pointed out that the numbers could have been understated.

Now, a year later, a British organization *ORB* has published new figures on Iraqi casualties. According to *ORB* data, 1.2 million Iraqis have died in the period 2003-

2007, and another million have been wounded. Also, according to an estimate, 4 million Iraqis have become homeless. It is important to emphasize that while collecting such data, those regions, such as Anbar and Karbala, where fighting is intense and more blood has been shed, have been excluded! Therefore the figures are likely to be below the actual numbers. It is worth pondering over that at least 100,000 people have died only as a result of US aerial bombing. If we add to these numbers the 500,000 children and the 1.5 million adults who died as a result of embargo on medicines, etc., after the *first* Gulf War, the figure of dead Iraqis exceeds 2.7 million. Does this not constitute genocide? Do the hands of US journalists become paralyzed when they have to write about this? Do the great comperes and anchor persons of the US and other Western channels become tongue-tied when they have to utter words about these brutal realities? Or is it that everybody has gone blind and cannot see? Where is their integrity?

All this bloodshed and misery has one fundamental cause. A few super-rich families on this planet want hundreds of billions, if not trillions, of dollars in their coffers by capturing oil reserves of Iraq and by selling defense equipment and war munitions.[1] At the same time a strong and rich Muslim country is being destroyed to "protect" Israel. Can a society in the world of today digest such a price that it has exacted from an entire nation? Will this kind of savage and brutal greed leave

---

[1]According to a study by Group Strategic Foresight of India, between 1991-2010, the war has cost the mid-eastern nations a loss of 12 trillion US dollars!

the souls and minds of a society executing it untouched and unaffected? The reason for the criminal silence of US media is due to the fact that it is owned by the very same elite that profits from worldwide plunder in which the US forces are employed. By keeping the US people ignorant of the true reality, and by stirring up their fears perpetually, they keep the US public in line. For the corporate owners the people of the US serve only one purpose - cannon fodder for unending wars of corporate profit. However Nature cannot be deceived and Nature plans better than all the strategists put together.

It was only a few days ago that a news item, which seems to have been consigned to sudden oblivion without comment, mentioned that the US stood at position number 20 in worldwide corruption rankings (Pakistan was 42nd). This should disturb all Americans, but it will disturb them only if they know about it. The media, however, won't let them know! This level of corruption in US is not a revelation for those who have studied the corrupt and corrupting corporate grip on the US society. The scale on which US rulers and the elite are plundering money that belongs to the people of the United States is simply staggering. As Charles Derber has put it so well in his *Corporation Nation* (published in 1998):

> Leaders symbolize what the country stands for. As corruption becomes routine in Washington in both parties, it trickles down as a corrupting influence in everyone's lives. It becomes harder to resist cheating, which up to 70 percent of American college students ad-

mit to, when the president and congressional leaders are being caught with their own hands in the cookie jar.

Democracy is the ultimate casualty, and the sapping of democratic life is the most serious contribution of corporate ascendancy to our spiritual decline. As democracy ebbs, Americans retreat into private cocoons, feeling helpless to make a difference. The sense of powerlessness is not morally ennobling. In a democracy, civic participation and the belief in one's ability to contribute to the common good is the most important guarantor of public morality. When that belief fades, so too does the vision of the common good itself.

The increasing helplessness of the American people has made the corporations even more arrogant and assertive. It has given the corporations greater courage and they have embarked, through their puppet US government, on a program of worldwide aggression, warfare, and plunder. This does not augur well for the US as well as for the rest of the world. In order to protect the US leaders from being tried for war crimes at some future date, the US Congress has silently passed, in 2006, the War Crimes Act, according to which the US leaders cannot be tried for actions that, in standard parlance, are termed war crimes!

Written October 2007 - unpublished

NOTE ADDED

Charles Derber has referred to the withdrawal of Americans into cocoons. In his book *The New Physics: The Route into the Atomic Age*, Armin Hermann writes:

> Since intellectuals practiced political abstinence, the radicals dominated the political scene. The German intellectuals have turned over, "without resistance", said Einstein, "the political government to the bli-nd and the irresponsible". Johannes Stark, Lenard's[2] best friend, gave up his research, as he proudly reported, "and joined ranks of combatants behind Adolf Hitler." In the face of ugly political events the silent majority of physicists locked themselves in their laboratories and studies. The louder the cry on the street, the quieter they became.

It was this passivity of the German intellectual elite that contributed to the rise of German totalitarianism. A similar trend can be seen on US campuses. Professor Thomas Nagy of George Washington University uncovered documents showing deliberate violations of Geneva Convention (see next chapter) by the US government during the first Gulf War. However when he tried to organize a protest during a visit, to his university, of Madeliene Albright, who was Secretary of State during the war, the faculty members of his university did not take part in the protest.

---

[2]Both, Stark and Lenard, were Nobel Laureates in Physics.

Chapter 13

An Open Letter to US Military

Odd that Bush and Cheney are so delighted at war when, during Vietnam, they were both what we used to call draft dodgers.

A World War II veteran

The war is not meant to be won, it is meant to be continuous. Hierarchical society is only possible on the basis of poverty and ignorance. This new version is the past and no different past can ever have existed. In principle the war effort is always planned to keep society on the brink of starvation. The war is waged by the ruling group against its own subjects and its object is not the victory over either Eurasia or East Asia, but to keep the very structure of society intact.

George Orwell 1984

When George Bush assumed office in 2000 after a rigged election, serious US analysts began pointing out that the Bush administration will, very swiftly, take the US into war. At that time many people were not inclined to believe such a prognosis. But the reality of Peak Oil and the breakup of the Soviet Union led the US strategists to adopt the point of view that the US must, within a short window of time available, become totally dominant on the globe and must not allow any adversary to raise its head again. In this context, oil is a two edged sword - the supply of oil ensures that your energy requirements are fulfilled, and that your transport is in motion. If the oil supply is cut off, life in the advanced world in particular will come to a standstill, cities will plunge into darkness and the industry will cease to produce. Therefore, if you can capture or control global oil reserves, you are in a highly advantageous position - you not only ensure your own oil supply, you can, by denying oil, paralyze your enemy completely. This is the real strategic reason behind the Iraq war and behind the US desire to conquer Central Asia and Iran. The eruption of US militarism after 9/11 is all connected with energy concerns and profits for the elite through both war and oil and gas; 9/11 was just the pretext for the wars in which the US is currently engaged.

The US leadership anticipated quick victories in the wars against Iraq and Afghanistan. Contrary to their expectation, they now face serious resistance on military and political fronts in both wars. Despite these serious difficulties the Bush-Cheney cabal has been vociferously threatening Iran. These threats of attacking Iran are motivated by various factors. The unstable situation in Iraq, the rapid depletion of oil resources and Iran's vast oil and gas reserves, and the interests of Israel are pushing US into a situation of possible war with Iran.

In his extremely important book *The Grand Chessboard,* Brzezinski had postulated the capture of Central Asia as the fundamental prerequisite for complete and sustained global hegemony. He had, however, emphasized that Russia, Iran and China must not be allowed to join hands. The US rulers have deviated from this script and in their haste the Bush-Cheney cabal has created conditions in which the three countries appear to be together. This situation has not only exacerbated US military and political difficulties in the region, it has also led to serious opposition to attacking Iran within the US.

Recently, in a signed statement, many important US personalities, including the music legend Willie Nelson, novelist Gore Vidal, the well known ex-Congresswoman Cynthia McKinney, Cindy Sheehan, Col. (Retd) Ann Wright, radio host Thom Hartmann and several others, have called upon the "US Joint Chiefs of Staff and all US military personnel" *not* to attack Iran. The signatories also include two rabbis. They have warned that any pre-emptive attack on Iran would be "illegal" and "criminal". They write:

> We, the citizens of the United States, respect-
> fully urge you, courageous men and women
> of our military, to refuse any order to pre-
> emptively attack Iran, a nation that repre-
> sents no serious or immediate threat to the
> United States. To attack Iran, a sovereign

nation of 70 million people, would be a crime
of the highest magnitude.

The Nuremberg Principles, which are part of
US law, provide that all military personnel
have the obligation not to obey illegal orders.
The *Army Field Manual* 27-10, sec. 609 and
UCMJ, àrt. 92, incorporate this principle.
Art. 92 says: "A general order or regulation
is lawful unless it is contrary to the Constitu-
tion, the law of the United States."

They go on to explain that the US is a signatory to the
UN Charter whose article II Section 4 states: "All members shall refrain in their international relations from the
threat or use of force against the territorial integrity or
political independence of any state...." Any international
treaty that has been ratified by the US automatically
becomes US law and, therefore, by attacking Iran, the
US leadership will violate both, international and the US
law. The letter further contends that the charges leveled
by the Bush administration against Iran have not been
proved. And, even if the charges of developing nuclear
weapons and aiding Iraqis against US were to be proved,
they would still not provide "justification for an illegal
war". The letter further states:

When you joined the military, you took an
oath to defend our Constitution. Following
the orders of your government or superiors
does not relieve you from responsibility under international law. Under the Principles
of International Law recognized in the Char-

ter of the Nuremberg Tribunal, complicity in
the commission of war crime is a crime under
international law.

The letter further points out that any attack on Iran
might prompt a retaliatory attack from "the formidable
Iranian military" on US troops in Iraq leading to possible
casualties or capture of US soldiers. "A US attack against
Iranian nuclear facilities could also mean the deaths, from
radiation poisoning, of tens of thousands of innocent Iranian civilians." The letter argues that the people of Iran
have no control over the actions of the Iranian government and that it would not be right to punish the people
for something in which they are not responsible. The letter further states as a result of bombings people of Iran
are likely to suffer terribly.

> Bombing raids would amount to collective pun-
> ishment, a violation of the Geneva Conven-
> tion, and would surely sow seeds of hatred
> for generations to come. Children make up a
> quarter of Iran's population.

The signatories of the letter are aware of the great difficulties that the US military personnel will face if they
have to conduct themselves in accordance with the law. If
they disobey illegal orders, their superior officers might
court martial them and if they carry out illegal orders
they face the possibility of trial in international tribunals.
They have advised military personnel to consult lawyers
so as to avoid getting into a situation where they may be
forced to act illegally.

We make this plea, also aware that you have no easy options. If you obey an illegal order to participate in an aggressive attack on Iran, you could potentially be charged with war crimes. If you heed our call and disobey an illegal order, you could be charged with crimes including treason. You could be falsely court martialled.

The people of the United States do not want war and are fed up with the rising cost of living. They are restless. The problem is that the "elected" representatives do not consider the people as their masters - their real masters are in the corporate elite, and therefore, they do not pay any attention to what the people want. In the meantime, the US leadership is heading fast towards global war which will lead to horrific destruction. If mankind survives a nuclear Armageddon it will subsist at a primitive level only. It was Einstein who had said:

I do not know how the Third World War will be fought, but I can tell you what they will use in the Fourth - rocks!

Waqt, October 13, 2007

Chapter 14

Geneva Convention and Iraqi Children

There is a hard core of the people in the United States who will not be moved whatever facts you present, from their conviction that this nation means only to do good, and almost always does good, in the world...

Howard Zinn

A war of collective punishment, a war of mass destruction directed at the civilian population of Iraq. The UN, at the insistence of the US, and contrary to international conventions and treaties, has created, in Iraq, a zone of misery and death - with no end in sight... The toll of these sanctions on an entire generation of Iraqi children is incalculable. What are the implications of Iraqi children growing up traumatized by hunger and disease, if they survive at all? How can the deeds of one leader or even an entire government be used to justify this un-

precedented, internationally sanctioned violation of human rights?... The devastating effects continue to harm the environment, agricultural production and health of the Iraqi people significantly.

Nafeez Mosaddeq Ahmed

The problem that the United States faces is that almost all of its invasions violate international law, and sometimes, as in the case of Iraq, in a blatant manner. So how do the political elite and the news media reconcile this contradiction? Simple: They ignore it. It is virtually unthinkable for a mainstream US reporter to even pursue this issue.

John Nichols and **Robert McChesney**

The American ruling elite and those civil and military officers who plan its global strategy are the cruellest people ever to walk this earth. The number of people killed as a result of their planned activity by far exceeds the number of people killed by Hitler, Genghis Khan, and Hulagu Khan. This chain of mass killings is on the increase instead of ending or abating with the passage of time. Recently, on October 17, President Bush has threatened Third World War if Iran is not prevented from going nuclear. If any international agreement or international law stands in the way of these brutal people, they simply trample it under their boots. However, they do take one precaution - they make sure that the truth is concealed from the forthright and kind American public. In this foul game, they have the complete support of the the so called "free" US media. In order to deceive the US public and the world at large, President Bush talks about "human rights" on an almost daily basis. His illustrious father indulged in the same game and so did his predecessor.

US is a signatory of the Geneva Convention but the manner in which this great document has repeatedly been torn to shreds by the US ruling elite is unprecedented. Those who are beating their breasts at a few deaths in Burma have murdered millions of men and millions of children literally. Those crying hoarse at "genocide" in the Sudan are themselves carrying out, unknown to their own people, genocide in cold blood. Article 54 of the Geneva Convention clearly states the following in regard to "protection of victims of international conflicts":

> It is prohibited to attack, destroy, remove, or render useless objects indispensable to the survival of civilian population, such as food-stuffs, crops, livestock, drinking water installations and supplies, and irrigation works, for the specific purpose of denying them for their sustenance value to the civilian population or to the adverse Party, whatever the motive, whether in order to starve out civilians, to cause them to move away, or for any other motive.

It was in 2001 that Thomas Nagy, an American Professor, pointed out the existence of five secret documents of the Defense Intelligence Agency (DIA), which establish beyond any doubt that the "US government intentionally used sanctions against Iraq to degrade the country's water supply after the Gulf War. The United States knew the cost that civilian Iraqis, mostly children, would pay, and it went ahead anyway." In 2001 the UN estimated that at least half a million (500,000) Iraqi *children* had died as a result of these sanctions. At least four of these five documents of the DIA can be located on the web even today.

The DIA documents date between January 22, 1991 and November 15, 1991. These documents bring to light the shocking fact that the Pentagon was continuously assessing the spread of disease among the Iraqi population as a result of the systematic degradation of the drinking water system and the sanctions on medicine and despite being fully aware of the fatal effect of these on children and senior citizens, continued this silent murder with great satisfaction. In fact the precise objective of these restrictions and the degradation of the drinking water system was increase in Iraqi civilian fatalities. When several years later an American journalist asked the Foreign Secretary during the Gulf War, Madeleine Albright, if the US government ever regretted such brutality she responded in the following words *"It was worth it"*! These words shall, forever live in infamy. This reply is reminiscent of Nazis - except that Madeleine Albright is Jewish! In fact, one writer has commented that the sentiments of Nazis at the murder of Jews were identical to those of Madeleine Albright at the murder of Iraqi children.

The first DIA document, dated January 22, 1991, was written during the Gulf War. After noting that on account of sanctions Iraq was having difficulties in obtaining chemicals, it goes on:

Failing to secure supplies will result in a shortage of pure drinking water for much of the
population. This could lead to increased inci-
dences, if not epidemics, of disease and to certain water-dependent industries becoming incapacitated including petrochemicals, fertil-
izers, petroleum refining, electronics, pharm-
aceuticals, food processing, textiles, concrete
construction and thermal power plants. Iraq's
overall water treatment capability will suffer
a slow decline, rather than a precipitous halt,
as dwindling supplies and cannibalized parts
are located at higher priority locations...
Iraq will suffer increasing shortages of purified
water because of the lack of required chemicals and desalinization membranes.

After giving a survey of Iraq's water resources and related matters the report concludes "Full degradation of
the water treatment system will take at least another six
months."

The next report, dated February 21, 1991 states:

For severe outbreaks to develop, a protracted
war or more extensive collateral damage will
have to occur. However conditions are favorable for communicable disease outbreaks,
particularly in major urban areas affected by
coalition bombing.

Thus almost a month after the first report the medical
experts working for DIA had pointed out that condi-

tions were ripe for "major disease outbreaks". The report lists the following "likely diseases in the next 60-90 days in descending order" - diarrheal diseases (particularly children), acute respiratory illnesses (colds and influenza), typhoid, hepatitis A (particularly children), measles, diphtheria, and pertussis (particularly children), meningitis, including meningococcal (particularly children), cholera (possible, but less likely). This is followed up by a list of most likely disease outbreaks in the 90-180 day period where again children are the most susceptible group. A report dated March 15, 1991, notes that "conditions in Baghdad remain favorable for communicable disease outbreaks" despite government efforts. In a report filed in May 1991 the outbreak of diseases in refugee camps is noted and it is predicted that communicable diseases will further increase owing to unclean water and the failure to maintain a clean environment. A June 1991 report points out that the medical system in Iraq has disintegrated and that medical facilities have been plundered and all important medicines are in great shortage.

In a write up in the June 23, 1991 issue of *Washington Post*, the writer states that a Pentagon officer was queried that the destruction of Iraq's electric power generation and supply system will lead to its economic bankruptcy. The reply of the officer is most revealing - he is reported to have said that this destruction will affect the water and sewerage systems of Iraq and that the US was not helping the people of Iraq but was enhancing the effect (i.e., loss of life) by a systematic and planned bombing of installations in conjunction with sanctions! This also establishes that the US was deliberately trying to increase the incidence of disease among Iraqi population. Some of the aforementioned reports expressed one concern and that was that the Iraqi government might try to exploit the deaths of children politically against the US! The death of children in itself was of no concern to the Bush cabal just as the deaths of Jews were of no concern to the Hitler cabal.

This was the state of affairs in 2001. Professor Nagy writes that these DIA documents establish that the US government was fully aware that sanctions against Iraq will lead to the degradation of the clean water supply system resulting in the outbreak of diseases and high increase in child mortality. No one should violate the Geneva Convention. As Professor Nagy wrote:

> But that is precisely what the U.S. government did, with malice aforethought. It "destroyed, removed, or rendered useless" Iraq's "drinking water installations and supplies". The sanctions, imposed for a decade, largely on the insistence of the United States, constitute a violation of the Geneva Convention.

In 2004 the infamous corporation Bechtel was awarded the contract for rebuilding the clean water supply system of Iraq! Recently, in August 2007, outbreak of cholera was reported in Northern Iraq. An October 3, 2007, update of WHO reveals that the disease has now affected nine provinces of Iraq and over 30,000 people have been affected. If the rate of 5,000 child deaths per month up to 2001 is extended to 2007 then another 360,000 children may have died. The demand for prosecuting the US leaders for violation of Geneva Convention must be raised worldwide, in every country and continent, regardless of race, color or religion. What is happening to Iraqi children today may happen to children of any country tomorrow.

Waqt, October 22, 2007

Chapter 15

The Billionaires

In Moscow in March 2001, attending an international economic conference... I was saddened to hear the Russian writers and business people in Moscow tell me that the population of Russia had shrunk from an estimated high of around 160 million people in 1991 to 145 million in a decade; that the life expectancy of a male had dropped in 2000 to around 48 years; that the population was expected to drop to 130 million by 2030; and that in nearby Republic of Moldavia, pieces of human cadaver were being sold in stores as meat.

Michael Ruppert
Crossing the Rubicon

By 1920 Morgan partner Thomas W.Lamont noted with obvious satisfaction that, as a result of the four years of war and global devastation, "the national debts of the world have increased by $ 210,000,000,000 or about 475 percent in the last six years, and as a natural consequence,

the variety of government bonds and the number of investors in them have been greatly multiplied."
William Engdahl
*A Century of War: Anglo-American
Oil Politics and the New World Order*

We implore, Most Merciful One, just as You turned Lot's wife into a pillar of salt, that You turn - all - the rich -into paupers and homeless, wiping out their entire savings, assets and mutual funds. Remove them from positions of power, and yea, may they walk through the valley and into the darkness of a welfare office. Condemn them to a life of flipping burgers and dodging bill collectors. Let them hear the wailing of the innocents as they sit in the middle seat of row number 43 in coach and let them feel the gnashing of teeth that are abscessed and rotted like the 108 million who have no dental coverage.
Michael Moore
A Prayer to Afflict the Comfortable
in his book *Stupid White Men*

There is absolutely no doubt that the gap between the rich and the poor is increasing by the day. This disturbing trend is a consequence of the policies adopted in the US in the past quarter century, the breakup of the USSR and the changes in China's economic policies. The unbridled chariot of imperial capitalism is trampling mankind under its feet. The grip of the superrich on this globe has become more comprehensive and firm than ever before in the history of mankind. The great champions of democracy, the "elected" representatives of the

15. The Billionaires

US Congress and the "elected" government of the US itself, are elected through corporate money and work for
the protection of corporate interests. The kindhearted
American public had voted the Democratic Party into
the Congress in recent elections because they wanted an
end to the wars abroad and wanted the US troops to
come home. However, the "elected" representatives have
joined hands with the superrich who funded them and
have abandoned those who voted them into office. This
is precisely the reason why in a recent Zogby survey, 89%
of the people expressed dissatisfaction with the Congress.
If 89% of the people are dissatisfied with the "elected"
representatives, one is led to question the claim of democracy.

A few months go the *Forbes* magazine published the
most recent list of billionaires of the entire world. The
number of billionaires has risen from 793 in 2006 to 943
in 2007. This is an approximately 35% increase in the
population of billionaires in one year. The largest number of billionaires is in the US - their number stands at
415. The second position is occupied by Germany which
has 55 billionaires closely followed by Russia where now
53 billionaires have emerged. In Asia, the largest number of billionaires are to be found in India which has 35
billionaires followed by China where, in a short span of
time, 20 brand new billionaires have emerged. Of the
38 Latin American billionaires, 30 reside in Brazil and
Mexico. The *Forbes* magazine did not mention any Pakistani billionaires probably because Pakistani billionaires
do not declare their real wealth. (It was almost a decade
ago that the *Wall Street Journal* had published a list of

thirteen Pakistanis who had *at least* one billion dollars in their foreign accounts.)

The 943 billionaires mentioned in the *Forbes* list own, between themselves, $3500 billion. While the billionaires are on the rise, 55% of mankind is eking out an existence in extreme poverty. In the past years the income of three billion people has either fallen or has stood still. The less than one thousand billionaires together have more money than the combined earnings of these three billion people! The emergence of Russian billionaires is a result of fraud, murder, deception and absolutely callous plunder of national wealth. Before 9/11, more than $300 billion at least were plundered and transferred out of Russia, breaking its back economically. Therefore when, in 2002, the US attacked Afghanistan, Russia was too weak economically to respond to US presence in its backyard. In fact, thoughtful writers have expressed the view that the US agencies were involved in the plunder of Russia and the purpose was to weaken Russia to an extent where it would not be able to respond to American aggression.

Wherever the billionaires advance, the shadows of suffering and poverty lengthen. Two-thirds of Latin Americans are living in extreme poverty and misery. They have no access to clean drinking water and basic medicine. The global advance of billionaires is being propelled by the political control of US government by the American billionaires. In the US things have come to such a pass that on the one hand the US government is giving one tax relief after another to the rich, it is, on the other hand, transferring the burden of war to the shoulders of the low income groups. According to figures released recently by the US Internal Revenue Service, at least $300-400 billion is concealed annually from the tax authorities. If this amount is spread over all the years starting from the 1980s, one may easily infer that trillions of dollars of black money is in the hands of a few Americans.

In an analysis, James Petras has pointed out that the emergence of new billionaires in various countries was a three phase process. In the first phase, the billionaires to be, successfully bribed government officials to win government contracts, tax exemptions and government support and protection against foreign competitors. In the second phase, as a consequence of these "liberalization" measures, they were able to purchase government assets at a very cheap rate, thereby ensuring profits for themselves. The so-called "privatization" policies were in reality a political sale comprising of four elements - cheap rates, selection of certain preferred buyers, illegal shares for those selling off national property and the promotion of a certain ideology. National banks, power production units, telecommunications, transport and mineral wealth were handed over at throwaway prices in the name of paying off government debts. This was the stage when millionaires were transformed into billionaires. In Latin America, these advances were made through corruption, and in Russia, through murder and gang warfare. In the third phase, the billionaires not only consolidated their empires, but also transferred their wealth abroad through different means. Through mobile phones, telecom, and similar so-called goods of public use and through inflated prices, these newly rich added more to their newly acquired billions. As Petras points out, these billionaires have brought great poverty and a fall in the standard of living of ordinary people. These billionaires have destroyed societies to accumulate their wealth. He points out that the anger of the White House against Hugo Chavez of Venezuela stems from Chavez's policies that run counter to what the US billionaires want. He is nationalizing energy and other public utility business and has also has taken over large estates. Chavez is not just challenging American hegemony - he is "reversing policies that create billionaires and mass poverty". That is what makes Washington, and the billionaires it serves, so mad.

Waqt, October 27, 2007

Chapter 16

Torture and the Bush Regime

The size of a lie is a definite factor in causing it to be believed, for the vast masses of the nation are in the depths of their hearts more easily deceived than they are consciously and intentionally bad. The primitive simplicity of their minds renders them a more easy prey to a big lie than a small one, for they themselves often tell lies but would be ashamed to tell a big one.
Adolf Hitler *Mein Kampf*

This [the US Constitution] is likely to be administered for a course of years and then end in despotism... when the people become so corrupted as to need despotic government, being incapable of any other.
Benjamin Franklin

A new book called "Administration of Torture", by two

114

ACLU attorneys, contains evidence (from FOIA requests) from over 100,000 newly released documents. It reveals how US military commanders carried out abuse and torture under orders from their superiors on scores of prisoners. The book quotes Major General Michael Dunlavey who had DOD responsibility for interrogation of "suspected terrorists". He and Guantanamo commander General Geoffrey Miller both told the FBI they got their "marching orders" from Donald Rumsfeld to use harsh methods at Guantanamo that presumably were meant for all other US-run torture prisons as well. It was also revealed that Rumsfeld was "personally involved" in over-seeing the torture-interrogation of Mohammad al Qahtani. He was falsely accused of being the 20th 9/11 hijacker, confessed under torture, and then retracted the testimony later as completely untrue.

Stephen Lendman

Power is not a means, it is an end. One does not establish a dictatorship in order to safeguard a revolution; one makes the revolution in order to establish the dictatorship. The object of persecution is persecution. The object of torture is torture. The object of power is power.

George Orwell

The British novelist George Orwell was an extraordinary writer. His everlasting satire on Communism, *Animal Farm*, comprised a mere one hundred pages or so. He foresaw very clearly the rise of totalitarian trends in industrial societies. About sixty years ago, he wrote a famed novel with the simple title *1984*. In this novel, the world was divided among three major powers, one of these named Oceania. In order to maintain control over its population, the leaders of Oceania had a system for keeping a watch on every citizen. George Orwell wrote:

> And in the general hardening of outlook that set in ··· practices which had been abandoned - imprisonment without trial, the use of war prisoners as slaves, public executions, torture to extract confessions ··· and the deportation of whole populations - not only became common again, but were tolerated and even defended by people who considered themselves enlightened and progressive.

Present day United States of America is fast becoming a realization of Oceania. Many aspects of the society quoted above can now be seen clearly in the US, whereas secret preparations for realizing the remaining aspects are going on, and have been going on secretly for years. Announcements of *Orange Alert* and *Red Alert* can now be heard frequently at US airports. These announcements keep the US public in a state of perpetual fear and anxiety and remind them of unknown and unseen enemies amidst them. Their postal correspondence, telephone calls and emails are under constant surveillance by agencies. Now, under the law, any one can be interned indefinitely if the President of the US so desires. Similarly, under Presidential orders, torture has also been allowed.

At a hurriedly called press conference in the White House in the first week of October 2007), President Bush announced: "This Government does not torture people."

He also claimed that the "interrogation methods" that have been allowed were "fully disclosed to appropriate members of the US Congress". In other words, these interrogation methods have been concealed from the vast majority of Congress members as well as the people of USA. Mr. Bush further stated that the US public expected that the government will protect them from further attacks. He thus held, in a sense, the people responsible for allowing the new interrogation methods because he followed it by introducing a new phrase - he said that the people of the US wanted "actionable intelligence". The implication of course was that this expectation of the people required new techniques of interrogation. He also went on to say, "These are highly trained professionals questioning these extremists and terrorists."

The claim by President Bush that the US Government does not torture people is a blatant lie. Actually, the US Government has redefined torture. According to President Bush's new definition, until and unless your methods render some organ non-functional, the methods will not constitute torture! Thus if beating you leads to a broken arm then it will be torture; otherwise not. Similarly, if your nose bleeds profusely under punches from your interrogator it will not constitute torture unless your bone is broken! Or your eye may be blue as a result of beatings but as long as the eye can perform its function this will not constitute torture. It is a reflection on the state of affairs in the United States, and on the mental state of the Congress, the courts and the government, that physical violence on prisoners or detainees will be acceptable and torture will not be considered torture by redefinition!

Those emerging from Guantanamo, or other secret prisons maintained worldwide by US authorities, complained of having been subjected to sleep deprivation, of having been denied the light of the day for prolonged periods, or of being forced naked into painful postures in freezing temperatures or of being confined to suffocating rooms. Certainly none of these "techniques" meet the Bush definition of torture. The case of Jose Padilla is heart rending. He was confined to a 7×9 square feet room, given mind altering drugs, beaten, denied a lawyer for two years, treated so badly that he became mentally incapacitated. On top of it no charges were brought up against him and he was detained merely on suspicion. All this does not constitute torture by Mr. Bush's new definition. Mr. Bush, who evaded the Vietnam war through the influence of his family connections, who was brought up on a fortune built significantly by his forefathers through black money, should try a drop of his own medicine! Jose Padilla was a US citizen and Mr. Bush should be ashamed. But he is not!

Under a planned strategy, the super billionaires of US, and their counterparts elsewhere, are fast transforming this globe into a vast prison for mankind. There is nowhere to run and nowhere to hide from their onslaught. The only way out is to fight them politically. If the people of the US and the rest of the mankind do not join hands, they will be completely enslaved by this cabal in a short span of time. The demand for prosecuting US leaders for war crimes and crimes against humanity must be raised from every country, regardless of color, creed or race.

The US government is aided and abetted by its "allied" governments. The involvement of the Australian government and many European governments in this filthy game, on grounds of prejudice, fear of or favor from US, is also beyond doubt. Columns in newspapers are not enough to pen down the horrific activities being carried out by "civilized" allies unknown to their people, particularly the people of USA. Whose names should one bring up for it are not only the "civilized" allies. To paraphrase an Urdu poet:

After being pierced by an arrow, I looked towards my hideout and ran into my own "friends".

Waqt, October 30, 2007

119

Chapter 17

The Darfur Problem

It is the function of CIA to keep the world unstable.
John Stockwell, a former CIA official

This war was not an issue of corporate greed. It was about power, and geopolitical power above all... The occupation of the oil fields of Iraq, the war in Kosovo and the Balkans, endless civil wars in Africa, financial crises across Asia, the dramatic collapse of the Soviet Union and the subsequent emergence of a Russian oligarchy, blessed by the International Monetary Fund and by Washington, all assumed coherence in a world where geopolitics, power and control dictated relations.
William Engdahl in *A Century of War: Anglo-American Oil Politics and the New World Order*

The US and British governments have been asserting for the past several years that the Sudanese government is perpetrating genocide in the western province of Darfur. In 2002, the US Congress passed the *Sudan Peace Act* which formally allowed for US intervention in "areas of Sudan not controlled by the Government of Sudan." Hostilities in Darfur erupted soon after, in the year 2003. Since then, the Western media, which for all practical purposes is "global" media, has been propagating the official genocide line faithfully. Is the civil war in Sudan really genocide?

According to the UN, WHO and the French NGO Médecins Sans Frontières, the fighting in Darfur is not genocide. The Sudanese government vehemently denies charges of genocide. Why then is the US-British coalition so vociferously pursuing the "genocide" line? What is the Darfur problem and why is the US so keenly interested in it, the same US which has, according to a recent survey, killed over 1.2 million Iraqis since 2003, wounding another one million and rendering about four million homeless? This is, in addition, to one and-a-half million Iraqis, including 500,000 children, killed between the first Gulf War and 2003 as a result of US backed embargo on medicine and other items.

Sudan is Africa's largest country area-wise. It has an area of 9,67,500 square miles which is 3.2 times the size of Pakistan. However, Sudan has a population of only 35 million, almost a fifth of Pakistan's population. Seventy percent of Sudanese are Muslims, twenty five percent animist and five percent Christians. The Darfur region is located in the West of Sudan bordering Chad. The Darfur province is about a fifth of Sudan's total area, approximately the size of France, but has a population estimated variously between 6 to 7 million only. The people of Darfur are ethnically the same as the bulk of Sudanese population. They speak Arabic and, like the mainstream Sudanese population, are Sunni Muslims. A Congressional Research Service brief (updated September 2004) prepared for the US Congress by Ted Dagne states:

> Darfur is home to an estimated 7 million people and has more than 30 ethnic groups, although these groups fall into two major categories: African and Arab. Both communities are Muslim and years of intermarriage has made racial distinction impossible.

This lack of racial distinction, acknowledged in an official US document, is sufficient to destroy the argument of genocide in Darfur. The South of Sudan, on the other hand, is populated by tribes that are predominantly Christian or animistic in their beliefs. Many of these do not speak Arabic.

Sudan is rich in natural resources. It has rich oil and gas reserves. Sudan has huge uranium deposits and the fourth largest deposits of copper in the world. It was found some years ago that the Darfur region has enormous untapped oil reserves that are comparable to those of Saudi Arabia if not more. Excluding the Darfur reserves, Saudi Arabia possesses 25% of the known global oil deposits. In a world that is heading fast towards oil depletion, this is news of the highest importance. And the world's largest consumer of oil is, by far, the United States of America. It is, therefore, no surprise that the US is so keenly interested in Darfur. To quote John Bart

Gerald:

> If the nations of the world agreed that a veri-
> fiable genocide were occurring, it would allow
> US to occupy Sudan and gain its assets. Th-
> ere is profit for the US in deciding that Su-
> dan's government has committed genocide.

Darfur and the entire region has had a serious water problem that has, for generations, been a source of unending conflict among various sections of the Darfur population. In particular, the settled and nomadic tribes
have fought over water for a long time. In November
2004, Brian Smith wrote: "Water is strategically important, given that the blue Nile and white Nile meet in
Sudan and constitute the lifeline of Egypt immediately
north. Recent pressure from Anglo-American interests
led Ethiopia, Kenya, Uganda and Tanzania to question
the old Nile treaties with Egypt, which has extensive interests in Sudan." The discovery this year of a mega-lake
under northern Darfur has made the Darfur region even
more valuable. A "1000 wells for Darfur" initiative was
recently agreed upon between President al-Bashir and
Egyptian born remote sensing expert Farouk El-Baz who
works at Boston University. However, it remains to be
seen how this project develops, if at all, and how the US
will exploit this find.

Oil was discovered in Sudan in 1978. In 1983, rebellion
in Southern Sudan broke out. The rebellion was led by
John Garang who, to quote Jay Janson, received "military training at the infamous Fort Benning, Georgia"
where the US Army Command College is located. Ac-

cording to the Federation of American Scientists, "The US government decided, in 1996, to send nearly 20 million dollars of military equipment through the frontline states of Ethiopia, Eriteria and Uganda to help the Sudanese opposition overthrow the Khartoum regime." John Garang led a so-called Sudanese Peoples Liberation Army and while the US continuously decried the abuse of human rights by the Khartoum regime, it kept mum about the abuses committed by John Garang in the areas that he controlled. According to a BBC report, "John Garang did not tolerate dissent and anyone who disagreed with him was either imprisoned or killed." John Garang was involved in training the rebels of Darfur.

In June 2006, Sarah Flounders wrote:

> US imperialism is heavily involved in the entire region. Chad, which is directly west of Darfur, last year participated in a US-organized military exercise that, according to US Defense Department, was the largest in Africa since World War II. Chad is a former French colony and both French and US forces are heavily involved in funding, training and equipping the army of its military ruler, Idriss Deby, who has supported rebel groups in Darfur.

According to a Jerusalem Post report of April 27, 2006 "US Jews Leading Darfur Rally Planning". This rally involved a host of other organizations allied with Zioinsts, particulary those related to Evangelical Christians. The prominent coverage given by US media to a rally (held April 30, 2006) that involved only 5000-7000 people contrasts with the meager coverage given by the same media to anti-war rallies involving hundreds of thousands of US citizens. This in itself indicates backing by the US establishment to mobilizing public opinion against the Khartoum regime. In fact, in November 1999 President Clinton signed a Bill authorizing funds to John Garang's army. Israel's Mossad has also been involved in supplying arms to rebels.

In 2005, hemmed in from three sides by proxies encouraged, trained and funded by US, the Khartoum regime signed a peace deal with the South allowing the US proxy John Garang to become first Vice President of Sudan. Garang died soon afterwards in a plane crash. This agreement gave concessions to the South allowing it to reclaim land and sell oil from that land. It is, therefore, clear that the conflict with the South had nothing to do with religion - it had to do with oil. This is equally true of the Darfur conflict.

Currently, China has agreements with Sudan and is the major importer of Sudanese oil. The US companies are essentially unable to do oil business with Sudan due to sanctions imposed by the US government. The US has been relentlessly pressuring Sudan for accepting a UN force. However, the Sudanese government is well aware that the UN will just be a cover for landing US and British troops on Sudanese soil with the object of overthrowing the Khartoum regime. It has, therefore, resisted. In fact, when US and UK forced a resolution through the UN Security Council in 2006 allowing for UN troops in Sudan, the Khartoum regime openly declared that it will attack any forces that attempted to land in Sudan. Instead the Sudanese government has allowed the African Union forces to be stationed there.

John Bart Gerald states:

> Over four million Sudanese became displaced according to a 1999 estimate and the subsequent diminished figures suggest the accounts are juggled. In the South of Sudan alone two million have died from war and starvation brought about by a rebellion and guerilla war.

This immense tragedy has been brought about by corporate US. As Michael Ruppert puts it:

> It is in the nature of CIA that if it finds a difference of the size of a pinhole, it widens it into an eight lane highway and keeps dressing it.

He also points out that the relocation of US and NATO forces has taken place only into regions which are rich in oil and gas, or which lie along routes from where oil and gas has to pass to reach the West. By capturing all major oil and gas fields in the world, the US will not only fulfill its energy requirements, it will, by denying these to its imagined enemies, cripple them completely. Therein lies the significance of the Darfur problem, the Afghan and Iraq wars and the expected Iran war.

The Nation, October 31, 2007

Chapter 18

The Decay of US Courts

*And in the general hardening of outlook that set in ...
practices which had been abandoned - imprisonment without trail, the use of war prisoners as slaves, public exe-
cutions, torture to extract confessions ··· and the deportation of whole populations - not only became common
again, but were tolerated and even defended by people who
considered themselves enlightened and progressive.*
                              George Orwell *1984*

*False flag terror attacks, a fake war on terrorism, rou-
tine political murders, stolen elections, and Republican
traffic in pedophilia remain causes for outrage and defiance, but they can no longer be useful avenues to justice:
the legal system is broken. It is broken for reasons greater
than what used to be called corruption. And it cannot be
fixed when a world war and unprecedented economic and*

ecological collapse are smashing down every wall between humanity and the unthinkable.
Michael Ruppert in *GlobalCorp* 2005

The October 2006 Military Commissions Act followed, appropriately called "torture authorization act". It gives the administration extraordinary unconstitutional powers to detain, interrogate and prosecute alleged terror suspects and anyone thought to be their supporters. The law lets the President designate anyone in the world an "unlawful enemy combatant", without corroborating evidence, and order they be arrested and incarcerated indefinitely in military prison outside the criminal justice system without habeas and without due process rights. US citizens aren't exempt. We're all "enemy combatants" under this law. Anyone charged under it loses all constitutionally protected rights and can be subjected to cruel and unusual punishment including torture.
Stephen Lendman

The US constitution is one of the greatest documents of human history. It places human rights and individual liberties on the highest pedestal. The founding fathers of the US, the architects of the constitution, always feared that US governments may, one day, turn hostile to the freedoms allowed for the citizenry by the constitution. The American constitution does not permit detention without cause - the famous writ of habeas corpus is enshrined in it. During the American Civil War, a supporter of the Southern states named Merryman was arrested in May 1861. Roger Tanney, the Chief Justice of the US Supreme

Court at the time, ordered that charges be brought up against Merryman, failing which he must be set free - to hold him without charges would be unconstitutional. Despite the fact that Lincoln was a lawyer, he suspended the writ of habeas corpus through a Presidential order, and ordered his general to arrest Merryman. When General Caldwater expressed his reservations on the matter, Lincoln left it to Caldwater's discretion. General Caldwater decided not to arrest Merryman and Lincoln too did not insist. After Lincoln's death, the US Supreme Court passed a historic judgement on the issue of the writ of habeas corpus.

The Constitution of the United States is a law for rulers and people equally in war and peace, and covers with the shield of its protection all classes of men, at all times, and under all circumstances. No doctrine, involving more pernicious consequences, was ever invented by the wit of man than that any of its provisions can be suspended during any of the great exigencies of government.

This is the famous judgement Ex parte Milligan U.S. 2 (1866). Such a judgement was passed when the US was a country preparing for a role of leadership in world affairs and was studded with courts, judges, generals and presidents of great stature. As remarked by someone, the US Supreme Court was then a real Supreme Court. All this is now a thing of the past.

The decline of integrity in the US no longer afflicts

the so-called elected representatives and media; it has touched the courts too and is spreading fast. In recent years US courts have given decisions that remind one of Third World courts. In particular, cases where wrongdoing on part of US government or its agencies is involved, the courts seem to go with the government. One of the crutches held by the US authorities goes by the name of State Secrets Privilege. Instead of being forthright that wrongdoing has been committed, the US courts have permitted wrongdoing by taking refuge behind this Privilege. This attitude of the courts has strengthened the tendency of the US government to commit wrongdoing and has emboldened it to the extent of disregarding the constitution.

One example of the foregoing is the case of Khalid Al Masri. Al Masri is a German citizen of Lebanese origin and he was picked up in 2003 while vacationing in Macedonia on the grounds that his namesake was an important Al Qaeda member. He was handed over to US authorities in 2004 who not only kept him in confinement but abused him sexually. He was chained eaglespread to the floor of a plane and transported to Afghanistan where he was transferred to a torture cell controlled by the US. Al Masri was not allowed access to a lawyer for two years! Nor was he permitted to talk to anyone. When Al Masri went on hunger strike the US authorities panicked - after all he was a German citizen and the Americans knew he was innocent. He was taken to Albania and released on an abandoned road! Has the world now become one vast prison, one vast hive of torture cells in US control?

In December 2005, Al Masri filed a case in a US District Court against the Homeland Security Chief George

Tenet. However, in May 2006 the District Judge accepted the stance of the US government that if the case were allowed to continue and judicial investigations carried out, they might lead to the revelation of state secrets. What are "state secrets" here? Abduction of innocent people, torturing them, preventing access to lawyers for years, preventing access to families for years, transporting them illegally from one country to another, from one torture cell to another hell hole? Are these the state secrets that will threaten US Security once brought to light?

In March 2007, even the Supreme Court rejected Al Masri's appeal. Now, in October 2007, US Supreme Court has driven the last nail in the coffin of rule of law - it has simply refused to hear Al Masri's case without giving any remarks! This attitude of the US Supreme Court has dealt a severe blow to its prestige in judicial and legal circles worldwide. But it appears that the US political and judicial leadership does not really care anymore about what the world thinks of them. In a sense the US Supreme Court has refused to touch the US government even when it indulges in outright torture and blatant and flagrant violation of human rights. Does that remind one of George Orwell?

Col Stephen Abraham has strongly criticized the manner in which prisoners at Guantanamo are being prosecuted. In a written affidavit, he has stated that whenever the results of prosecution are not to the liking of the officers, they get upset and convey to those carrying out the prosecution that their conclusions are wrong! The superior officers seem to think that if we conclude that a prisoner at Guantanamo is innocent, then we have surely made a mistake somewhere. Therefore, instead of setting him free we must reinvestigate and prosecute anew. A major of the US army who has refused to divulge his name out of fear, has stated that many innocent people have been confined in Guantanamo. For instance, a Sudanese hospital administrator named Adil Hammad has been in Guantanamo for the past five years despite having no connection whatsoever with Al Qaeda. He has stated that whenever an investigator concludes that a particular prisoner is not involved in fighting against America, the superior officers change the outcome of the investigation. This is the height of injustice. Those who criticized the Soviet concentration camps have today interned innocent people indefinitely. The Bush cabal has revived memories of Stalin.

The US Supreme Court has allowed the US government to wield its dagger under the cloak of state security. The Supreme Court seems oblivious to the fact that the US rulers, drunk with power, stand completely naked before the world. They have not even bothered to cover themselves with a fig leaf!

Waqt, November 2, 2007

Chapter 19

Cheney and 9/11

It's not just private, èlite control over the legal system, nor private evasion of the rule of law. It's a crisis-induced transition from a society with a deeply compromised legal system to a society where force and surveillance completely supplant that system. Although the apparatus is about terrorism, the real one is about energy scarcity.

The United States is the greatest threat to world peace, and has been for a long time, and not merely because it is a superpower. Equally important, the United States is also far more disposed to use its power than any other powerful nation currently is. Though Americans are culturally and emotionally blind to the fact, the mere intrusion of US power is, in and of itself, destabilizing.
T. D. Allman

Oil supplies are finite and will soon be controlled by a handful of nations; the invasion of Iraq and the control of its pipelines will do little to change that. One can only

hope that an informed electorate and its principled repre-
sentatives will realize that the facts do matter, and that
nature - not military might - will soon dictate the ulti-
mate availability of petroleum.

Alfred Cavallo

There is no free lunch for the creature comforts delivered
by the corporation. The ravaging of nature, the erosion
of economic security, the destabilization of the family, the
commercialization of all human relationships, the corrup-
tion of democracy, and the dissipation of spiritual mean-
ing in the face of rampant materialism - these are all part
of the cost of the corporate system as we know it. And
they add up to a very high price to pay for the bounty of
the great American shopping mall.

Charler Derber *Corporation Nation*

Ideology - that is what gives devildoing its long sought
justification and gives the evildoer the necessary steadfast-
ness and determination. That is the social theory which
helps to make his acts seem good instead of bad in his
own and others' eyes, so that he won't hear reproaches
and curses but will receive praises and honors.

Alexander Solzhenitsyn

Whenever US governments wish to shove the US into a
great war, its agencies, through planned effort, arrange
for incidents that lead to the loss of innocent American
lives. The resulting anger generated in the US public,
is diverted against the "enemy". Such incidents have to
be arranged because the American public abhors war and

predominantly favors peace. The US entry in both World Wars involved the staging of such incidents. That is why many thoughtful Americans and other people worldwide believe that 9/11 may be a similar kind of planned incident. The internet has a lot of material on this subject. In fact, in July 2002, I had completed editing a 700 page book on 9/11 which, although it had been composed, was withdrawn by the publisher at the last moment on account of some pressures.

The book on 9/11 that has sold the most copies was written by Michael Ruppert - *Crossing the Rubicon:The Decline of the American Empire at the End of the Age of Oil*. This 675 page book was published in the last part of 2004. However, prior to the publication of this book, Ruppert edited a web newsletter *From the Wilderness* (FTW). In this newsletter, he presented his deep and lucid analysis of 9/11. His life was endangered on account of his work and several attempts on his life were made as a result of which he left USA in 2006, fearing that the agencies might kill him. Soon after his newsletter FTW also ceased.

Michael Ruppert has argued that the deaths that occurred in 9/11 were the result of the planning of the US Secret Service and the CIA. According to him, planning for 9/11 started during the Clinton era. Therefore, these deaths constitute *murder*. He argues that in order to establish murder the law requires three things - did the suspect possess the "means, motive, and opportunity to commit the crime." He argues that it was only the US government that possessed the means, motive and opportunity to carry out 9/11. Ruppert says:

In the end the only "suspects" found to meet all of these criteria will not be al Qaeda and Osama bin Laden. They will instead be a group of people working within certain government agencies, including the White House, for the benefit of major financial interests within the United States and other countries. This group will specifically include parts of the administration of George W. Bush and before it, the administration of William Jefferson Clinton. However the only possible unifying thread will be the intelligence community and, in particular, the United States Secret Service and the Central Intelligence Agency.

In fact, a few months before 9/11 Dick Cheney was, through a Presidential Order, placed at head of a chain of command connected to the Secret Service. Agencies under his control had at their disposal, all the means that enabled them to watch the movement of the hijacked planes all the time, and to take action in time. Under the law, the US Secret Service is empowered to assume control of the US Supreme Command in a national emergency. It is also established that from 8.15 AM (at most 8.45 AM) onwards the Secret Service was playing its role in decision making. The first plane was hijacked at 8.15 AM.

The real motive behind 9/11 was the rapid depletion of global oil fields and Cheney was well aware of this situation, at least from 1999 onwards, if not before.

In November 1999, Cheney delivered a crucial, but little
known speech, before the London Institute of Petroleum.
In this speech Cheney gave a deep analysis of the global
oil situation. He said that in order to survive in the oil
business you have to continually find new oil reserves. He
stated that in the early 1990s there was an expectation
that "significant amounts of world's new resources would
come from Soviet Union and China." He further stated:

> Oil is unique in that it is so strategic in na-
> ture. We are not talking about soapflakes or
> leisurewear here. Energy is truly fundamental
> to the world's economy. The Gulf war was a
> reflection of that reality. It is the basic, fun-
> damental building block of the world's econ-
> omy ··· Our constituency is not just oilmen
> from Louisiana or Texas, but software writers
> in Massachusetts and especially steel produc-
> ers in Pennsylvania ···
> Well the end of the oil era is not here yet, but
> changes are afoot, and the industry must be
> ready to adapt to the new century and to the
> transformations that lie ahead ···

The opportunity for 9/11 arose because the air force was
conducting war games in which hypothetical events similar to 9/11 were to be dealt with. The agencies used this
cover to carry out the real 9/11. Pilots who had been
training for the exercise for a long time could not distinguish between the simulated events and the real 9/11. In
fact, false blips were introduced on radar screens of the
Federal Aviation Authority to create confusion, thereby

making it impossible to tell the real from the fake.

Michael Ruppert's book is replete with evidence and proofs in favor of the hypothesis stated at the outset. He has charged Dick Cheney by name, and with proofs, with responsibility of the 9/11 murders. Probably the US courts do not have *suo moto* powers, or has the US Supreme Court degenerated to the level of Third World courts? For the past few months it is being reported that Dick Cheney is advocating an attack on Iran. After 9/11, Dick Cheney clearly stated that the war against "terrorism" "will not end in our lifetimes". He has also expressed the apprehension that "terrorists" armed with nuclear weapons might attack the USA. Parallel to all these, dictatorial laws are being passed in the US. Is it because the criminal gang feels that as long as the US is in a state of war, the people will not be able to pay attention to its crimes and no case will be filed against them?

Waqt, November 6, 2007

Chapter 20

Canadian Sovereignty?

The corporations don't have to lobby the government any more. They are the government.
Jim Hightower
While free markets tend to democratize a society, unfettered capitalism leads invariably to corporate control of government.
Robert Kennedy Jr
The World is at the crossroads of the most serious crisis in modern history. The US has launched a military adventure which threatens the future of humanity. It has formulated the contours of an imperial project of World domination. Canada is contiguous to "the center of the · empire". Territorial control over Canada is part of the US geopolitical and military agenda.
Prof. M. Chossudovsky

The destruction of the Soviet Union also destroyed the

balance of power in the world. In the resulting unipolar world the US leadership embarked on a swift and intense program of taking the entire world in its iron grip. It was almost five decades ago, in 1959, that the North American Aerospace Defense Command (NORAD) was established. NORAD had the express objective of defending North American air space against any aggressor - believed to be the Soviet Union at that time. Then in 1994 the North American Free Trade Agreement (NAFTA) was signed that benefitted the great US corporations. Under NAFTA all restrictions on trade between Canada, US and Mexico were lifted and free trade between these countries commenced. After 9/11, in 2002, the US unilaterally set up the Northern Command (NORTHCOM). It is important to bear in mind that the Canadian Prime Minister at that time, Jean Chretien, did not agree to Canada joining NORTHCOM. As a result a binational group was set up and was entrusted with the task of improving the defenses of both, the US and Canada. This binational group is under complete US control since it works under NORTHCOM whereas NORTHCOM is controlled by the US Department of Defense. Shortly after setting up NORTHCOM, the US unilaterally declared that the jurisdiction of NORTHCOM extended from the Carribean in the south to the extreme north in Canada and covered all US and Canadian air and sea space as well as geographical territory. On 9/11, NORAD was conducting a vast military exercise in which the US and Canadian airforces were defending their territories against a possible Russian attack. According to Michael Ruppert, the entire 9/11 episode was secretly embedded in this exercise by the agencies and was carried out under this cover.

Is the merger of Canada with the US the real purpose behind establishing NORTHCOM? This question was first raised by Prof. Chossudovsky of Ottawa University in an article published in November 2004. All negotiations about NORTHCOM were held, not in Canada, but at a US air base in Colorado, USA. These "negotiations" lasted two years. As a result of what was agreed in the binational group, Canadian sovereignty received a very serious set back. Firstly, Canadian borders will be controlled by US forces and information about Canadian citizens will be shared with Homeland Security. Secondly, US troops and special forces can enter Canada without permission and arrest any Canadian citizen (the reciprocal arrangement is also allowed but everyone knows that there is no chance of Canadian forces entering the US to arrest a US citizen). By using the label "NORTH", the NORTHCOM, i.e., US forces will not only be able to extend their control over entire North America, but will also be able to set up "northern" military bases on Canadian soil. The US elite has its eye on the vast resources of Canada, a country larger in size than the US. According to Professor Chossudovsky, Canada will cease to exist as a sovereign state as a result of these arrangements. All these bodies and agreements, NAFTA, NORTHCOM and SPP, were set up on the direction of the Council on Foreign Relations. The Mexican Council on Foreign Relations and the Chief Executive Council of Canada were also involved in this process.

Alongside NORTHCOM, a Security and Prosperity Partnership (SPP) was also established. The purpose behind its establishment is the promotion and protection of the vested interests of the super rich elite of the US, while at the same time transforming Mexico, US and Canada into a "fortress". In this set up, the Mexican and Canadian citizens will be reduced to the status of slaves of the US elite, which has already shackled the people of the US. According to Stephen Lendman, under the SPP "many secret working groups have been set up to formulate treaties that will not be subject to discussion, and once signed, even the elected representatives of the countries will not be able to change them." All this is astonishing but in view of the extent and depth acquired by US domination in the last century, all this is not just possible, it is happening. As Lendman puts it:

> It's a corporate-led coup d'etat against the sovereignty of three nations enforced by a common hard line security strategy already in play separately in each country... It's a scheme to create a borderless North American Union under US control without barriers to trade and capital flows for corporate giants, mainly US ones. It's also to insure America gets free and unlimited access to Canadian and Mexican resources, mainly oil, and in the case of Canada, water as well. It's to assure US security as a top priority while denying Canada and Mexico preferential access to their own resources henceforth earmarked for US markets.

In the twentieth and the current century, the US has become a hungry giant, perpetually devoring global resources, and doing so through the use of force. This giant consumes oil, and unless tens of millions of barrels of oil reach its stomach, it cannot be appeased. To meet its addiction to oil, pipes from all over the globe, from Asia, Africa and South America, connect with its body. It has created and promoted perpetual conflict, bloodshed and restlessness in every corner of the globe. This giant can only be tamed through the combined efforts of the people of the USA and the rest of the world.

Waqt, November 9, 2007

Chapter 21

DU and Bush War Crimes

(DU denotes depleted Uranium)

This country is in the grip of a President who was not elected, who has surrounded himself with thugs in suits who care nothing about human life abroad or here, who care nothing about what happens to earth · · · The so-called war on terrorism is not only a war on innocent people in other countries, but also a war on the people of the United States: a war on our liberties, a war on our standard of living. The wealth of the country is being stolen from the people and handed over to superrich. The lives of our young are being stolen. And the thieves are in the White House.

Howard Zinn

Any president engaged in lying and empire-building must

have some of the traits of a psychopath : · · To murder innocent people in order to aggrandize the American Empire would be extremely difficult if not impossible for someone who feels empathy, remorse and guilt and who is incapable of lying. It might even be suggested that having at least some psychopathic traits is a qualification for the job.
David Model

Everyone seems to be dying of cancer. Every day one hears about another acquaintance or friend of a friend dying. How many more die in hospitals that one does not know? Apparently, over thirty percent of Iraqis have cancer, and there are lots of kids with leukemia. The depleted uranium left by the U.S. bombing campaign has turned Iraq into a cancer-infested country. For hundreds of years to come, the effects of the uranium will continue to wreak havoc on Iraq and its surrounding areas.
Nuha Al Radi artist and author *Iraq Diaries*, Sept 2004, prior to her death due to leukemia

---

While the US scientists and scholars have played a key role in the intellectual evolution of mankind, the wealthy US elite and its agents, the rulers of the US, have committed the greatest crimes against humanity. These horrific crimes continue unabated with silent intensity. With some exceptions, the "free" US media has maintained complete silence on these crimes. The reason for this silence has to do with the vested interests of media owners - their interests lie in suppressing humanity. Many conscientious and aware Americans do raise their voice against these crimes but the torment and agony of these

American citizens does not seem to have any effect on the pet journalists of media owners. This insensitivity is drowning the United States of America and with it the rest of the world.

One of the most diabolical advances in weaponry is the use of uranium that can no longer be used in reactors. This is known as depleted uranium. Depleted uranium is radioactive. After a certain processing, it can be converted into the hardest material on earth. A steel bullet will not penetrate a steel tank. However, a bullet made of depleted uranium will penetrate through the steel body of the tank and explode inside the tank. Uranium has the property that when heated it burns intensely. In powder form uranium automatically catches fire when heated.

The US has used depleted uranium in Yugoslavia, Iraq and Afghanistan. There was no need to employ depleted uranium in these wars. Depleted uranium was probably employed for two fold reasons. Firstly, the US always tests its new weapons in such wars (if an Iran war takes pace new weapons will be tested). Secondly, when a human being kills within himself all regard for human life and his diabolical tendencies take him in their grip, he relishes torturing and tormenting men and enjoys their helplessness. President Bush and his predecessors, including his father, are precisely such a tribe and embody man's darkness. They are all traders of death who have nurtured further such traders in the Third World.

Wherever depleted uranium is used in warfare, it generates radioactivity. Burnt uranium will keep radiating for millions of years. Radiations emitted from uranium do not travel far from the source. But if, perchance,

146

these radioactive particles happen to enter your body either through inhalation or through contaminated water intake, then till your dying day and afterwards, they will keep on disrupting basic structures in your body such as DNA, etc. Their effect is to produce deadly disorders such as cancer that lead the exposed individual to his grave. The US authorities have spread this radioactive debris in various parts of the world and concealed this fact from its people.

According to various estimates, about 500 - 600 tons of radioactive debris lies scattered in various parts of Afghanistan whereas the radioactive debris in Iraq exceeds that of Afghanistan many times. Not only does this radioactive debris kill people, it leads to defective births. According to one report, defective babies are being born in Afghanistan in affected areas - some are without eyes. some have missing limbs, some have faces distorted by flesh that hangs, some have highly deformed reproductive organs and so on. Congressman Denis Kucinich was one of the few politicians to raise his voice against the use of depleted uranium weapons. He stated:

> One of the most serious abuses of human rights has come through the Pentagon's development of, production of, and use of, depleted uranium munitions. These munitions have created an unending toll of casualties wherever they've been used, and they have created for the United States a great moral dilemma about when we are ready to recognize that the mere use of such munitions constitutes an offense

against humanity. And when are we going to
recognize our responsibility to not just stop
making these munitions but to help create the
cleanup wherever they've been used, to help
provide medical care for any person who's been
adversely affected by it, and to do the long
range studies that must be done in order to
calculate the human health effects and to ame-
liorate those effects in the long term.

The problem is that the US does not have the capability to clean such debris. Where radioactive debris is
despatching people of other countries to death, nature
has exacted its revenge and 11,000 American soldiers have
died due to such exposure. In addition, according to one
estimate, 325,000 US military personnel had been rendered permanently disabled until 2000. In 2006, an estimated 519,000 former US soldiers were in need of constant medical attention and had been rendered useless for
military service. All these unfortunate men and women
were victims of the two Gulf wars. Ordinary Americans
are, as usual, unaware of this shattering reality.

Evidence presented before an international tribunal
on US war crimes, convened in Tokyo in 2004, is heart
rending. Read the following testimony presented before
the international tribunal given by Sayed Gharib at Tora
Bora.

What else do the Americans want? They
killed us, they turned our new borns into horrific deformations, and they turned our farm
lands into grave yards and destroyed our hom-

es. On top of all this their planes fly over and spray us with bullets $\cdots$ we have nothing to lose $\cdots$ we will fight them the same way we fought the previous invaders .

Is there an eye that is not wet after reading these lines? Is there a human being who is not angry at this silent and endless genocide perpetrated by the Bush-Cheney cabal?

Voices are being raised worldwide against the use of depleted uranium weapons and, as declared by the Tokyo tribunal, the US leadership is guilty of most horrible war crimes. They must be given exemplary punishments. The US leadership is so drunk with power that it has become completely oblivious of the fact that those very laws of nature that have brought the US to the pinnacle of power and dominance will also bring it down, and quite rapidly. People of the Third World are paying the price of being weak but punishment that is visiting the world in the form of the present US leadership is also coming to its logical end swiftly. The problem is that the leadership of the United States of America will not only burn the world, it will also burn the US itself in the process.

To paraphrase a mystic Punjabi poet

May the streets be deserted and may my beloved be the only one in the deserted streets

However, the deserted streets will be radioactive.

Waqt, November 14, 2007

NOTE ADDED

Following is the opinion of of Justice Niloufer Bhagwat, given at the conclusion of the proceedings of the International Criminal Tribunal for Afghanistan at Tokyo, on 10 March, 2004 (The People versus George Walker Bush, President of the United States of America).

Verdict

1. I find the Defendant, George Walker Bush, President of the United States and Commander-in-Chief of United States Armed Forces guilty - under Article 2 of the Statute of the International Criminal Tribunal for Afghanistan and under International Criminal Law, for waging a war of aggression against Afghanistan and the Afghan people

2. Under Article 3, Part I, clause (a), (b), (c), (d), (f), (g) and Article 3, Part II, clause (a), (b), (c), (d), (e), (f), (h), (i), (k), (l), (n), (o), (p), (q) of the Statute of the International Criminal Tribunal for Afghanistan, under International Criminal Law and International Humanitarian Law, in respect of War Crimes committed against the people of Afghanistan by the use of weapons prohibited by the laws of warfare causing death and destruction to the Afghan people, maiming men, women and children

3. Under Article 4, clause (a), (b), (d), (e), (f), (h) and (i) of the Statute of the International Criminal Tribunal and International Humanitarian Law, for

Crimes Against Humanity committed against the people of Afghanistan, resulting in inhumane acts affecting large sections of the population caused by the military invasion, bombing, and lack of humanitarian relief

4. Under Article 3, Part I, clause (a), (b), (c), (f), (g) and Article 3, Part II clause (f), (k), (p), and (q) of the Statute of the International Criminal Tribunal for Afghanistan, under International Criminal Law and the Hague Convention and Geneva Convention (III) of 1949 in respect of the torture and killings of Talban and other prisoners of war who had surrendered and their torture and inhumane conditions of detention and deportation of innocent civilians. In respect of the transport of prisoners in sealed containers and their death due to suffocation and filing of rifle shots at the container for creating holes for ventilation with the prisoners inside and for conditions at Sheberghan prison; the Defendant is entitled to benefit of doubt at this trial. However, the issues are left open for trial, before any other court/Tribunal as the evidence before the Tribunal is not conclusive on the involvement of United States forces;

5. Under Article 3, Part I (c) and (g); Article 3 Part 2 (a), (b), (c), (d), (e), (h), (i), (l) and Article 4 (b), (l) of (n), (p), (q) of the ICTA in respect of the serious humanitarian situation resulting from the refugee exodus in Afghanistan due to the bombing of civilian population and civilian infrastructure in a country already affected by serious famine resulting in mass exodus of people and death from bombing, hunger, displacement, disease and absence of humanitarian relief

6. Under Article 3, Part II, clause (o), (p) and under

Article 4 clause (a), (b) and (l) of the statute of the International Criminal Tribunal for Afghanistan, and under International Criminal Law and International Humanitarian Law; in respect of the DU weapons used on the people of Afghanistan to exterminate the population and for the crime of "Omnicide" the extermination of life, contamination of air, water and food resources and the irreversible alteration of the genetic code of all living organisms including plant life as a direct consequence of the use of radioactive munitions in Afghanistan affecting countries in the entire region;

7. Under Article 3, Part II, clause (o), (p) and under Article 4 (a) and (i) of the Statute of the International Tribunal for Afghanistan, under International Criminal Law, for exposing soldiers and other personnel of the United States, UK and other soldiers of coalition forces to radioactive contamination by the use of DU weapons, hazarding their lives, their physiology, and that of their future progeny by irreversible alteration of the genetic code.

Chapter 22

Bush Marches Towards Dictatorship

My country is dead. Its people have surrendered to tyranny, and in so doing, they have become tyranny's primary support group; its base constituency; its defender. Every day they offer their endorsement of tyranny by banking in its banks and spending their borrowed money with the corporations that run it. The great Neocon strategy of George H.W. Bush has triumphed. Convince the American people that they can't live without the "good things", then sit back and watch as they endorse the progressively more outrageous crimes you commit as you throw them bones with ever less meat on them. All the while lock them into debt. Destroy the middle class, the only political base that need be feared. Make them accept, because of their own shared guilt, ever-more repressive police state measures. Do whatever you want.
Michael Ruppert *By the Light of a Burning Bridge*

Brzezinski's book *The Grand Chessboard* may be called a script for complete global domination by the US. Published in 1997, this book contains numerous observations that throw light on the mindset and future plans of the US elite. For instance, there is a map in which the precise region, currently torn by strife and war, or under the shadow of imminent war, including Pakistan, Afghanistan, Central Asia, Iran, Iraq, Saudi Arabia, Egypt, Turkey etc., has been encircled and marked as "The Global Zone of Percolating Violence". Many states of the region have also been referred to as the "Eurasian Balkans" implying that their maps are likely to be redrawn.

The US leadership has, throughout the twentieth century, employed documented and proven deceptions to arouse the American people into entering major wars. These deceptions involved the loss of innocent American lives. US entry into the two world wars was possible because the US authorities were able to deceive their people into believing that certain belligerent actions were perpetrated against US citizens despite the desire of the US to keep aloof from the conflict between Eurasian powers. Events like Pearl Harbor were carefully planned and secretly manipulated by US agencies, and the reality successfully hidden from the great mass of US people permanently. Both wars resulted in the US victory and the consequent emergence of the US as a global power. Therefore, such tactics have paid off in the past.

Now with the global balance of power altered in favor of the US, the American elite is likely to employ similar tactics once again, and it may already have done so, to initiate a long war with the intent of dominating the globe for a long time to come. The Project of the New American Century (PNAC) commissioned by Dick Cheney asserts that the US must pre-empt the emergence of any major challenge within the short window of time that it has obtained after destroying the USSR. The first phase in this war is the so called "war against terrorism", aimed at capturing the most vital global resources, viz. oil and gas.

Brzezinski writes:

> But the pursuit of power is not a goal that commands popular passion, except in conditions of a sudden threat or challenge to the public's sense of domestic well being. The economic self-denial (that is, defense spending) and the human sacrifice (casualties among professional soldiers) required in the effort are uncongenial to democratic instincts. Democracy is inimical to the cause of imperial mobilization.

This key observation explains the shift of American rulers towards dictatorial legislation. A vast apparatus for suppressing the people of the US, is already in place in the form of various organizations like FEMA (Federal Emergency Management Authority). FEMA had carried out an exercise a few years ago as to how to intern 400,000 people at short notice. Now the necessary legislation has been quietly put in place, with the so called "free" US media observing a complete silence, and even complicity, in the entire exercise. The shackles that bind, mostly innocent, prisoners in Guantanamo are now also ready for the US public and minorities. The US public at large is not yet aware as to what is in store if it dissents with the policies of the elite. The eruption of American militarism abroad and the speedy enactment of dictatorial laws at home are, therefore, two faces of the same coin.

On October 17, 2006 President Bush signed a John Warner Defense Authorization Act of 2007 which practically demolishes the legal bar against the use of military in quelling any disorder without the permission of Governor of the State. This bar was enacted through the famous Posse Comitatus Act (PCA) of 1878, which makes the use of military force in US unlawful except where permitted by the Constitution or Congress. Violation of PCA is punishable. either through a fine,. or imprisonment up to two years, or both.

The new law signed by President Bush contains the following clause:

> The President may employ the armed forces, including the National Guard in Federal service, to restore public order and enforce the laws of the United States when. as result of natural disaster, epidemic. or other serious public health emergency, terrorist attack or incident, or other condition in any State or possession of the United States, the President determines that domestic violence has occurred to such an extent that the constituted authorities of the State or possession are incapable of ("refuse" or "fail" in) main-

156

taining public order, in order to suppress, in any State, any insurrection, domestic violence, unlawful combination, or conspiracy.

President Bush has previously interpreted the law in his own way, and will, if needed, do so in the case of the above law as well. The US Supreme Court is now complicit with the US Government in cover up of its unconstitutional acts and has allowed the Bush regime an astonishingly broad latitude under cover of national security considerations.

One Senator who has criticized the new law is Patrick Leahy of the Democratic Party. This is the same Patrick Leahy who received an anthrax letter when he asked the infamous Attorney General Ashcroft as to how had he undermined the Fifth Amendment. That was enough to close down the Congress and silence Leahy. He said that the new law makes it "easier for the President to declare martial law". In a story filed on October 26, 2006, Frank Morales pointed out, "The law also facilitates militarized round-ups and detentions of protestors, so called 'illegal aliens', 'potential terrorists' and other 'undesirables' for detention in facilities already contracted for and under construction by Halliburton". Dick Cheney, whom Michael Ruppert holds responsible for executing the 9/11 attacks, was CEO of Halliburton prior to becoming vice president. Halliburton has also been accused of drug running in the Iran-Contra affair.

The passage of the Military Commissions Act of 2006 (MCA) by the Congress has dealt a death blow to fundamental rights such as the right against detention without trial, the right to a speedy trial in front of an impartial jury, the right to appeal, etc. These habeas corpus laws were a pride of the US constitution. Thomas Jefferson wrote "··· *freedom of the person under the protection of habeas corpus; and trial by juries impartially selected"* and other such principles constituted *the bright constellation which has gone before us, guided our steps through an age of revolution and reformation.* In fact, habeas corpus was essentially enshrined in Magna Carta as far back as 1215. With one stroke of pen on October 17, 2006, Mr. Bush has undone all that.

There has been some disinformation about the repeal of habeas corpus laws. An impression has been conveyed that this is only for aliens. But this is incorrect. The clauses refer to "any person" not just aliens. This law also states:

> [N]o court, justice, or judge shall have jurisdiction to hear or consider any claim or cause of action whatsoever ··· relating to prosecution, trial or judgment of a military commission under this chapter, including challenges to lawfulness of military procedures.

Of course; confessions extracted by torture are now valid material under the new law and the US superior courts have made a mockery of justice in several cases.

Jose Padilla, a US citizen by birth, was kept in confinement in a 9 × 7 square feet cell for three and a half years, denied a lawyer for two years, beaten, abused, given mind altering drugs until he became a pulp of a man, but he did not receive any justice in the 21st century United States of America. He was declared "enemy combatant" by President Bush. The judge who dealt with Padilla's case is currently a candidate for Attorney General.

Khalid Al Masri, a German citizen of Lebanese descent, was picked up in Macedonia in 2002 while on vacation on grounds that he had the same name as an Al Qaeda member. He was chained eagle spread to the floor of an aircraft, taken to Afghanistan, routinely beaten and sexually abused. Finally, when he went on hunger strike and it became clear that he was the wrong man, he was taken and dumped on an abandoned road in Albania. He filed a case against George Tenet and several companies in a US court in 2005 but on the basis of State Secrets Privilege he was denied justice.

The US elite is determined to wage endless war to become pre-eminent for the next millennium if not for all times to come. The use of nuclear weapons is highly likely - Mr. Bush has already talked of the possibility of WW III in connection with Iran. Dissent at home will certainly not be tolerated in times to come. A couple of billion deaths do not matter for the achievement of the hitherto elusive permanent pre-eminence. It may come as a shock to people that the number of avoidable deaths since 1950 stands at 1.3 billion! The dominant fraction comes from wars manipulated by US agencies and fought by US or its proxies. The US may be the most powerful nation on earth but it is not, as remarked by Michael Ruppert, more powerful than the whole world put together. The earlier this lesson is imbibed the better.

The Nation, November 18, 2007

Chapter 23

New Espionage Laws in US

The United States is no longer the nation its citizens once thought: a place, unlike most others in the world, free from censorship and thought police, where people can say what they want, when they want to, about their government... Until the citizens of this land aggressively defend their First Amendment rights of free speech, there is little hope that the march to censorship will be reversed. The survival of the cornerstone of the Bill of Rights is at stake.
Angus Mackenzie, *Secrets*

If you tell a lie big enough and keep repeating it, people will eventually come to believe it. The lie can can be maintained only for such time as the State can shield the people from the political, economic and/or military consequences of the lie. It thus becomes vitally important for the State to use all its powers to repress dissent, for the

160

truth is the mortal enemy of the lie, and thus by extension, the truth is the greatest enemy of the State.

Joseph Goebbels

There was of course no way of knowing whether you were being watched at any given moment. How often, or on what system, the Thought Police plugged in on any individual wire was guesswork. It was even conceivable that they watched everybody all the time. But at any rate they could plug in your wire whenever they wanted to. You had to live - did live, from habit that became instinct - in the assumption that every sound you made was overheard, and, except in darkness, every movement scrutinized.

George Orwell *1984*

In 1978 the US legislature passed the Foreign Intelligence Surveillance Act (FISA) that allowed US agencies to keep an eye on written, telephonic, and other communications within the US. After 9/11 the US authorities started surveillance of US citizens and others but concealed this fact from the public. An unlawful aspect of the new surveillance activity pertained to what has been called data mining. Under data mining, US agencies started accessing and storing records of emails and telephonic conversations, including their length or duration, of tens of millions of US citizens. This meant that the US agencies were in possession of information pertaining to personal contacts, friendships and personal relationships that they were not supposed to possess under the US constitution.

It was in December 2005 that the *New York Times*

made a sensational revelation. The *New York Times* not only revealed the existence of such a program but also that differences had developed in the Bush administration over this sensitive matter. Bush promptly defended such internal surveillance. It is worth noting that the Bush administration has never formally admitted the existence of such surveillance. According to the *New York Times*, the US government has completely concealed the existence of such a massive surveillance program and has never admitted to it. Such surveillance is an open violation of the fourth amendment to the US constitution. The fourth amendment states:

> *The right of the people to be secure in their persons, houses, papers, and effects, against unreasonable searches and seizures, shall not be violated, and no Warrants shall issue, but upon probable cause, supported by Oath or affirmation, and particularly describing the place to be searched, and the persons or things to be seized.*

In August 2007, the US Congress passed the Protect America Act of 2007. The Democratic Party cooperated fully with the fascist government of George Bush and thus violated the mandate that the people of the US gave the Democrats in the Congress. The fundamental reason for this cooperation lies in the fact that both parties work for the interests of the wealthy elite that remains behind the scene but controls both parties. The new law permits US agencies to look into or intercept electronic communications without a warrant. A deliberate ambiguity has been left in the law: if it is thought "reasonable" that the other end of a communication is probably outside the US, then the agencies may intercept it. On account of this ambiguity, the US agencies may intercept any communication involving US and non-US citizens because all email communications at least take place through business centers located inside the US. As Joe Kay puts it, "Some sections of this bill in themselves constitute an enormous and unconstitutional increase in spying, but this law gives far greater powers to the US government to spy on its citizens."

Addressing the Congress, President Bush stated, "The need for action is quite clear. Director McConnell has warned that if the changes in the FISA are not made permanent our professional dealing with security will be deprived of very important weapons. Without these weapons it will be extremely difficult to determine what our enemy is doing in recruiting and training individuals who are to be entered in our country. Without these weapons it will be easy to harm our country." Former Federal prosecutor Edward Lazarus has stated that surveillance without warrants is a grave threat to the US constitution which keeps the principle of division of powers in view. Through this law the administration has largely usurped the powers of the judiciary and the legislature. Lazarus states that "Division of powers in the constitution was the real defense against tyranny and the well known Yale expert in law Professor Stephen Carter has expressed this in a single sentence - tyranny does not incapacitate a nation in one moment but gradually takes it in its grip." Lazarus says that tyranny is spreading in the US with the speed of a cheetah.

Waqt, November 18, 2007

Chapter 24

Blackwater: Hired Murderers

When a republic's most venerable institutions no longer operate as they were intended, it becomes possible for small cabals to usurp power, and, while keeping the forms, corrupt the function of these institutions for their own ends. Looking at things that way, the George W. Bush presidency has been both result and symptom of the decadence of America's constitutional mechanisms.

T. D. Allman

Although a tyranny, because it needs no consent, may successfully rule over foreign peoples, it can stay in power if it destroys first of all the national institutions of its own people.

Hannah Arendt *The Origins of Totalitarianism*

Private corporations have penetrated war so deeply that they are now the second biggest contributor to coalition forces in Iraq after the Pentagon, a Guardian investigation has established...

The investigation also discovered that the proportion of contracted security personnel in the firing line is 10 times greater than during the first Gulf war. In 1991, for every private contractor there were about 100 servicemen and women; now there are 10. The private sector is so firmly embedded in combat, occupation and peacekeeping duties that the phenomenon may have reached the point of no return: the US military would struggle to wage war without it... The myriad military and security companies thriving on this largesse are at the sharp end of a revolution in military affairs that is taking us into unknown territory - the partial privatization of war...

There are other formidable problems surfacing in what is uncharted territory - issues of loyalty, accountability, ideology and national interest. By definition, a private military company is in Iraq or Bosnia not to pursue, US, UN, or EU policy, but to make money.

Ian Traynor in *"The Privatization of War - $30 Billion goes to Private Military"*, The *Guardian*, UK, December 10, 2003

There is a very deep alliance between a particular Jewish lobby and the Evangelical Christian sect. This sect believes that until and unless the Temple of Solomon is erected in place of the Al-Aqsa mosque, the Promised Messiah will not descend on earth. This sect is an extreme right wing sect and its members are involved in planning warfare and bloodshed against Muslims worldwide. The leaders of this sect do not like ordinary sec-

166

ular Americans and, therefore, never have much success in elections. Despite this, the Evangelical Christian sect has a very powerful influence in the US government, in particular in the Republican party. One of the reasons is that this company funds the Republican party very liberally.

The infamous Blackwater, a firm of mercenaries, has gained global notoriety after engaging in a killing rampage in Iraq. It is owned by an Evangelical Christian named Erik Prince, who also heads it. Erik Prince is a former Navy seal.[1] The Prince family has spent a lot of money in building extremism in the Republican Party. Blackwater USA was set up in 1996. Its offices and training grounds are located in a marshy region of North Carolina known as the Great Dismal Swamp. It owns an area of about 7,000 acres here. Blackwater claims that this 7,000 acre territory is the biggest military training facility in USA. In November 2006, Blackwater purchased another 80 acres about 150 miles north of Chicago and set

---

[1]On August 21, 2010 the website infowars.org reported: "Erik Prince, the founder of the notorious security company Blackwater/Xe, has left the United States and is settling with his family in Abu Dhabi, the capital of United Arab Emirates. Prince 51, is not facing any criminal charges for now, but his company now known as Xe Services LLC, has been implicated in a series of scandals related to operations in Iraq, Afghanistan, and elsewhere, court documents say." On December 17, 2010, the web newspaper Huffington Post (www.huffingtonpost.com) reported: "An investment group with ties to the founder of the company formerly known as Blackwater announced Friday that it has bought the security firm, which was heavily criticized for its contractor's actions in Iraq. USTC Holdings said in a statement that the acquisition of the company now called Xe Services includes its training facility in North Carolina.

up a subsidiary company by the name Blackwater North. It is also trying to acquire land in California for training purposes but the local people are opposing this move. Blackwater has 20,000 mercenaries and 20 airplanes and helicopter gunships. Most of the employees of Blackwater are former US soldiers but it also employs Filipinos, Chileans, Bosnians, etc. According to one estimate, this company trains about 40,000 people annually.

The creation of Blackwater was made possible by the thinking of the mysterious and ruthless Vice President of US Dick Cheney. Dick Cheney was Secretary Defense during the first Gulf War. During the last days in office, he directed the notorious firm Halliburton to carry out an analysis about privatizing US military bureaucracy. After being relieved from the Department of Defense, Dick Cheney himself became head of Halliburton and also joined the extreme rightwing think tank American Enterprise Institute (AEI). It was AEI that commissioned the report of the Project of New American Century about rebuilding America's defenses in which a blueprint for complete global conquest by the US was laid out. Before 9/11, Rumsfeld declared "war" against the US military bureaucracy. He stated that Pentagon will be run like private enterprise. After 9/11 the use of PMCs (Private Military Companies) has increased and that has brought great profits to Blackwater. It is estimated that about 48000 mercenaries are currently active in shedding blood in Iraq. Most of these belong to Blackwater. The US has a wonderful law called Freedom of Information Act (FOIA). Under this law the US government is bound to provide information to its citizens on any government activity provided the release of that information does not threaten national security. However, the private sector is exempt from this law and therein lies one of the real advantage of the use of PMCs in military operations. Apart from profiteering, the casualties can be concealed from the US public.

· Since January 2007 news has been circulating that Blackwater is ready to play its role in the civil war in Sudan. Last year President Bush was forced to lift restrictions against Sudan because the country has a sizable Christian population. According to a news report, Blackwater is getting ready to train the rebel forces in southern Sudan. It is reported that Blackwater has handed over to the US authorities a plan for training rebel forces. Blackwater mercenaries are also being used in Afghanistan. Apart from combat and bloodshed, Blackwater has also been entrusted with the job of protecting US VIPs in sensitive regions. For example, they were entrusted with the job of protecting Negroponte and Khalilzad. In addition, the protection of embassy personnel in countries like Iraq and Afghanistan is entrusted to Blackwater. Pentagon has awarded a five year, $1 billion contract to Blackwater for protection of embassy personnel. An amount of $320 million has already been received by Blackwater.

Blackwater mercenaries have been involved in incidents where they have fired on unarmed civilians or armed personnel without provocation. On September 16, 2007, these mercenaries killed 17 Iraqis. Investigations have established that they fired without provocation. Five investigations into this incident have been conducted. On October 2, 2007, Erik Prince appeared before a congressional committee to answer questions about the conduct of Blackwater employees in Iraq and Afghanistan. When the Iraqi government initiated proceedings against Blackwater employees involved in the shooting of 17 Iraqis, the State Department declared Blackwater exempt from such trials. Ironically, the Department of Justice has stated that the State Department has no jurisdiction in declaring anyone charged with crime exempt from punishment or trail.

The senior positions in Blackwater are occupied by people who have, in the past, worked in important positions in the US government. For instance, Cofer Black, a former head of the counter terrorism division of the CIA is Vice President of Blackwater. Similarly, former Inspector General of the Department of Defense and former head of the near east in CIA Robert Richer also works for Blackwater. In October 2007, Blackwater USA changed its name to Blackwater Worldwide in view of its increasing involvement in global operations.

The privatization of US military operations is a deeply disturbing development for USA and others. The US public has no control whatsoever over this kind of fighting force. Apart from profiteering, Blackwater is imbued with a missionary zeal for promoting "Christianity" and making it dominant worldwide. What more can one ask when profits and "religious" duties reinforce each other. In his farewell address, President Eisenhower had warned the US public against the rise of a military-industrial complex which had influence in the corridors of power and whose increased influence was a threat to American values. Jeremy Scahill, who has written a book on Blackwater, states that Blackwater embodies all the aspects of this uncontrolled threat pointed out by Eisenhower. In the wake of the growing involvement of the US in the Middle East, Central Asia and elsewhere, the role of Blackwater is growing, and a time will soon come when the out of control Blackwater will pose a grave threat to US itself.

Waqt, November 21, 2007

Chapter 25

Enemy of the Poor: Greenspan

The country is governed for the richest, for the corporation, the bankers, the land speculators, and for the exploiters.

Helen Keller

The United States has only one party - the property party. It's the party of big corporations, the party of money. It has two right wings; one is Democrat and the other is Republican.

Gore Vidal

The ruling elite knows who their enemies are, and their enemies are the people at home and the people abroad. Their enemies are anybody who wants more social justice, anybody who wants to use the surplus value of society for social needs rather than for individual class greed, that's their enemy.

Michael Parenti

*George Bush and corporate America are intent on elimi-
nating taxes on all capital incomes. Nor do they care if
record budget deficits are the result. Many of their rightwing friends, including those in the Congress, actually
want larger deficits. They see chronic, record deficits as
producing the budget crisis necessary to use as an excuse
to privatize Social Security and dismantle what remains
of the Roosevelt New Deal programs of the 1930s.*

Jack Rasmus

*The Federal Reserve Bank is a consortium of twelve pri-
vate banks which are "NOT" part of the United States
Government. These private banks purchase paper notes
from the U.S. mint for printing cost then lend back the
money plus interest to the people through member banks.
The profits go into the share holders of the bank's pocket's.
Sometimes the bank pays an arbitrary 'franchise fee' to
the U.S. The first two private National Banking Systems
lasted about 20 years before being eliminated. The current Federal Reserve Bank, private National Bank, has
lasted nearly 100 years. The cost to the U.S. public is
hundreds of billions of dollars every year while holding
the country in a constant state of debt. There have been
assassination attempts on every President who attempted
to eliminate these private National Banks. The Federal
Reserve Bank has not once been audited and never pays
any income tax on their astonishing income. The bank is*

173

supposed to bring stability to the economy, however, al-
most every major market crash can be attributed to the
Federal Reserve Bank, including the Great Depression.
Destroy The Evil Federal Reserve That Is Causing America's Financial Problems - posted on rense.com

Alan Greenspan, former Chairman Federal Reserve, has
published his biography recently. He has received an advance of $8.5 million, and it has also been agreed with
the publisher that Greenspan will receive royalty provided more than 1.9 million copies of the book are sold.
Greenspan is 81 years old now and was Chairman of the
Federal Reserve for twenty years (1987-2006). This was
a very painful period for the people of the US and it
was mainly due to the policies of Greenspan who acted
in the interest of his masters in the elite. Many of the
difficulties faced by lower income groups in the US today
are the direct result of the policies of the Federal Reserve under Greenspan's chairmanship and continue even
as these lines are being written. News of an impending
crisis in the housing sector are now being heard and this
is also, to a fair extent, the result of policies adopted under Greenspan.

The US Federal Reserve is a private bank which has
the power to issue and control circulation of US currency.
Usually such powers are given to banks owned by the
state. The creation of this bank was the result of a
heinous intrigue which will be described in some other
column. This intrigue was conceived on Jekyll island
in the state of Georgia in the US. Seven of the richest
families on the planet colluded in this intrigue. They

put their heads together for nine days in complete secrecy and decided to collaborate instead of competing, to jointly control the wealth of the people of the United States of America. This unconstitutional Act was passed on the night between 22nd and 23rd December at 1.00 AM when most Congressmen had either gone for Christmas or were dosing.

Greenspan was born in 1928 and grew up in New York. He is Jewish and his parents hailed from Hungary. He did his bachelors and masters in economics from New York University. He has a PhD from Columbia. In order to obtain a PhD one normally has to do course work and research and then write up a thesis based on this research. Greenspan did no research nor did he write up a thesis, but he was awarded a PhD in 1977 by Columbia University.

In 1955 Greenspan set up a private advisory firm with the name Townsend Greenspan and Co. This proved to be a failure. According to writers the predictions of this firm on financial and economic matters were often wrong and its analysis incorrect. Greenspan also became an adviser to politicians. During Nixon's election campaign, he became a coordinator for internal affairs, and during Ford's time, he was appointed Chairman of the committee on economic affairs. In 1982, he was appointed chairman of a Commission constituted by Reagan for dealing with pension issues facing the US. It was in this capacity that Greenspan played a key role in transferring wealth of the poor to the rich. The fact of the matter was that there was no financial problem with Social Security. Steve Lendman wrote in 2007:

There was just one problem. It was a hoax,
but who'd know as the dominant media stayed
silent. They let the Commission do its work
that would end up transferring trillions of public dollars to the rich. It represents one of the
greatest ever heists in plain sight, still ongoing and greater than ever, with no one crying
foul to stop it. The Commission issued its
report in January, 1983, and Congress used
it as the basis for the 1983 Social Security
Amendments to "resolve short-term financing problem(s) and (make) many other significant changes in Social Security law" with the
public none the wiser it was a scam harming
them.

As a result of the' recommendations of the Greenspan
Commission, tax deduction from the salary of low income
people began, while the rich got tax rebates. For the first
time in the US history, the rich got tax rebates while tax
on lower income groups was increased simultaneously.

A deduction of 6.2% is made from the salaries of low
income employees and is transferred to Social Security
and medicare. Additionally, half the amount being paid
to old and physically disabled or mentally handicapped
people was taxed as a result of his recommendations.
People were told that as a result of action of the recommendations of the Commission, Social Security will be
safe for the next 75 years. But, as Lendman has pointed
out, there was no problem with Social Security - it 'was
all a ploy to transfer wealth to the rich. The taxation on

the rich was reduced from 70% to 28% over a three year period!

One of the jobs of the Federal Reserve is to regulate business in the US and keep it within the law. Greenspan's tenure witnessed some huge crashes in the stock market. The bursting of the "dotcom bubble" is well known. "Bubble" refers to a psychological environment created on the basis of false propaganda in which people are made to believe that a certain business will bring large and quick profits so that people invest money in that particular business. Afterwards big companies in this business declare themselves bankrupt and the Directors of the company divide whatever money people have invested, amongst themselves, making fabulous sums. Ordinary people who have invested their lifelong savings in the business get nothing (this is the "pump and dump" activity). Greenspan deliberately let this bubble grow - despite being aware of the situation he contributed to the growth of the bubble through his statements. Earlier in 1987 also the stock market went through a serious crisis.

The accentuation of horrifying inequalities in US society are a consequence of Greenspan's policies spread over two decades. At this point, 1% of the US population owns 33% of its wealth. The upper 20% own 84.7% wealth whereas the lower 80% of the population owns a mere 15.3% of the wealth of the United States of America, and the debt burden on the shoulders of these masses is increasing by the day.

Waqt, November 24, 2007

NOTE ADDED

It may be useful to quote Eustace Mullins's biographical sketch of Greenspan quoted at the end of his book *The Secrets of the Federal Reserve: The London Connection*. This book, which is available on the net, reveals the control of the US as well as the global money supply, and of the global politics, by a few families to its deepest level. An earlier version of the book that did not mention the "London Connection", was refused publication by 18 New York publishers whereas the 19th publisher told Mullins that no New York publisher will publish his book! A German edition printed in 1955 was seized under court orders and all 10,000 copies burnt! As George Orwell puts it: "During times of universal deceit telling the truth becomes a revolutionary act." Sadly Eustace Mullins passed away in February 2010 and in him the world has lost a great friend of, and fighter for humanity. The US has lost a man of outstanding integrity during times when integrity is most needed. It goes as follows:

> Alan Greenspan (1926-): Appointed President Reagan to succeed Volcker as Chairman of the Board of Governors of the Federal Reserve System in 1987. Greenspan had succeeded Herbert Stein as chairman of the President's Council of Economic Advisors in 1974. He was the protege of former chairman of the Board of Governors, Arthur Burns of Austria (Bernstein). Burns was a monetarist representing the Rothschild's Viennese School

of Economics, which manifested its influence in England through the Royal Colonial Society, a front for Rothschilds and other English bankers who stashed their profits from the world drug trade in the Hong Kong Shanghai Bank. The staff economist for the Royal Colonial Society was Alfred Marshall, inventor of the monetarist theory, who, as head of the Oxford Group, became the patron of Wesley Clair Mitchell, who founded the National Bureau of Economic Research for the Rockefellers in the United States.

Mitchell, in turn, became the patron of Arthur Burns and Milton Friedman, whose theories are now the power techniques of Greenspan at the Federal Reserve Board. Greenspan is also the protege of Ayn Rand, a weirdo who interposed her sexual affairs with guttural commands to be selfish. Rand was also the patron of CIA propagandist William Buckeley and the National Review. Greenspan was director of major Wall Street firms such as J.P. Morgan Co., Morgan Guaranty Trust (the American bank for the Soviets after the Bolshevik Revolution of 1917), Brookings Institution, Bowery Savings Bank, the Dreyfus Fund, General Foods, and Time, Inc. Greenspan's most impressive achievement was as chairman of the National Commission on Social Security from 1981-1983. He juggled figures to convince the public that Social Security was bankrupt, when in fact it had an enormous surplus. These figures were then used to fasten onto American workers a huge increase in Social Security withholding tax, which invoked David Ricardo's economic dictum of the iron law of wages, that workers could only be paid a subsistence wage, and any funds beyond that must be extorted from them forcibly by tax increases. As a partner of J.P. Morgan Co. since 1977, Greenspan represented the unbroken line of control of the Federal Reserve System by the firms represented at the secret meeting on Jekyll Island in 1910, where Henry P. Davison, righthand man of J.P. Morgan, was a key figure in the drafting of the Federal Reserve Act.

Within days of taking over as chairman of the Federal Reserve Board, Greenspan immediately raised the interest rate on Sept. 4, 1987, the first such increase in three years of general prosperity, and precipitated the stock market crash of Oct., 1987, Black Monday, when the Dow Jones average plunged 508 points. Under Greenspan's direction, the Federal Reserve Board has steadily nudged the United States deeper and deeper into recession, without a word of criticism from the complaisant members of Congress.

Chapter 26

The WGA Strike

People of privilege will always risk their complete destruction rather than surrender any material part of their advantage.

John Kenneth Galbraith

The question here, really, is what have we done to democracy? What have we turned it into? What happens once democracy has been used up? When it has been hollowed out and emptied of meaning? What happens when each of its institutions has metastasized into something dangerous? What happens now that democracy and the Free Market have fused into a single predatory organism with a thin, constricted imagination that revolves almost entirely around the idea of maximizing profit?
Arundhati Roy *Listening to Grasshoppers* 2009

... the termination of the New Deal social contract represented an economy-wide initiative by leading corporations-

26. The WGA Strike

some exposed to new competitive pressures and some pro-
tected from it - who no longer found themselves compelled
to make a deal with unions or communities. Contractors
constitute only one category of the virtual workers who
make up America's new contingent labor force. The oth-
ers include roughly three million temps; a million leased
workers, who-like temps-are rented by the hour, day, week
or month; and nearly 25 million part-time workers. Col-
lectively, contingent workers now make up between one-
fourth and one-third of all American workers. "If there
was a national fear index," says economist Richard Be-
lous about these new charter members of the anxious class,
"it would be directly related to the growth of contingent
work."

Charles Derber in *Corporation Nation*

The Union of American writers, Writers Guild of America (WGA) has been on strike since November 5. WGA
comprises of 12,000 writers whose creations include writing scripts for different programs, for TV drama, for TV
comedy, in addition to scripts for movies. The decision
to go on strike was arrived at through voting in which
approximately 6,000 members cast their votes and 90.3%
of these voted in favor of strike. This was the biggest
vote in the history of WGA. The WGA has demanded
not only better royalty on DVD profits, but also royalty
on income from internet and ipod. The alliance of owners
of TV channels and Hollywood film makers is known as
the Alliance of Motion Pictures and TV Producers. As a
result of the WGA strike, recording of new TV programs
has stopped and popular programs on TV channels have

182

either been suspended or are being gradually stopped - mostly old recordings are now being repeated. After initial sessions, negotiations failed and were stopped. According to latest information, the negotiations will resume on November 26.

The WGA strike is a result of increased profiteering by owners, of the economic situation precipitated by the war and the rising cost of living. Nineteen years earlier the WGA had gone on strike but today the WGA faces a much more formidable and ruthless adversary. In the past fifteen years or so, US TV channels and studios have become the property of five or six big corporations. In a previous column the details about these corporations were given. The most prominent and powerful among these are Time Warner, Disney World, Viacom, NBC Universal and News Corporation. Each of these earns billions of dollars every year in profits. Without the writers, these corporations would hardly have made any profits whatsoever. Without the TV writers, hardly any programs of interest would exist to be aired. The words of these writers are the drops of blood whose circulation gives life to these corporations. Those who give life to these corporations, without whose work the corporations would cease to be, are paid nominally, and are forced to submit the products of their creative efforts at the feet of the gods who own these corporations. Who has given these god-like powers to men like Rupert Murdoch, Michael Eisner, Ron Meyer and others of this tribe? The WGA not only has the support of the people of the US, but also masses worldwide because this is a fight against the poisonous and destructive influence on human culture, of the incredible concentration of wealth in a few hands.

On account of the fundamental importance of the writers to the TV and movie world, famous actors, actresses, comedians and other people belonging to showbiz join the striking writers from time to time, to show their solidarity with them. In fact the renowned comedian Jay Leno has openly stated that he cannot inject effective humor in his show without the script writers. One striker said that the writers, though employees, are the real creative force - people think that producers and directors make movies and films, but without the writers no film or movie has a backbone.

According to one survey, the WGA strike has support of people across the racial spectrum. Of the 69% people in Los Angeles who were aware of the strike, only 8% favored the corporations. Among the Hispanics, 74% favor the WGA strike, whereas 79% blacks and 65% whites support the strike. Ramon Valle, who has quoted these figures, writes that the biggest surprise for the strikers is the fact that 61% of the LA Republicans are in favor of this strike.

Both the political parties of US are currently busy in election campaigning. Three of the leading candidates from the Democratic Party, Obama, Hillory Clinton and Edwardes have apparently expressed solidarity with the striking writers. The fact of the matter is that the Democratic leadership is indebted to those very corporate owners against whom the strike is being conducted. According to one estimate, the Democratic Party has received donations worth 14 million dollars from owners of TV, music and film. In addition to this, individuals connected with the ownership of this industry have donated more than 11 million dollars to the Democrats. This indicates that the Democratic Party too works for the protection of corporate interests. The donations mentioned above are not giveaways - these have been given by hardcore businessmen who will not give a dime unless they expect a return on it. Could not these $25 million be given by these ruthless, selfish and greedy media owners to the writers?

The fact of the matter is that salaries given to the executives in these corporations are shameful. For instance, Time Warner has appointed Jeff Bewkes as Chief Executive in order to break this strike. He will be paid more than $10.75 million annually in salary and bonuses. Most striking workers earn less than 600 dollars per month. At the end of the first week of the strike, NBC Universal issued an ultimatum to the strikers that they will be dismissed if they did not return to work. For the sake of record, according to data that is available, the income of Time Warner, Disney World, and News Corporation in the year 2003 was $39.6, $10.27 and $20.19 billion respectively (a billion equals 1000 million). Viacom is bigger corporation than News Corporation[1]. CBS, which is a subsidiary of Viacom has issued a threat similar to the one issued by NBS. Twentieth Century Fox, owned by fascist media owner Rupert Murdoch has also issued a similar ultimatum to striking writers. Murdoch owns News Corporation and Twentieth Century Fox is a subsidiary of News Corporation. At the time of writing, the

---

[1]This is no longer the case. See chapter 11.

185

26. The WGA Strike

WGA is firm on its stand.

One of the most shameful aspects of this episode is the role of the US media. This important news has been suppressed by the leading newspapers. It is astonishing that newspapers have not given this strike the prominence that it deserved. This was a strike of all writers connected with the media and these writers are part of the media world - they were not outsiders who did not deserve attention of the newspapers. The real reason for this cold treatment lies in the fact that the same corporations own the leading newspapers, and the editors would lose their jobs if they were to give prominence to news of strike against the owners of their papers.

An apprehension is being expressed about the possibility that the WGA leadership might bow down before the bullying of corporate media owners. In fact, the leadership of the auto industry workers struck a "deal" with the owners and dealt a severe blow to the interests of the auto workers. We can only express solidarity with the striking workers and pray for them. Without their creativity the world would become quite colorless, lifeless, dull and poor. The destruction of the creative force of American writers will be a deep loss for mankind. May God protect them and keep them safe from the satanic designs of the corporate media owners.

Written December 2007 - unpublished

Chapter 27

Project for "American Century"

They have pillaged the world. When the land has noth-
ing left for men who ravage everything, they scour the
sea. If the enemy is rich, they are greedy; if the enemy
is poor they crave glory. Neither East nor West can sate
their appetite. They are the only people on earth to covet
wealth and poverty with equal craving. They plunder, they
butcher, they ravish, and call it by the lying name of "em-
pire". They make a desert and call it "peace".

Roman historian **Tacitus**

How many of these war millionaires shouldered a rifle?
How many of them dug a trench? How many of them
knew what it meant to go hungry in a rat-infested dugout?
How many of them spent sleepless, frightened nights, duck-
ing shells and shrapnel and machine gun bullets? How
many of them parried the bayonet thrust of an enemy?

187

27. Project for "American Century"

How many of them were wounded or killed in battle?
Out of war nations acquire additional territory, if they
are victorious. They just take it. The newly acquired ter-
ritory promptly is exploited by the few - the self-same few
who wrung dollars out of blood in the war. The general
public shoulders the bill.
And what is this bill? The bill renders a horrible
accounting. Newly placed gravestones. Mangled bodies.
Shattered minds. Broken hearts and homes. Economic
instability. Depression and its attendant miseries. Back-
breaking taxation for generations and generations.

Brig. Gen. Smedley D Butler
in *War is a Racket* 1935, reprinted 2003

The ideal set up by the Party was something huge, ter-
rible, and glittering - a world of steel and concrete, of
monstrous machines and terrifying weapons - a nation of
warriors and fanatics, marching forward in perfect unity,
all thinking the same thoughts and shouting the same slo-
gans, perpetually working, fighting, triumphing, persecut-
ing - three hundred million people all with the same face.

George Orwell 1984

In 1997 two Zionists Robert Kagan and William Kristol set up an organization by the name of Project of
New American Century (PNAC). On June 3, 1997 Rumsfeld, Jeb Bush (brother of President Bush), Paul Wolfowitz and other members of the Neocon cabal affixed
their signatures on the guiding principles of this organization. These war mongers subsequently became members
of the Bush cabinet or came to occupy important posi-

tions in the Bush administration. This group actually represented and defended several vested interests. This cabal included other shining stars. Richard Pearl, James Bolton, Zalmay Khalilzad, James Woolsey, William Bennet, Dan Quayle and others were the leading lights of this "American" project. It is also important to note that Rumsfeld, Wolfowitz, Richard Pearl, Bolton, Kagan, William Kristol, Elliot Abrams, Zakheim and others are Zionist Jews. All of them are them are an integral and important part of this "American" project.

Dick Cheney was Secretary Defense in the cabinet of President Bush Sr while Wolfowitz was his Under-Secretary. Soon after the disintegration of the Soviet Union in 1992 Wolfowitz began actively advising the US government about moving aggressively for setting up a New World Order in view of the fact that the US had emerged as the sole superpower on the globe. Further, even if the US allies did not cooperate in this venture the US should impose its will on the rest of the world unilaterally. It was during these years that Wolfowitz began advising and urging US conquest of Iraq so that the resources of the Gulf region, in particular an item as strategic as oil, remained in US control.

The US elite has inducted many pet thinkers into its "stable". These thinkers work continuously, day in and day out, thinking up strategies for the protection and promotion of the vested interests of this elite. On many occasions their edifying thoughts appear in journals like the *Foreign Affairs*. If needed, these articles are expanded and published in the form of books that are given wide publicity and are presented as books of great intellectual worth. This is part of the strategy to influence the minds of the US public in a desired manner apart from adding to the income of these thinkers and writers. Zalmay Khalilzad is a part of this set of pet thinkers of the elite. He published a book in 1995 in which he openly urged that the US must pursue an aggressive policy to capture all global resources. After this publication William Kristol and Paul Kagan published two articles in *Foreign Affairs* in which it was advocated that the US must set up a "benevolent global hegemony". Brzezinski has also advocated the same point of view in his book *The Grand Chessboard* which was published in 1997 and was developed out of his articles in *Foreign Affairs*.

In 1998, leaders of PNAC wrote to President Clinton urging him to remove Saddam from power. This letter urged President Clinton to remove Saddam even if the US failed to secure the support of the Security Council for the purpose. It is quite clear that the letter was written keeping in view Iraq's oil wealth and military power. It is a cornerstone of the thinking of the US establishment that no Muslim country should be rich and militarily strong at the same time - military and financial power must not be allowed together in any Muslim country. And if a Muslim country has this dual potential or capability, it must be destroyed.

It was in the year 2000 that the infamous report associated with PNAC came to light - it was titled *Rebuilding America's Defenses*. Although the report has three authors, 27 names are given at its end. These are names of individuals who took part in the project. Of these, at least 16 are Zionists. A perusal of the 90 page report reveals that it represents the interests of the defense industry, of oil companies and of Zionists. It aims at beguiling the people of the US by placing before them a dream of American greatness through global conquest and shoving the nation into a state of perpetual war, thereby serving the real interests of the elite. After going through the report one feels its title should read *Rebuilding America's Defenses for Global Conquest.* Wherever oil resources exist, these must be captured, and wherever there are other resources, these too must be snatched from local people.

This report calls upon the US government to develop the ability to transport forces rapidly to any region and to simultaneously fight and win many wars. Previous US strategy involved fighting two major wars simultaneously since Russia and China are the two other powers. The report writers appeared to have foreknowledge that the Republicans would win the next election, even if through rigging, and the report would be adopted by the US government. The report also calls upon US to play the role of a global policeman. This is an apparently highly attractive objective for the American people - they would love the US to play a role in eliminating conflict and promoting peace worldwide. In reality, the US will become a global gangster. Unknown to the US people, it will snatch whatever resources the poorer countries have and will suppress their voice. Ask the people of Iraq where, in the past 16 years, 2.8 million Iraqis have lost their lives.

Four "missions" have been proposed in the above report. All these pertain to increasing US forces and arming them with more modern equipment. In the first mission of the report it is clearly stated that the US should not only maintain it nuclear weapons, but enhance its nuclear power, while at the same time ensuring that other countries do not develop weapons of mass destruction. The report talks of American Peace - *Pax Americana* - on the globe. In reality *Pax Americana* would be a state of affairs where the US will have captured global resources and suppressed mankind. "Pax - Americana", "American Peace", "American century", "Global dominance", "New World Order", "Globalization" - all these terms are different names for the same state of affairs in which the US people will be conscripted as fodder for war and in which mankind will eke out a pitiable existence in poverty and suffering. A few superrich families will rule this plundered planet. Will this happen? Time will tell.

Waqt, December 5, 2007

Chapter 28

Kennedy's Assassination

The American press, with very few exceptions, is a kept press. Kept by the big corporations the way a whore is kept by a rich man.

Theodore Dreiser

Fundamentally the founding fathers of US intelligence were liars. The better you lied and the more you betrayed, the more likely you would be promoted. These people attracted and promoted each other. Outside of their duplicity, the only thing they had in common was the desire for absolute power. I did things that, in looking back on my life, I regret. But I was part of it and I loved being in it... Allen Dulles, Richard Helms, Carmel Offie, and Frank Wisner were the grand masters. If you were in a room with them you were in a room full of people that you had to believe would deservedly end up in hell... I guess I will see them there soon.

James Angelton Head CIA counter-terrorism wing and chief suspect in Kennedy's murder, on his deathbed. Quoted in **Joseph Trento**'s book *Secret History of the CIA*

Tom Nogouchi's autopsy on RFK stated unequivocally that the shot, which killed RFK, was fired from less than one to no more than three inches behind his right ear. Every soul in the pantry that night stated categorically that Sirhan never got closer than three feet to Bobby and was directly in front of him... To this day Sirhan has absolutely no recollection of the events that night. He was hypnotized and he was a patsy, firing loud blanks to distract the witnesses from the real assassin Thane Eugene Cesar. Please, somebody sue me! Let's go to court.

Does CIA produce mind-controlled assassins? Well aside from the reams of material released under FOIA from CIA which say they do, stop for a minute to look at one LAPD document from SUS files. Sirhan Sirhan was hypno-programmed using hypnosis, drugs, and torture by, among others, the Reverend Jerry Owen and CIA mind-control specialist William Bryan hypno-programmed Sirhan at a stable where he worked months before the shooting. Also working there was Thomas Bremer brother of Arthur Bremer who, in 1972, shot Presidential contender George Wallace. Read it for yourself and ask yourself what you believe about the existence of democracy in this country and what you believe about the fate of ANY Presidential candidate not sanctioned by the powers that be before the "race" is run.

Michael Ruppert in *Bobby I Didn't Know*

Four successive assassinations in the US in the 1960s have had a profound effect on the US as well as world history. The first of these was the assassination of President John F Ken-nedy. Kennedy was murdered on November 22, 1963 in Dallas, Texas, as he stood in his car waving to cheering crowds. This sensational murder threw the world in a turmoil. Who were the men behind this murder? This question has not yet been answered definitely. With the passage of time many of those who knew have left this world. However, under US law, many new facts and much information have come to light which have enabled researchers to uncover, to a very large extent, the hidden hands behind this assassination.

The second of these assassinations was the murder of the black leader Martin Luther King who waged a peaceful and effective struggle for the rights of the black community and was trying to earn for the black community a dignified place in US society. The black community stood united under his leadership. This murder deprived the blacks of a most beloved and effective leader. Four decades have passed since his murder, and because of this murder the blacks in the US are still in the wilderness. The third assassination of this series was that of another black leader Malcolm X and the fourth and final murder in this chain was that of Robert Kennedy who would have been most likely elected President and exposed the true killers of his brother. The true perpetrators behind these assassinations have never been brought to light and the truth has been denied to the people of USA.

195

28. Kennedy's Assassination

President Kennedy's murder was the result of a deep intrigue and researchers have now concluded that certain powerful elements within the CIA were involved in this plan. Apart from this the mainstream US media has played the same role that it has always played - misleading the public and planting incorrect things in their heads. The media has been very successful in this matter. It was Oliver Stone's movie *JFK* that shook the US public. This movie conveyed, to people of the US, the fact that the murder of President Kennedy was the result of an intrigue in which elements of the US establishment were fully involved. *JFK* was a very powerful movie, and the public reaction it evoked forced the US Congress to pass, what is known informally as the JFK Act. An Assassinations Records Review Board (ARRB) was set up under this Act that declassified about 2 million pages of documents pertaining to President Kennedy's murder during the period 1994-1998. Despite this, numerous documents remained classified because the US agencies claimed that their declassification might affect ongoing projects. One might wonder as to what kind of operations were still continuing three decades after the murder of John Kennedy that could be affected by declassification of these documents.

Nonetheless researchers have done an admirable job by minutely studying and analyzing the declassified documents and have pieced together the intrigue against President Kennedy. One of the conclusions that emerges from these studies is the role of the US media. It is quite clear that the US media has suppressed the truth about Kennedy's murder in subservience to the elite that owns it and you will not find revelations about this murder on the TV or in leading newspapers. A handful of courageous researchers launched a magazine named *Probe* that published results of these researches. This magazine has now ceased publication but articles published in the *Probe* may be viewed on the internet.

By a strange coincidence, a US citizen was making a film of the Kennedy motorcade when Kennedy was shot - this is the famous *Zapruder* film. It has captured the moments when Kennedy was hit and the subsequent moments. The film shows, without any doubt, that the President was hit by a bullet that came from the *front* because his head jerked backwards under the impact. Even an imbecile can infer that the bullet came from the front but the US media has repeated only one thing again and again and again and that is that Kennedy was killed by Oswald. The location from where Oswald is alleged to have shot Kennedy, however, was *behind* Kennedy. The fact is that bullets at Kennedy were fired from several locations and came from different directions. One may gauge the frightening power of the US elite from the fact that even today the average American believes that Oswald was the sole individual who fired at and shot Kennedy. As Michael Ruppert wrote:

> Only by taking the actual text of the Warren Commission report, the photographs, the medical records that have been released over the decades, and then comparing them, can a lone, crazed citizen arrive at any conclusions.

The conclusion is that Kennedy was killed by a bullet that came from the front and that he was fired at by more than one assassins.

The documents declassified through the JFK Act reveal that the US establishment was fully determined, from day one, to conceal the real facts about his murder and that it had complete cooperation of US media in this matter. In the foreword of their book *Assassinations* James DiEuginio and Lisa Pease write:

> Articles in *Probe* revealed how the press actively but clandestinely cooperates with the intelligence community, and then conceals the truth about that cooperation.

It is quite clear from the record that James Angleton, the head of the counter intelligence wing of the CIA, played a key role in this intrigue. Richard Helms also figures prominently in this regard. Later on it was Richard Helms who assumed charge as Director CIA! The real reason for Kennedy's murder was his decision to recall US "advisers" from Vietnam. After assuming charge as President, the first decision that Lyndon Johnson took was to reverse Kennedy's directive in this regard. Johnson thus ensured a deeper and wider involvement of the US in Viet Nam so that the defense industry and the big banks could make fabulous money, regardless of the outcome of the war.

Researchers have pointed out to another fact not shown in Oliver Stone's movie. It has to do with the Federal Reserve, a private bank that has the power to issue US currency. This unconstitutional power was usurped with great cunning, through the US Congress. The passage of the Federal Reserve Act gave unsurpassed power to the wealthiest families on the planet, who conceived of, and colluded in this heinous scheme, over the US people, the US economy and over the politics of the United States of America. Kennedy wanted to restore this power to the Treasury and had ordered printing of four billion dollars worth of treasury bills with the instruction that once printed, the-se would be put into circulation and the Federal Reserve notes would be withdrawn. This would have meant the end of the control of the elite over the US and, therefore, over the globe. Steve Lendman writes:

> Just months after the Kennedy plan went into effect, he was assassinated in Dallas in what was surely a coup d'etat disguised to look otherwise and may well have been carried out at least in part to save the Fed System and concentration of power it created that was so profitable for the powerful bankers in the country.

Rothschild had once said *"Give me control of a nation's money and I care not who makes the laws"*.

Waqt, December 15, 2007

Chapter 29

Attack on Iran and WWIII

The US is signatory to nine multilateral treaties that it has either blatantly violated or gradually subverted. The Bush administration is now outright rejecting a number of those treaties, and in doing so, places global security in jeopardy, as other nations feel entitled to do the same.
Project Censored 2005

The analysis, called TIRANNT, for "Theater Iran Near Term," was coupled with a mock scenario for a Marine Corps invasion and a simulation of the Iranian missile force. U.S. and British planners conducted a Caspian Sea war game around the same time. And Bush directed the U.S. Strategic Command to draw up a global strike war plan for an attack against Iranian weapons of mass destruction. All of this will ultimately feed into a new war plan for "major combat operations" against Iran that

military sources confirm now [April 2006] exists in draft form.
... Under TIRANNT, Army and U.S. Central Command planners have been examining both near-term and out-year scenarios for war with Iran, including all aspects of a major combat operation, from mobilization and deployment of forces through postwar stability operations after regime change.
William Arkin, Washington Post, 16 April 2006

The overwhelming majority of mankind ekes out an existence where it has to work day in and day out for a little bread. On the other hand a thousand or so billionaires, who own most of the global wealth, are ceaselessly intriguing to amass greater wealth. Some of the billionaires are not usually mentioned in the *Forbes* magazine. It is rare to find, if at all, the names of the Rothschilds and the Morgans and the Rockefellers in these lists. No war on earth is fought without economic or strategic objectives. A handful among these billionaires "decide" which country should go to war, which country be dismembered, whose resources be captured or plundered or which countries should unite. When European politicians failed to unite Europe, the Bilderberg Group took over and set up the European Union within two years. The meetings and decisions of this group are surrounded by complete secrecy.

The elite of the US, the pre-eminent power of today, poses the greatest threat to mankind. The elite owns the US defense industry, its major banks, oil and gas companies and major western media. The elite has its organizations that take "decisions" on war and peace, and the proceedings of the more important organizations are kept secret at all costs. President Bush, Dick Cheney, Congressmen and other US leaders are either part of the elite or work for it. The US elite now has the desire to capture the resources of the entire globe. This sentiment was expressed openly by Brzezinski over three decades ago. The war criminal Henry Kissinger has gone to the extent of saying that the increasing population of the Third World constitutes a "threat" to the "strategic" interests of the US. This implies that the world be rid of this "threat", i.e., the "extra" population. Informed researchers have alluded to a secret plan to reduce the present global population by one to two billion! Thinking appears to have been done on this "problem" and probably plans to achieve such an objective do exist.

On October 16, President Putin had stated that with regard to Iran we "should not only reject the use of force, we should not even think of it". The very next day President Bush made an astonishing observation in response to a question. He said that if you wish to avoid third world war then Iran will have to be stopped from acquiring knowledge needed to build nuclear weapons. A lot of people do not rate the mental abilities of President Bush very highly, but he has repeatedly defended his statement. Therefore, we may infer that it was not a chance remark that slipped through his mouth but, more likely, it represented the thinking of think tanks of the US establishment, think tanks that work for the elite.

Therefore, the following question arises: what are the factors with regard to Iran that could turn the US-Iran conflict into a third world war? Sixty to 70 percent of global oil resources are confined to a small region consisting of western Iran, southern Iraq and north-eastern part of Saudi Arabia. These three areas are contiguous. Also the second largest gas reserves in the entire world are located in Iran. Forty percent of the global oil consumed passes daily through the Persian Gulf. The Strait of Hormuz is a mere 34 mile wide strip flanked by the Iranian and Omani coastlines on the two sides. A two mile wide shipping lane has been allocated for the movement of oil tankers in the Strait of Hormuz. A further two mile sea strip has been left open on the sides of this lane. Iran has mounted Russian and Chinese missiles on motor boats or launches and in event of war the delivery of this oil can be affected. It is important to note that 70 percent of oil passing through this region goes to the far east while the remaining thirty percent goes to Europe.

China has signed a 70 billion dollar agreement with Iran under which Iran shall supply liquified gas to China for the next 30 years. Oil to China passes through the narrow Malacca Straits where it can be intercepted easily by the US navy. On account of this China has been considering an alternative - oil be offloaded on Burmese ports and delivered by a pipeline through Burma. This explains the noise made by the US government and media against the Burmese rulers - the pressure is being exerted to prevent this. Another project under consideration is the delivery of oil to China through a pipeline from northern Iran through Central Asian states. It is also important to bear in mind that the break up of the Soviet Union not only destroyed the economy of Russia, the US agencies, through a heinous plan, looted and plundered several hundred billion dollars from the Russia so that it would not be in a position to respond to the US attack on Afghanistan. Russian economy is now in a much better state and this is primarily due to export of oil. The Central Asian states also have gas and oil resources and the US has established a foothold in the region. The Shanghai Cooperation Organization (SCO) has, however, demanded in the past two or three years that the US forces quit the region and this demand is supported by the leadership of the Central Asian states.

The northern region of Iran is connected to Turkey as well as Central Asia. The Central Asian region is not just resource rich - it is strategically located - one can reach any part of the Eurasian land mass more easily from Central Asia than from any other region. The US strategist Brzezinski has clearly stated in his book *The Grand Chessboard* that the power that controls Central Asia will rule Eurasia. This is not his personal thinking - it reflects the thinking of the US establishment. The US establishment has never bothered about the loss of human life to achieve its strategic and economic objectives and it has never thought US victory in such a war is not certain. In his book Brzezinski has emphasized that China, Russia and Iran must not be allowed to join hands. In its impatience, the Bush-Cheney leadership has aggravated matters from this point of view and the three countries are fairly close now. Alex Leitner has raised the question as to whether it would be possible that the US may attack Iran after assuring Russia that its interests will be protected. This is not possible because, on the one hand, the US is waging war on "terror" in different places while on the other hand, it is training Muslims in Chechnya and Daghestan with the object of breaking them away from Russia. Once the US incapacitates Iran it will be able to maintain its forces on Iranian territory as well as in Central Asia and thus pose an even more serious threat to both Russia and China. Further, it will be in a position to prevent delivery of oil to China through land and sea and to block Russian oil exports thus devastating both countries economically. An important question arises: what will happen if countries stop selling and buying oil in dollars? At this point Iran is selling and buying oil in Euros and yen mostly, even though worldwide most oil transactions are conducted in dollars. The Chinese are also thinking of converting dollars into Euros. This trend is unacceptable for the US. The US wishes to maintain the Middle East in its grip and then to extend this grip to Central Asia so that it will in a position to strangulate both China and Russia. Attacking Iran will be the key step in this endgame and if the Russians and the Chinese stand idly by, they will be inviting their own death.

Waqt, December 8, 2007

Chapter 30

Mysterious Organizations

"We are now at the year 1908, which was the year that the Carnegie Foundation began operations. And, in that year, the trustees meeting, for the first time, raised a specific question, which they discussed throughout the balance of the year, in a very learned fashion. And the question is this: Is there any means known more effective than war, assuming you wish to alter the life of an entire people. And they conclude that, no more effective means to that end is known to humanity, than war. So then, in 1909, they raise the second question and discuss it, namely how do we involve the United States in a war"

Norman Dodd in 1982. Once member of US Congressional Special Committee for Investigating Tax-Exempt Foundations

Briefly the role of the American public was talked about by

Charlie Rose with Kissinger who paused to pick his words carefully. Kissinger told his interviewer, Rose, that the United States is a nation whose public has no clue about American foreign policy. **Mahdi Darius Nazemroaya** researcher in his article *War and the "New World Order"*

The "Goals 2000" program, developed during the presidency of George H.W. Bush to revamp the nation's public school system, was born at the April, 1970, Bilderberger meeting in Bad Ragaz, Switzerland. The purpose of the new educational philosophy was the "subordination of national ambitions to the idea of the international community." Because our schools are "too nationalistic," children, in the future, will be indoctrinated to consider themselves "world citizens." Prior to the 1971 meeting in Woodstock, Virginia, Prince Bernhard said that the subject of the meeting was the "change in the world role of the United States." After the weekend conference, Kissinger was sent to Red China to open up trade relations, and an international monetary crisis developed, which prompted the devaluing of the dollar by 8.57% (which made a tremendous profit for those who converted to the European Currency). In 1976, fifteen representatives from the Soviet Union attended the meeting which was held in the Arizona desert, and it was believed that at that time the plans were formulated for the "break-up of communism in the Soviet Union." **David Rivera** in *Final Warning: A History of the New World Order*

30. Mysterious Organizations

Those who work for secret organizations, or own fabulous wealth, or study issues deeply, are well aware of the fact that things are not as they appear to be. More often than not, very small but very powerful groups with vested interests, arrange for the presentation of an incorrect or distorted picture before the people with the object of controlling their minds so that their vested interests could be protected. In this context many of the tax-exempt Foundations of the US are most astonishing organizations that appear, on the face of it, to aspire for public good and are known for welfare work, but which, in reality, are the true hidden enemies, not just of the US people, but of mankind at large.

· What are these Foundations and what is their real work? Ford Foundation, Carnegie Foundation, Rockefeller Foundation, Guggenheim Foundation and many others conceal the real wealth of the wealthiest families on the planet and are dedicated to the use of this money for acquiring control over the entire globe. They aspire to set up a One World Government whose reins would be in their hands. They are most remarkable in that their true face and intentions are hidden from the world. Their wealth is greater than that of those billionaires who are mentioned in the media, particularly in magazines like the *Forbes Magazine*. The families behind these Foundations wield real power - they control the US government and perhaps all European governments. Authors employ the term "Elite" for this handful of fabulously rich and powerful families. Robert Gaylon Sr writes in his book *Who's Who of the Elite*:

It is impossible for any armed group to defeat the military capability of the elite. It is my opinion that they **own** the US military, NATO, the Secret Service, CIA, the Supreme Court and many of the lower courts. They appear to control, directly or indirectly, most of the State, county and local law enforcement agencies. To ignore this is pure lunacy.

In order to exercise control over the entire globe, the elite not only has international military and political organizations, they also have at their disposal, countless think tanks that work day and night to think out strategies to perpetuate and promote their hold. Bilderberg Group, Council on Foreign Relations (CFR) and the Trilateral Commission are three apex bodies in which, in addition to the US, European and Japanese billionaires are also represented. Gaylon Sr. writes that these are the groups that decide as to when and where wars should start, which countries will take part in the wars and which ones will not, who will provide funding for the wars, and who will rebuild regions destroyed by these wars. Above all, these groups determine as to which countries will have their maps redrawn. These organizations also decide who will be allowed to contest elections for the posts of President, Prime Minister, Chancellor, Governor General, and similar important offices in important countries. The stock markets, banks and media also belong to the elite.

In his very interesting article "The Grand Deception" Edward Griffin has provided highly important but deeply disturbing information. The elite works under a philosophy that could be called collectivism. It believes that by controlling and influencing the minds of mankind it can guide humanity and in this guidance lies the real well being of humanity. It has many converts and these converts believe that by silently penetrating various organs of society such as educational institutions, labor unions and government agencies, they must acquire control over them. They also believe that by silently penetrating and capturing the centers of powers of society they should quietly steer society towards collectivism. Nobody will know that they are being manipulated and, therefore, with a minimum of bloodshed, the collectivist objectives will be achieved. These people plan ahead - their planning stretches over decades and even centuries.

When, at the turn of the twentieth century, the superrich families faced heavy taxation as a result of the policies of the US government, they resorted to a cunning tactic. They set up Foundations and manoeuvered for the passage of a law whereby Foundations would be tax-exempt. Then they transferred their wealth into accounts of these Foundations and it must be remembered that the elite also owned these banks. Then they further ensured that, by law, the activities and accounts of these Foundations would not be subjected to any scrutiny or investigations by any agency or by anybody. The sole exception to this was the cunning proviso that only the US Congress could order an investigation into the activities and accounts of tax-exempt Foundations. Since most of the Congress has been under the thumb of the elite for most of the time, these Foundations have never been scrutinized, except on one occasion, in the entire twentieth century in democratic USA! This remarkable exception took place in 1954 when, on the insistence of some vocal Congress members, an investigation was ordered into the "un-American" activities of tax-exempt Foundations. The investigation was eventually subverted but not everything could be consigned to complete oblivion. A Congressman by the name of Norman Dodd was made the head of an investigative committee on which the Speaker of the Congress nominated certain members who had voted *against* the investigation! In 1982, some years before Norman Dodd's death, Edward Griffin recorded. in camera, his interview, that sheds extremely valuable light on the activities, methods and evolution of these mysterious and dangerous organizations.

Norman Dodd revealed that when he contacted the Carnegie Foundation, he was told that the Foundation office worked under directives, and was asked to send some representative who could go through the records and then, if required, copies of the record of interest could be provided. Dodd nominated an extremely bright lady, a lawyer by profession, to go through the records. The proceedings of the various meetings of the Board of Trustees were so shocking that the lady lawyer could not believe her eyes. For instance, from day one (1908) the Board members discussed as to what was the most effective strategy for moulding the mindset of the US public so that they could be put on the path of collectivism. After detailed discussions, it was decided. that the best way to mould the minds of people was through war! The subsequent discussions then focussed on how to take US into a war. It is, therefore, recorded in the proceedings of the Board of Trustees of the Carnegie Endowment Fund for Peace that efforts be initiated to push US into a war! It was decided that the State Department be penetrated and loyal hands of the elite be planted there! How the US was pushed into World War I is a fascinating story that will be told some other time.

At the conclusion of World War I, it was decided to control the US educational system. The Carnegie, Guggenheim and Rockefeller Foundations joined hands to achieve this objective. For this purpose, history books needed rewriting so that the collectivist philosophy could be promoted. It was decided to approach leading historians to rewrite history. When these historians refused to do so, it was decided that the Foundations should have their own "stable" of historians. After a process of short listing the Carnegie Endowment selected 20 young men with an appropriate psychological profile, gave them scholarships and sent them to the UK where they worked for their degrees in US history under the supervision of designated Professors. When these 20 scholars returned, an amount of $4.5 million was entrusted to them (in 1922) to set up the American Historical Association. They were given jobs in universities and thus the process was initiated. Soon these young men became established leaders of the academia in the field of US history. The entry of the US into World War II was also a result of manipulation and the War against "Terror" is no exception. As the poet-philosopher Iqbal put it: *The stars are not what they appear to be*

Waqt December 11, 2007

NOTE ADDED

While reading the quotes below one must remember that bodies like the Trilateral Commission, Bilderberg Group and the Council on Foreign Relations (CFR) are funded by the wealthiest families on the planet through various Foundations set up by them. The Trilateral Commission was established in 1972-73 as a result of David Rockefeller's initiatives.

The Trilateral Commission does not run the world, the Council on Foreign Relations does that!
Winston Lord Former US Ambassador to China and former President CFR

David Rockefeller is the most conspicuous representative today of the ruling class, a multinational fraternity of men who shape the global economy and manage the flow of capital... Private citizen David Rockefeller is accorded privileges of a head of state... He is untouched by customs or passport offices and hardly pauses for traffic lights.
Bill Moyers - journalist and former CFR member, writing in 1980

In 1973 David Rockefeller met with 27 heads of state, including representatives from Soviet Union and China; and in 1974, had a meeting with Pope Paul VI, who afterwards called for the nations to form a world government.
David Rivera in *Final Warning: A History of the New World Order*

The presidency of the United States and the key cabinet departments of the federal government have been taken over by a private organization dedicated to the subordination of the interests of the United States to the international interests of the multi-national banks and corporations. It would be unfair to say that the Trilateral Commission dominates the Carter Administration; the Trilateral Commission is the Carter Administration.

Craig S. Karpel in November 1977 issue of *Penthouse* magazine

In my view the Trilateral Commission represents a skillful, coordinated effort to seize control and consolidate the four centers of power: political, monetary, intellectual and ecclesiastical. All this is to be done in the interest of creating a more peaceful, more productive world community. What the Trilateralists truly intend is the creation of a worldwide economic power superior to the political governments of the nation-states involved.

Senator **Barry Goldwater**

Here comes our greatest difficulty. For the governments of the free nations are elected by the people, and if they do something the people don't like they are thrown out. It is difficult to reeducate people who have been brought up on nationalism to the idea of relinquishing part of their sovereignty to a supernational body...

Prince Bernhard of Netherlands, a founder of Bilderberg Group

Chapter 31

CIA and Drugs

The story begins at Yale, where three threads of American social history espionage, drug smuggling and secret societies entwine into one.
Kris Millegan,
Fleshing Out Skull and Bones

The most talked-about event in Barry Seal's much-talked about life concerns the persistent rumor, around shortly after his assassination, that he had been murdered when he threatened to make use of a videotape of a Drug Enforcement Agency (DEA) cocaine sting which had netted George Bush's two sons, Jeb and George W.
Daniel Hopsicker, in his book
Barry and the "Boys" - The CIA, The Mob and America's Secret History

What began as a strategy for containment of Soviet Union has become more and more nakedly a determination to control the oil resources of the world. The pursuit has progressively deformed the U.S. domestic economy, rendering it more and more unbalanced and dependent on heavy military expenditures in remote and ungovernable areas - most recently Afghanistan. It has also made the United States an increasingly belligerent power, fighting wars, especially in Asia, where it turns time after time to assets prominent in the global drug traffic.

Peter Dale Scott *Drugs, Oil, and War*, 2003

Through his writings, Michael Ruppert has exposed the central role of the CIA in drug trafficking and the role of black money in keeping giant US corporations alive. There is a deep connection between "Big Oil" and drug money. This money is used not only to keep US corporations alive, it is also used for ousting governments and promoting conflict worldwide. His articles appeared in his web newsletter *From the Wilderness* (FTW). This remarkable newsletter ceased after repeated attacks from elements that were probably connected to or instigated by the US agencies and, in order to save his life, Ruppert was forced to leave USA. In his book *Crossing the Rubicon*, this hideous game being played out by the US elite, its puppet government, and its agencies, has been thoroughly and powerfully exposed.

Drug trade generates money in two ways. Firstly, from the cultivation of crops to conversion of these in drug form, and from its trafficking to its sale there are fabulous profits. Secondly, money is involved in the form of agencies that are set up to "prevent" drug trafficking and to the construction of correctional facilities or jails and associated economic activity. According to one estimate, about $30 billion are spent annually on construction of jails. This money comes out of the pockets of taxpayers but the profits go to construction companies and to private companies that run many of the US jails and provide food, etc., to prisoners.

Can you guess how much money is generated by the global drug trade? According to one French publication in the year 2000, seven years ago, $500 billion US worth of drug money was being converted to white money annually. Michael Ruppert gave a similar estimate in the year 2004 - he estimated that drug money generates cash with $400-500 billion annually. He was once told, on conditions of anonymity, by an expert who worked for the US government and whose job was to keep an eye on the global cash flows: *"Its much much higher than that. Every conference that I go to is attended by the CIA, and we all round off the figure to around $700 billion."* In Pakistani rupees this comes out to be 42,000 billion ruppees[1]. This is far in excess of expenditure of governments of developing countries. For example, the estimated *expenditures* of the Pakistan government during the current fiscal year is 1,079 billion rupees. Therefore, roughly speaking, drug money generated annually, is sufficient to meet the annual *expenditures* of governments of approximately 40 developing countries, each with a population of 150 million!

---

[1] The conversion rate at the time this column was written (2007) was 60 Pak rupees to a dollar. Now it is close to 80 Pak rupees to a dollar. In any case, this is more than four times the current Pakistani GDP of $170 billion.

According to Ruppert, CIA began drug trafficking during the Vietnam war. In those days, it used to smuggle drugs out of Laos and this fact was a deep secret. Two drugs that bring the greatest profits are cocaine and heroin. In US alone, 400-500 metric tonnes of cocaine are consumed every year. On the other hand the total consumption of heroin worldwide is in the range 400-500 metric tonnes. Sixty percent of heroin consumed in the US also comes from Columbia. The rest of the heroin that is consumed in the US and the rest of the world comes entirely from Afghanistan.

In view of the above, Afghanistan is not just important because it is a possible route for transport of oil and gas. On account of its heroin, Afghanistan is profoundly important for the US corporations. In their ignorance, the Taliban banned cultivation of poppy and strangulated US corporations. This is what, according to Ruppert, became the immediate possible cause of the US attack on Afghanistan. President Carter was not wrong when he stated that there were lesser drugs on the streets when US was spending four to five billion dollars annually on DEA (Drug Enforcement Agency), and now, despite a DEA budget of over $20 billion the use of drugs was on the increase. In his painful book *Powderburns*, a former DEA agent Celerino Castello has narrated the horrific details of the collusion between US agencies and the drug mafia. In a nutshell, his book establishes that the US agencies are sabotaging the war against drugs through collusion with the drug mafia. Whenever an honest DEA officer wants to do something effective against the drug mafia, his job and his life are put on line. It is out of fear that many officers remain quiet about this fact.

Writing about Edgar Hoover, Michael Levine has stated that eight US Presidents were aware that Hoover was running a private police force in violation of every law of the land; however, all these Presidents decided to remain quiet about this. He further states that if a single individual could so terrorize eight Presidents of the United States of America, one may well imagine what kind of a club the CIA wields over our the current crop of US leaders. Black money from drug trade comes to corporations which show this as their profits, enhance their stocks, and earn further profits. The deep connection between CIA and the Wall Street will be described in another article.

Col. Oliver North, who played a key role in promoting the Iran-Iraq conflict, was involved in the famous Iran-Contra affair. Under a secret project, drugs were smuggled into US and sold to the blacks in San Francisco in particular. The proceeds were used to purchase equipment that was sent to Iran. Similarly, when a particular lobby was engaged in Clinton's character assassination, he ordered that the Inspector General's report on the connection between CIA and drug trafficking be made public. The report clearly established the involvement of CIA in drug trafficking. After redefining the word "agent", the report concludes that while CIA agents were not involved in drug trafficking, various contractors and pilots used by the CIA were indeed involved. During Clinton's time as Governor of Arkansas, drug trafficking took place under official patronage. Even today one may locate on the web, an excellent article titled "The Crimes of Mena: Gray Money". Investigative reporters provided evidence that the Government of Arkansas invested $60 million of black money in business through a company located in Barbados, West Indies.

Michael Ruppert has pointed out that during investigations into money laundering the names of Hewlett Packard, Ford, Sony, General Motors, General Electric, etc., had come to light. Similarly, the US airplane Hercules C 130 cannot be exported without permission of the State Department. The CIA first secured 28 such planes for the Forest Department for use in extinguishing forest fires. Then these were handed over to private companies. It transpired later that these companies worked for the CIA. These planes were then seen in Panama, Mexico, Angola and even Middle East. In 1994 cocaine worth $1 billion US was seized from one of these planes. Ruppert writes:

> The use of drug trade to secure economic advantage for an imperialist nation is at least as old as the British East India Company's first smuggling of opium from India into China in the late 1600s (the defense of that British practice, Scott points out, was John Stuart Mill's motivation for writing the tract "On Liberty"). They did it for 300 years. When something works that well, the ruling elites rarely let go of it.

Waqt, December 19, 2007

Chapter 32

CIA and Wall Street

You know how I got to be incharge of counter-terrorism? I agreed not to polygraph or require background checks on Allen Dulles and 60 of his closest friends...They were afraid that their own business dealings with Hitler's pals would come out. They were too arrogant to think that the Russians would discover it all...You know the CIA got tens of thousands of brave people killed... We played with lives as if we owned them. We gave false hopes. We - I - so misjudged what happened.
James Angelton on his deathbed. Quoted by Joseph Trento in his book *Secret History of the CIA*

George Herbert Walker Bush is now a paid consultant to the Carlyle Group, the 11th largest defense contractor in the nation, very influential on Wall Street. "Buzzy" Krongard is there. John Deutsch, the former CIA director, who retired a couple of years ago, a few years ago, is now on the board of Citibanc or Citigroup. And his number

*three, Nora Slatkin, the Executive Director at CIA is also
at Citigroup. And Maurice "Hank" Greenburg, who is
the chairman of AIG insurance, which is the third largest
investment pool of capital in the world, was up to be the
CIA director in 1995 and Bill Clinton declined to nominate
him. So there is an inextricable and unavoidable
relationship between CIA and Wall Street.*
Michael Ruppert in a radio interview Guns and Butter,
The Economy Watch with Kellia Ramares and Bonnie
Faulkner Aired on KPFA 94.1 FM, Berkeley, CA Friday,
October 12, 2001

*Under pressure from interested outsiders, decisions were
made by the United States, after World War II in Burma
and again in Laos in 1959-65, to back armies and governments
that were supporting themselves through the drug
traffic. This has led to a linked succession of wars, from
Vietnam to Afghanistan, which have suited the purposes
of international oil corporations and U.S. drug proxy allies,
far more than the those of either the U.S. government
or its people. Those decisions were also major causes
for the dramatic increase in drug trafficking over the last
half century.*
Peter Dale Scott in *Drugs, Oil, and War*, 2003

What is the relationship between CIA and Wall Street?
In order to understand this relation one would do well to
bear in mind that the wealthiest families of the planet
decide the fate of mankind from behind the curtain. Col.
Fletcher Prouty was a key officer in the US establishment
and gave briefings to the US Presidents in the period 1955

to 1964. In his excellent book *The Secret Team*[1], Prouty has narrated an incident involving Churchill. He narrates that one night during World War II, when the allied forces carried out very heavy bombing of Rotterdam, Churchill came up to the bar in the room of the duty captain, before going to his own underground bedroom. Talking to himself Churchill muttered

> "Unrestricted submarine warfare, unrestricted air bombing - this is total war." He continued sitting there, gazing at a large map, and then said, "Time and the Ocean and some guiding star and High Cabal have made us what we are."

Prouty remarks that during the dark days of the war, who could have known better than Churchill, of the existence of a "High Cabal". This "High Cabal" wields staggering power and is successful because it has discovered the value of anonymity.

Wall Street is located in the city of New York in the United States of America. Major banks, corporations and other business organizations have offices in Wall Street. Financial decisions taken in Wall Street determine global fiscal trends. The great global game is, to a very large extent, a game of money. This money is concentrated in a few hands and these hands are perpetually active to make more money. The US government, to a large extent, is a "front" of these wealthy families and is subservient to them. This subservience has intensified with the passage

---

[1]The book has been placed on the web for free download.

of time. In order to keep the wealth of the world in these few hands, US agencies are ceaselessly active in promoting conflict and bloodshed worldwide with the object of weakening and impoverishing resource rich countries so that the resources could be apportioned for this wealthy cabal whose most important center is named Wall Street.

The third chapter of Michael Ruppert's eye-opening book on 9/11, "Crossing the Rubicon" is titled "CIA is Wall Street and Drug Money is King." CIA came into existence as a result of the National Security Act of 1947. The author of this Act was Clark Clifford. He subsequently became the President of a bank - First American Bank Shares. Decades later Clark Clifford was indicted in the BCCI scandal, a bank set up by a Pakistani. The case of Clark Clifford reveals the pattern of relationship between the CIA and Wall Street. Senior officers of the CIA move back and forth between the CIA and the Wall Street. Whenever they commit a crime, they are never jailed. In recent years, the CIA has opened a university for its agents at a secret location where these agents are especially taught the subject of Finance.

Allen Foster Dulles and John Foster Dulles were two brothers who owned a very influential firm in Wall Street named Sullivan and Cromwell. Both brothers did intelligence work during World War II. Allen became CIA Director while John became Secretary of State during the Eisenhower regime. Allen Foster Dulles had worked at an executive position in the Standard Oil Company owned by the Rockefeller family. President Kennedy dismissed Allen Foster Dulles from the position of Director CIA. When Kennedy was murdered, presumably on the direction of the "High Cabal", Allen Foster Dulles was appointed as member of the investigative commission, Warren Commission as it came to be known, that was to look into the assassination of John Kennedy. When someone pointed out that the Warren Commission report was full of contradictions Allen Foster Dulles remarked "The American people don't read"! The real purpose of Warren Commission was to mislead the American public on the assassination, and to hide or distort facts, instead of uncovering the truth.

The father of the present President Bush was also a former Director of the CIA. The elders of this family were, according to investigative writers, involved in business with the Nazi industrialist Thyssen and converted black money into white through banking. The Bush family has been in the oil and intelligence business for decades now. In a revealing article "Bush Cheney Drug Empire" Michael Ruppert has pointed out possible links of Bush and Cheney with the drug business.

Similarly, Bill Casey was the Director of CIA during the Reagan era. It was Casey who, according to informed writers, brought the idea of using students of madrassas in the Afghan war. Casey had a hand in the Iran-Contra affair in which drug money was used to purchase equipment for shipment to Iran in order to prolong and sharpen the conflict. Casey was a former head of the Securities and Exchange Commission. He was also a founder and board member of a firm named Capital Cities. When the TV channel ABC aired programs showing the involvement of the CIA in money laundering through a firm in Hawaii, Casey and the CIA Counsel General Stanley

Sporkin put tremendous pressure on ABC to stop airing the program. In the ensuing conflict the stocks of ABC fell and it was purchased by Capital Cities! Michael Ruppert states that after it was purchased by Capital Cities, the ABC network became known as the "CIA network". Bill Casey was also connected to the mafia. Stanley Sporkin worked for the Securities and Exchange Commission for years and eventually became its Council General. Bill Casey and Stanley Sporkin were very closely connected. Sporkin too, according to writers, was involved with Iran-Contra and was in constant contact with Col. Oliver North. This is the infamous Oliver North who, as was proved in court, had lied to the Congress. Sporkin became a judge in Washington D.C. where he, in contravention of all ethical norms, remained a protector of illegitimate interests of the CIA.

Another CIA Director John Deutch was also connected with the US elite business community. After finishing his assignment with the CIA in 1996, he became a member of the Board of Directors of the famous banking giant Citigroup. Material is available on the web about money laundering by Citigroup. The Mexican bank Banamex was also purchased by this group. Banamex was involved in conversion of black money from drugs into white money. Similarly, an Executive Director of the CIA at the time of 9/11, connected to the Wall Street, was Alex "Buzzy" Krongard. Executive Director is the number three position in the CIA and all secret operations are overseen by the Executive Director. Krongard was the head of the Alex Brown Investment Bank prior to assuming his position as Executive Director of the CIA. The mysterious stock trading of shares of the American Airlines just before 9/11 took place through this bank. The matter of these "Profits of Death" has been completely suppressed and concealed from the US public. The real ruling cabal of the US is scared of the US public and maintains itself by keeping the public in the dark.

Professor Peter Dale Scott of the University of California has written wonderful books on "deep politics". He mentions that "secret collusion and violation of the law" are an integral part of the "deep" political system. Professor Scott has also stated that six out of the first seven Directors of the CIA belonged to "social register" of New York and that all seven Deputy Directors during the time of President Truman and Walter Bedell Smith came from the financial and legal circles of the Wall Street. In an earlier column, the connection between CIA and drugs was described. Wall Street amasses huge amounts through drug money. This money is invested in different profitable projects. If the firms were to borrow money from banks for such projects they would have to pay high interest. Michael Ruppert has, therefore, referred to drug money as the "steroid" of the US finance system. This "medicine" is provided to the Wall Street by the CIA. In fact, the protection of the interests of the Wall Street is the real function of the CIA. The US finance system has now become one of the most corrupt finance systems of the world. According to researchers, six trillion dollars[2]

---

[2]This is $6000 billion! It will do well to remember that this is more than 35 times the current GDP of Pakistan ($170 billion). Pakistan is a country with a population of around 170 million in 2010. All this money has gone to a handful of people and the

have been stolen from the hard working, patriotic, honest and humane people of the US. There is no one who will check this cabal of thieves and now this cabal aims at conquering the world through the US armed forces.

Waqt, December 25, 2007

---

vast majority of the US population has no knowledge of this crime simply because the media is owned by the elite.

Chapter 33

Capturing Africa

Later in the book her husband Bill, a veteran war correspondent and author, recounts the attitudes of French agents who financed wars in Indochina with opium. He said about the French, "They said that to save France, you had to destroy the human garbage. If the garbage sustained its drug addiction by spending huge amou-nts of money, and if that money financed wars in Indochina against communism - well, then you got some benefit from the human garbage!"

Michael Ruppert
My Dream and the Color of Suffering

The wealthiest families of the planet rule the world from behind the curtain. The government of the United States of America and Western governments work for the protection of the interests of this wealthy elite. These families maintain mankind in a state of perpetual conflict and war. War serves two purposes. Firstly, it brings enormous profits through sale of equipment and ammunition. Secondly, entire governments become their captives because governments have to borrow money from banks owned by these families to meet war expenses. These ruthless families do not allow mankind a moment's respite. The sole objective of this elite is to make more money and to hold complete control over the politics and resources of the entire globe in order to protect their wealth. The grip of these families is usually identified as US or Western dominance. The fact of the matter is that the American people are fed up with perpetual war, rising cost of living and the growth of dictatorial powers of the US administration. Yet it is not possible for them to free themselves from the clutches of the elite. According to one estimate, the US public owes $45 trillion in debt to the elite and this amount is increasing by the day on account of interest.

According to Professor Michel Chossudovsky of Montreal University, the War on Terror is a fraud. This war is being fought only in those regions that are rich in oil and gas or through which oil and gas are transported. As the dependence of USA on imported oil increases, the US is placing its forces worldwide with the objective of securing and apportioning the global oil and gas resources for itself. In order to secure its objectives the US has set a chain of "commands". These "commands" have been entrusted with the "responsibility" of establishing US hegemony in various parts of the globe. We read about CENTCOM in the newspapers. The first "responsibility" of CENTCOM was the Middle East. Later its sphere of "responsibility" was extended to cover Central Asia as well as the coastal countries of East Africa. Similarly NORTHCOM (i.e., Northern Command) is "responsible" for maintaining US control over the land, air space and sea of Canada, the US and Mexico. In a similar vein, we have European Command (EUCOM) that has been set up to maintain control over most of Europe, Israel and many countries of Africa.

In January 2007, through a Presidential order, President Bush directed the setting up of AFRICOM. AFRICOM is expected to come into practical shape by September 2008. AFRICOM will look after entire Africa with the exception of Egypt, and will ensure that the oil and gas wealth of Africa come under the exclusive control of the US. During the cold war US interest in Africa was essentially dictated by rivalry with the USSR. However with the gradual depletion of US oil fields and the increase in demand for oil in the country, the US has developed an "interest" in every region that possesses oil and gas. In May 2001, a report was prepared on the direction of Vice President Dick Cheney which concluded that in the coming years the US will have to increasingly depend on oil from other countries. A few months later the US State Department declared that oil and gas in Africa was of "strategic" value to the US. Whenever the term "strategic" is invoked, it implies that the US has a right over everyone else and will use all means and methods, including the use of force, for securing the "strategic" items. Local people, who are real owners of those items, hold no significance in this regard.

It is not surprising that the US has military pacts and formal arrangements with 32 African countries. If you look at the map of Africa, you will notice the "Horn" of Africa in the east. The coastal countries here include Sudan, Eriteria, Djibouti, Somalia and Abyssinia. The US has promoted perpetual conflict in Sudan while entering into military agreements with the remaining countries. About 2000 US troops are stationed in Djibouti. Whenever the US wants to get hold of energy sources, it first enters into an agreement to train local forces against "terrorism". By setting up bases in the coastal countries in the "Horn" of Africa, the US can target oil traffic through the Red Sea, or protect it. On the other hand if you start from the Western side of Africa and move along the coast to South Africa you will notice the following countries with most of whom the US has entered into pacts or agreements on the pretext of fighting "terrorism": Algeria, Mauritania, Sierra Leone, Cote de Ivory, Ghana, Togo, Benin, Nigeria, Gabon, Angola, Namibia and South Africa. US forces are present throughout this coastal region of Africa at various locations. All these countries will now be entrusted to AFRICOM. The problem, however, is that "terrorism" does not exist in these countries. That is why an employee of the US State Department likened the US policy against terrorism in these countries to a hammer in search of a nail! The propaganda about "terrorism" is a ploy to deceive the US public and other people worldwide. In fact, close analysis reveals the presence of US hands in regions where there is "terrorism", be it Chechnya or Kososvo.

The US Air Force, Navy and the US Army are one of the largest consumers of oil in the entire world. In fact by virtue of their massive oil consumption the US forces would rank 35th if one were to make a list of countries that consume oil, treating the US forces as a "country". The US Department of Defense owns over 10,000 airplanes, 4,000 helicopters, 140,000 vehicles, 28,000 armored vehicles and 285 warships. With the exception of 80 submarines and warships that are nuclear powered, all other run on oil. An anonymous American writer has stated "Oil is money. More than that it is an essential component of modern life on which people living in the important centers of power of the world have become dependent. Oil is the blood that gives life to modern military civilization of the West." For acquiring this "blood", the US elite sheds human blood worldwide. This is the essence of US foreign policy.

Waqt, January 1, 2008

Chapter 34

120 years of US "Jihad"

Every ten years or so, the United States needs to pick up some crappy little country and throw it against the wall, just to show we mean business.
Michael Ledeen

Why don't all those damned oil companies fly their own flags on their personal property - maybe a flag with a gas pump on it.
Brig. Gen. Smedley D. Butler

I helped make Mexico, especially Tampico, safe for American oil interests in 1914. I helped make Haiti and Cuba a decent place for the National City Bank boys to collect revenues in. I helped in the raping of half a dozen Central American republics for the benefits of Wall Street. The record of racketeering is long. I helped purify Nicaragua

*for the international banking house of Brown Brothers in
1909 – 1912. I brought light to the Dominican Republic
for American sugar interests in 1916. In China I helped
to see that Standard Oil went its way unmolested.*
Brig. Gen. Smedley D. Butler
in *War is a Racket* 1935, reprinted 2003

*I wish you to kill and burn; the more you kill and burn
the better you please me.*
Gen. "Howling" Jake Smith
during the US war to occupy Philippines 1898-1910

*From 1945 to 2003, the United States attempted to over-
throw more than 40 foreign governments, and to crush
more than 30 populist-nationalist movements fighting against intolerable regimes. In the process, the US bombed
some 25 countries, caused the end of life for several million more to a life of agony and despair.*
William Blum

The unprecedented US global dominance is thought provoking for anyone with an interest in history. There are
three factors that have led to this dominance. Firstly, a
planned and sustained effort to become the world leader
in science and technology. This effort began in the 1870s.
Secondly, immense productivity based on technology and
capitalism. Thirdly, perpetual "jihad" to ensure its economic and financial interests. US has been using its forces
abroad almost continuously since 1800. In the period
1800-1889 US intervened in other countries, or sent its
forces abroad, at least 86 times in Central and South-

ern America, in Asia, in Europe, and in Africa. Zoltan Grossman has collected very interesting information on US military interventions during the period 1890 -2000. Congressional briefs and other analysis and data are also available on the web and in book form. The result of his researches, and of others, is given in the following.

Since 1890 there has not been a single year in which the US troops have not been used, at home or abroad, or stationed abroad, for the protection of US corporate interests. Use of US forces abroad from 1890 onwards began with neighboring regions i.e., Southern and Central American republics, spreading to small island states in the Pacific, and then across to the states on the other side of the Pacific Ocean as well as in Africa. The US had, even before 1890, intervened militarily in the four major continents - Americas, Asia, Africa and Europe. The US fought an undeclared war with France in Dominican Republic in the period 1798-1800. Interestingly, the first US foray in Africa took place in Tripoli in the period 1801-1805. In Europe, the US intervened in Greece in 1827 to hunt for pirates. The first US intervention in Asia took place in 1832 in Sumatra where US forces landed to punish natives for plundering a US ship. Today, the US forces are present in all continents in the vast majority of UN member countries. In fact, a June 30, 2009, chart of "Active Duty Military Personnel Strengths by Regional Area and by Country" lists 150 countries outside CONUS (this is an abbreviation for the Continental United States) in which US military personnel are present. This is 78% of the entire UN membership of 192! The number of military personnel on active duty varies from a mini-

The Grand Deception

mum of one for places like Fiji, Gabon, Mali and Guyana to an unspecified number in Afghanistan. Kuwait and Iraq that certainly runs to well over 200,000 and maybe actually close to 300,000. *Excluding* Iraq, Kuwait and Afghanistan, the number of active duty US military personnel stationed abroad has been quoted as 285,773. This also does not include mercenaries like Blackwater employees, nor does it include the hordes of civilian intelligence and other agents that flock to countries of interest in various garbs such as personnel of bodies like USAID, etc., in order to assist US forces. The number of overseas US military bases stood at 737 in 2005.

The number of bases and personnel quoted above could be misleading and even inaccurate in a sense. As noted by Chalmers Johnson in his book *Nemesis: The Last Days of the American Republic*, the number of 737 overseas bases does not cover the actual number of bases occupied by the US. As he states, the 2005 Base Structure Report does not mention Camp Bondsteel in Kosovo, one of the largest ever military bases built.[1] Similarly, the number of 737 bases does not include at least 106 bases in Afghanistan (as of 2005) and other bases that the governments collaborating with the US are too scared to reveal. Similarly, the US bases in Britain are disguised as RAF bases. Also, the US military also employs a large

---

[1] Interestingly this base was built and maintained by a Halliburton subsidiary, the former Kellogg Brown and Root Corporation, now disguised as KBR Corporation. Of course Dick Cheney was Chief Executive of Halliburton and KBR which were, as Ruppert has noted in his article "Bush-Cheney Drug Empire", involved in drug business during the Iran-Contra era at least.

number of local personnel in its overseas operations and these should be included in the count.

In 1890, the US troops were sent to Argentina to protect the interests of the Government of Argentina. In 1891, the US marines clashed with nationalist rebels in Chile as well as with revolting black workers in Haiti. In 1892, US Army was employed to suppress the silver miners' strike in Idaho and, in 1893, US troops simply annexed Hawaii - the kingdom was brought to an end. In 1894, US troops occupied Bluefields in Nicaragua and the same year successfully quelled a rail strike in Chicago, killing 34 strikers.

The first US adventure, after 1890, into the far end of the Pacific region took place in 1894-95. In 1894-95, US troops and Navy reached China during the Sino-Japanese war. From 1894 to 1896 the US forces stayed on the Korean Peninsula, across the Pacific, while the Chinese and Japanese were at war. At the same time, in 1895, US marines landed in Panama, then part of Colombia, at the end of the Pacific closer to home. This was the first step towards eventual separation of the Province of Panama from Colombia, and its establishment as an independent Republic which would then allow the US to build the Panama Canal serving its economic and military interests. This target was achieved at the turn of the century. In 1896, US troops occupied the port of Corinto in Nicaragua. In the period 1898-1900, the US forces were involved in crushing the famous *Boxer rebelion* in China, a rebelion that was quelled by the government of China with the help of foreign forces.

In the year 1898, a US warship exploded while in the

harbor off Havana. At that time Cuba was a Spanish colony. The US wanted to annex all Spanish colonies and, therefore, used this as a pretext for war against Spain. The US annexed Cuba, and even today, has possession of the now infamous *Guantanamo* base on Cuban soil. Just as in today's wars, the rhetoric of human rights and democracy was used as a propaganda tool by the US leaders! This was the beginning of a series of conquests of Spanish colonies by the US. It had already annexed Hawaii. These campaigns lasted for a good part of the first quarter of the twentieth century. US troops landed in Nicaragua in 1898 and again in 1899, in 1907 and in 1910 when they occupied Bluefields and Corinto. It was also in 1898 that the US snatched Guam from Spain, and to date, Guam is a US military base.. The same year US participated in the struggle for power in Samoa. At home also, the US forces were used in crushing the Creek Indian revolt in Oklahoma. In the period 1899-1901, the US army occupied the Coeur d' Alene mining region in Idaho.

With increasing confidence the US began using its troops for longer term campaigns aimed at securing its hold wherever there was opportunity. On the one hand, US troops were being employed to subjugate the South American countries whereas on the other hand they were involved in a brutal war in faraway Philipinnes. During the period 1901-1914, the US was active in breaking up Colombia. In 1903, US warships were sent to support the US corporate sponsored rebellion to detach Panama from Colombia. It was a mere 5 days after the "independence" of Panama that the US signed a treaty for building the

Panama Canal linking the Atlantic and Pacific Oceans. This was an immensely important strategic and economic gain. At the other end, the US fought a brutal war to wrest Philippines from Spain. In 1903, US marines intervened in Honduras and during 1903-04 its troops were employed in Dominican Republic in aid of US corporate interests. The US was again to fight rebels in Dominican Republic in 1914 over Santo Domingo.

In the Philippine war, fought roughly from 1898 to 1910, over 600,000 Filipinos were killed. The quote from General "Howling" Jake Smith at the start of this chapter reveals the true face and bloody nature of this conflict. This was the first time the US had killed in hundreds of thousands and the taste of blood was to stick in its corporate mouth. It was well on its way to becoming the most murderous power ever to stalk this earth. All this was being done for one reason - the US was increasingly under corporate control and empire building and corporate interests became one. While this was going on, the US marines were stationed in Korea during the Russo-Japanese war in 1904-05.

Dictated by its corporate interests, the US continued its interventions in its South and Central American backyard. In the period 1906 to 1909, US marines interfered in Cuban elections. The US was to interfere in Cuba again in 1912. In 1907, during the war with Nicaragua, the US troops landed in Honduras, where they were to return in 1912 to protect the US economic interests.

The US began stationing troops on a long term basis wherever its economic interests dictated. It troops remained in China from 1911-1941 continuously. In 1912, the US began a 21 year occupation of Nicaragua which ended in 1933. After revolts in Haiti, the US troops remained in the small country for 20 years, from 1914-34. From 1914-1918, the US carried out a series of interventions against nationalists in Mexico. An eight year occupation of Dominican Republic was carried out by the US from 1916-1924. From 1917-1933, a 16 year long occupation of Cuba was carried out by the US converting Cuba into a protectorate.

Woodrow Wilson was reelected in 1916 on the promise of keeping US out of World War I. Five months later banking interests forced him to declare war on Germany. As the fiery and highly principled Brigadier General Smedley D. Butler wrote, "The 4,000,000 young men who put on uniforms and marched or sailed away, were not asked whether they wanted to go forth to suffer and die." The US entry into war was made possible by the sinking, by German U boats, of a passenger ship carrying munitions. The whole incident was managed and preplanned and an advertisement sent to about 50 papers in the US by the German embassy warning passengers not to board that particular ship, was killed by the State Department.

It is astonishing that the US troops landed five times on Russian soil in the period 1918-1922 (to assist or to oppose the Bolshevik revolutionaries?) On the other hand, in Panama the US forces performed "police" duties during 1918-1920 after election unrest, returning again in 1925 to quell a general strike. The US interference in the affairs of other countries purely for corporate interests is incredible. In 1919, US marines were in Honduras during elections and returned again in 1924-25 on account of election strife. At home, in 1920-21, US troops were employed to quell the strike of mine workers in West Virginia. In 1922, the US forces fought the Turks in Izmir and from 1922-27, and then 1927-1934, US troops were deployed all over China. What business did US have in China? And of course El Salvador also received its share when in 1932, warships were sent there to help quell a revolt.

In one of the most shameful incidents in US history, US Army was employed against its own World War I veterans who were demanding an early payment of their war bonuses. The veterans were marching on Washington DC and were fired upon, resulting in two deaths. Hundreds of war veterans were injured. The US corporations are incredibly brutal and insensitive to human values and the attack on US war veterans establishes this poignantly. Having thousands of US soldiers killed in World War I, it dumped them and secured a fresh crop of soldiers, who were then to sacrifice themselves during World War II. Generals George Patton and MacArthur were the stalwarts who dealt with these unfortunate war veterans.

US entered WWII in December 1941 after having manipulated Japan into attacking Pearl Harbor. For the first time in human history, atomic bombs were dropped on a country with horrendous consequences. Hiroshima and Nagasaki, the two cities of Japan, were utterly destroyed. However, the US Strategic Bombing Survey concluded that the Japanese would have surrendered even without the use of the atomic bombs. At the end of the war, US troops were stationed in Europe and Asia permanently. The European powers and Japan had exhausted themselves and the US and the USSR emerged as the new superpowers, generating a fresh worldwide struggle for control of resources. It may also be added that during the allied bombing of Dresden, spearheaded by the US, 100,000 civilians were killed - this was a city without any military targets. At home, the US troops quelled the Black rebellion in Detroit in 1943.

In 1946, the US issued a nuclear threat to Soviet Russia to keep its hands off Iran. It was, therefore, natural for USSR to accelerate its nuclear program so that the US would not threaten it any more. All the incidents pertaining to nuclear threats or deployment of nuclear bombers described in the following are based on the work of Zoltan Grossman. In 1947, US deployed nuclear armed bombers as a threat to Uruguay. In 1948, during the Berlin airlift, bombers with atomic weapons were deployed showing the increased US reliance on the use of its newly acquired nuclear power. On account of repeated US nuclear sabre rattling, the monopoly of the US on atomic weapons had to be broken. This generated a race for nuclear weapons which, today, hangs as the biggest threat to the very survival of human species on the planet.

From 1948 to 1954, the CIA directed a war against the native Huk rebellion in the Philippines. Starting from 1948 to date, the US has been providing military and economic support to Israel using it as its military arm to control Muslim oil resources. US and Israel became very close after 1957 as a result of the clandestine efforts of the mysterious CIA operative James Jesus Angleton who became Head of counter-intelligence in CIA and whose name surfaces again and again in declassified documents in connection with the murder of President Kennedy. Israel has been receiving, on an average, $3 billion of free annual aid, i.e., grant from the US for many years now.

From 1950 to 1953, the US fought in the Korean war that decimated the country. The US used the nuclear threat twice, once in 1950 and once in 1953, during the Korean war. US troops have been in South Korea since then. In the Korean war, two million people died.

The US oil companies intervened through the CIA in Iran and overthrew an elected government in 1953, just because it wanted a reasonable share of profits in oil sales of oil owned by Iran! The US then installed a highly repressive regime that murdered hundred of thousands of Iranians. The ensuing quarter century of US backed killings, horrific torture and tyranny led to the Iranian revolution. As a result of the blood shed by the US backed regime in Iran, its siphoning off of Iranian oil resources for decades, resentment against US in Iran persists even today and US has implicity threatened the use of nuclear weapons against Iran.

In the year 1954, the US began another involvement, this time in Vietnam. It offered the French colonial forces the use of US nuclear bombs. This involvement was to lead to millions of deaths and eventually an ignominious defeat in 1975. This was the Vietnam involvement that, under the machinations of defense corporations and the financial elite, became a full-fledged war. The US employed napalm bombs, carried out carpet bombing, used chemical weapons, burnt lush down green forests, and did everything in its power, including the employment of psychological warfare, to terrorize the population. Two million people died in this war in which the people of Laos and Cambodia also experienced US savagery. In the year 1954 the CIA engineered a coup in which President Jacobo Arbenz of Guatemala was overthrown because his reforms threatened a US company known as United Fruit. The US moved bombers to Nicaragua and gave nuclear threat. Professor Peter Dale Scott states that the "symbiosis of the fruit companies, their local client rulers, the US military, and organized crime became more institutionalized with the passage of years." The threat of using nuclear force was again employed in the Suez crisis in 1956. In 1958, a nuclear threat was issued to Iraq forbidding it from invading Kuwait. In 1958, the US marines occupied parts of Lebanon. The same year, 1958, a nuclear threat was given to China against attacking Taiwan. And again, in 1958, US troops were sent to Panama to quell protests.

In 1961, the US deployed nuclear armed bombers during the Berlin Wall crisis. The same year the US tried to oust the Cuban government of Fidel Castro by using exiles, trained by the US agencies, as an invading force. This was the Bay of Pigs fiasco. The discovery of Soviet nuclear missiles led to a nuclear confrontation in which the Soviet Union backed off. This led President Kennedy to the desire of peaceful coexistence with the Russians and to order a recall of US advisers from Vietnam. This meant there will be no more wars, something that meant the eventual death of the the defense industry and of banking cartels from whom money, with heavy interest, for war expenditures is borrowed. No wonder Kennedy was killed in Dallas, Texas, in 1963 in what, according to researchers, was a CIA operation showing who the true masters of the CIA are. His orders to recall "advisors" from Vietnam were reversed as soon as President Johnson took office - in fact the reversal of JFK's orders was the first order issued by him.

In 1964, US troops shot protestors in Panama demanding the return of the Panama Canal. The Dominican Republic was bombed and US troops landed there during an election campaign. One of the bloodiest CIA operations was the ouster of the populist President Sukarno of Indonesia in 1965, followed by a purge in which about a million people were massacred - CIA supplied lists of labor leaders, peasant leaders and others to be eliminated.[2] Under US encouragement Suharto occupied East Timor in the seventies and almost a third of the population of East Timor was killed. In its Central and Southern American backyard, US continued its interventions, intervening militarily in Guatemala in 1966-67.

So wide and terrifying is the subversive power of the US elite, for whom the entire US government works, that

---

[2]I remember watching, while I was a Fulbright scholar in the US during 1988-89, a TV interview of Richard Helms who headed the CIA during the Indonesian operation. Helms was sad and regretted the bloodshed they had caused in Indonesia and said that it should not have been done - and then qualified it by saying that it was an era of confrontation with Communism. This kind of regret is expressed by many chiefs of subversive agencies once out of office, but it is always a bit late as the loss of lives is irreversible. A similar regret about his past conduct was expressed by James Jesus Angleton on his deathbed. He was the head of CIA counter intelligence wing, and an ally of Richard Helms in the murder of John F. Kennedy.

while it was busy shedding blood in Asia and shattering to smithereens the independence of Central and Southern American countries, it was also busy in the African continent too. The US agencies engineered the murder, in 1960, of Patrice Lumumba, the first elected leader of the Democratic Republic of Congo, through a plane crash. The corrupt tyrant Mobutu eventually assumed power in 1965, and Congo has been bleeding ever since. At home, in Detroit, 43 people were killed as US forces fought blacks in 1967. The very next year the greatest black leader ever produced by America, Dr Martin Luther King was shot dead. Declassified documents again point to the CIA. A total of 21,000 US soldiers were deployed in various cities to prevent a reaction from the black community - the blacks were furious.

From 1969-1975, the US killed approximately 2 million people by bombing Cambodia, by starving it, and by helping create disorder and chaos. Once again, in 1973, US was on nuclear alert during the Mideast war. And in Africa it undermined Angola by backing rebels trained by white ruled South Africa from 1976-1992. I have not been able to find a count of those who died in this CIA promoted strife.

Zoltan Grossman has pointed out that when, in 1980, the Iranians stormed the US embassy, nuclear threat was used and the Soviets were warned not to get involved in the revolution. In 1981, two Libyan jets were shot down by the US. Again in the period 1981 to 1992, the US kept on interfering in El Salvador using its military and its "advisors" aiding the government in its war with rebels. During the Iran-Iraq war, which was instigated, promoted and prolonged by the US, it carried out the infamous Iran-Contra operation in which drugs were smuggled by the CIA from Nicaragua and sold in predominantly black areas in San Francisco and the money used to ship arms to Iran so that it could keep fighting Saddam's forces. The war resulted in at least 1.2 million dead and millions were displaced. Two rich and strong Muslim countries became paupers - and who earned the profits of war? From 1981-1990, the US subjected Nicaragua to civil war by aiding the Contra invasions because the elected government was not to US liking. In 1982-1984, the US stationed forces in Lebanon and fought against the PLO - the US Navy bombed Muslim and Syrian positions. Grenada was bombed and invaded in 1983-84. Two Iranian jets were shot down in 1984, Libya was bombed in 1986 and Iran was bombed in 1987-88 in support of Saddam. In 1986, US troops assisted in raids on regions where cocaine was produced in Bolivia. Two Libyan jets were downed by US in 1989 and troops were sent to Virgin Islands. The same year US intervened in an attempted coup in Philippines providing air cover against revolting forces. In 1989 President Bush announced the Andean initiative on the war on drugs. He announced that the military and law enforcement assistance will be provided to the Andean nations of Colombia, Bolivia and Peru to combat drug traffickers. The Special Forces and military advisers were duly sent to the three countries. The US ended the decade of 1980s by killing 2,000 plus citizens of Panama. The 27,000 strong US forces ousted the nationalist government of Panama. This happened in 1989-90.

The US began the 1990s of the last century by initiating a war against Iraq that is going on today after going through different phases. After the Iraqi invasion of Kuwait in 1990, the US moved forces into the region. Beginning January 16, 1991, it bombed and blockaded Iraq, killing over 200,000 people. In order to encourage and strengthen fissiparous trends in Iraq, the US imposed no-fly zones over Kurdish and Shiite territories. It imposed an embargo on chemicals and medicine knowing full well that children and older people will suffer. It systematically degraded the clean water system of Iraq causing incalculable suffering and blatantly violating the Geneva Convention. Till 2000, half a million Iraqi children had died. In 2007 the count of Iraqi dead including the first and second Gulf Wars stood at 2.8 million! About 4 million have been displaced. All for the sake of oil and for Israel whose entire population probably equals the number of Iraqis killed and displaced since 1990.

The years 1990-1992, saw involvement of US forces in Somalia, a country that has continued to face US aggression from time to time since then. UN forces led by the US were stationed there during the civil war and were involved in action. In the same period, i.e., 1990-1992, the US and NATO forces blockaded Montenegro and Serbia. From 1993 to 1995, Serbs were bombed in Bosnia by US forces and its planes patrolled the no-fly zone in the civil war. In the year 1995. Serb airfields were attacked. Across the ocean the US forces restored President Aristide of Haiti three years after having been ousted in a coup. This was in the period 1994-96.

Simultaneously, the US was involved in the African continent. In 1990, a reinforced rifle company was sent to protect the US embassy in Liberia. After widespread disturbances in Kinshasa in Zaire (former Congo) in September 1991, US C141 aircraft were employed to airlift Belgian and French troops. In 1992, US troops were involved in Sierra Leone in evacuating Americans after a coup. In 1992, the US also got involved in Somalia where they stayed from December 1992 to May 1993 assisting in UN operations. In Zaire, the US was involved in instigating revolt or "revolution". A brutal and most ugly war, provoked, aided and abetted by the CIA and the French intelligence, utilizing tribal factors, was waged in this region. The US marines were present in Hutu refugee camps from where the insurrection began. As Chossudovsky puts it, "The civil war in Rwanda and the ethnic massacres were an integral part of US foreign policy, carefully staged in accordance with precise strategic and economic objectives." The war began in 1990 and the horrendous ethnic massacres took place in 1994. The US was brutally ousting the French and the Belgians and at the same time wanted to use Uganda and other states in the adjoining regions to launch movements into the oil rich Sudan. A UN report leaked in 2010 points out that about *six million* men, women and children were killed by Rwandan and Ugandan troops, both countries being run by US client rulers. As Glen Ford wrote on September 1, 2010, in his article "Rwanda Crisis Could Expose US Role in Congo Genocide":

US allies Rwanda and Uganda bear primary responsibility for the deaths of as many as six million Congolese. Now a leaked United

Nations report has confirmed that Rwanda's crimes in Congo may rise to the level of genocide, since Paul Kagame's forces killed Hutu elderly, children and women without regard to nationality. Rwandan President Paul Kagame's "mentors and funders in the US government · · · must be held equally accountable." The Tutsi Rwandan military stayed in eastern Congo to exploit the rare minerals of the region, employing slave labor and selling the bounty to multinational corporations. They were joined by the Ugandan military, who also set themselves up as soldiers/enterpreneurs on Congolese soil. The Rwandans and Ugandans remain in the region, uniformed African gangsters in league with Euro-American corporations in a killing ground that may have swallowed up possibly six million Congolese. Some estimate Congolese "excess deaths" in areas controlled by Rwanda, alone, at three and a half million. Their blood and stolen heritage has made Kigali, the Rwandan capital, a bustling beacon of capitalist enterprise - a "free market" success story.

Carnage on such a scale could not have occurred were it not for the connivance of the United States, which has nurtured Kagame at every juncture.[3]

---

[3]One reason for US interest in the region is that the US has less than half the cobalt stockpiles that will be needed during war. Instead of 85 million tons it has 40 million tons of not so

In 1995, the US deployed 1,800 strong contingent Somalia to assist withdrawal of UN forces. In 1996, US forces were fired upon while in action in Liberia. President Clinton stated that the US troops had to be deployed for evacuation and also to respond to "isolated" attacks on the US embassy. Also, in 1996, US deployed troops in Bangui, Central African Republic, for evacuation of US "private citizens". They were also involved in extracting foreigners from Albania the same year and were also employed in Rwanda and Zaire. In 1997, military personnel were deployed in Gabon and Congo to protect US citizens and others. For the very same purpose in the very same year (1997), US troops were sent to Freetown, Sierra Leone.

The year 1998 also saw continuous US troop deployment and action abroad. In 1998, the US attacked and destroyed a pharmaceutical plant in Sudan, falsely alleging that it was manufacturing nerve gas! The real purpose was to increase fatalities in Sudan by denying medicine to the people of Sudan, a country that had been in a state of civil war, on and off, since 1983. This civil war is carried out by US proxies. President Clinton told the Congress that he had authorized air strikes against camps and installation in Afghanistan and Sudan which were being used by Osama bin Laden and his organization. The year 1998 saw US troop involvement in Guinea-Bissau for evacuation purposes as a result of a military mutiny. Troops were also deployed in Liberia in 1998

---

pure cobalt. Extremely pure cobalt is found in huge quantities in the Katanga Copper Belt that runs from southeastern Congo into Northern Zambia. Cobalt is necessary to make powerful jet aircraft engines

for possible rapid evacuation that could be required on account of civil disturbances. In the same year, US carried out an intense four day bombing of Iraq because the weapons inspectors reported that there were obstructions from Iraq. The bombings of US embassies in Kenya and Tanzania in 1998 led to US troop deployment in the two countries. The troop deployment in Kenya continued into 1999 pending repairs at the embassy building. In 2000, the US sent troops to Sierra Leone for "peace keeping" operations - ammunition and other supplies were delivered. In the African theater, the US military involvement has continued to date. In 2002-2005, the US troops were spread in various countries under the deception of countering terrorism and for evacuation in disturbed regions. In 2002, US military was sent to Cote d'Ivoire in response to a rebellion and to evacuate US and other nationals. In December 2002, US forces arrived in the Horn of Africa after having received training in North Carolina as well as aboard USS Mount Whitney. In May 2003, US troops were in Djibouti and then in Liberia. About 4,350 US troops were sent to Liberian waters later in the year to support restoration of order in the country and to provide humanitarian assistance. In 2004, US troops were deployed in the Horn of Africa "in support of global war on terrorism". In a Presidential report to the Congress, sent in November 2004, the US troop deployments in Kenya, Ethiopia, Eritreaand Djibouti on the African continent are mentioned. A similar report in 2005 mentions Yemen, Kenya, Ethiopia and Djibouti where military deployments are involved in the enhancement of "counter-terrorism capabilities" of these nations.

In 2005-2006 US troops were used for humanitarian aid to Kashmiris hit by a devastating earthquake. In 2006, the US troops evacuated US citizens in view of the ongoing conflict between Israel and Hezbollah in Lebanon. Airstrikes were conducted by the US in Somali territory against some Al Qaeda suspects in 2007. And in 2008 US transported Georgian troops from Iraq during a conflict in South Ossetia. US also trained Georgian forces and provided them with ammunition.

When the Bush administration took charge in 2000, it moved speedily towards war. Using the mysterious 9/11 incident as a pretext, it launched wars against Afghanistan in 2002 and later, in 2003, on other pretexts against Iraq. These wars are still going on and, in Afghanistan, the US faces a possible defeat. In these wars full US machinery was employed causing very high "collateral damage" - the euphemism for loss of human life and property. Depleted uranium was also employed leading to long term misery for the people of both countries.[4] Both wars are

---

[4]In fact, on account of the use of depleted uranium and probably other secret nuclear devices, cancer has increased in both countries. A study of the city of Fallujah, Iraq, covering the period 2005-2009, indicates that cancer rates in Fallujah are higher than in Hiroshima and Nagasaki. The study has been published in the *International Journal of Environmental Studies and Public Health* under the title *Cancer, Infant Mortality and Birth-Sex Ratio in Fallujah, Iraq 2005-2009*. The city of Fallujah is experiencing a higher rate of cancer, leukemia, sexual mutations and infant mortality compared to the people of Hiroshima and Nagasaki. Fallujah was punished collectively on a scale beyond imagination for its heroic resistance.

The war criminals in Washington aside, the silence and complicity of the US media in this crime is proof that the media does not

being waged for control of oil and gas resources and for connected geo-strategic reasons but the people are being told that there was and is a threat to their culture and civilization. The two wars have affected the standard of living of the people and the economy of the US seriously but the defense industry and the banks have made fabulous sums. So has the oil industry. The debts will be repaid generation after generation by the people of the US. The number of deaths in these wars have been described in other chapters of this book. During the course of these wars, Pakistan has been repeatedly attacked by drones. These attacks began in 2004 and have continued even at the time of writing these lines (2010) causing loss of civilian life and generating deep resentment. Pakistan's sovereignty has been seriously compromised by the presence of US soldiers and Blackwater mercenaries on Pakistani soil. The overwhelming majority of Pakistani people have turned against the US military presence in the region and attribute sabotage in the country to this presence. Pakistan has lost about 40,000 people in the so-called "War against terror" apart from suffering billions of rupees of losses to its economy.

The US rulers have continued the policy of war. The

---

have any interest in revealing the truth - to the contrary it keeps the people of US utterly misinformed and misleads them. The reporters and editors are well aware as to who owns the media and who pays them. This corporate control of the media has made the decline of integrity of US people faster at every level and they are unable to arrest it. This does not augur well, either for the people of the US or for the world because we will all become canon fodder for perpetual wars that will bring profits to the High Cabal mentioned by Churchill.

34. 120 years of US "Jihad"

Congress has very recently decided to send another 30,000 troops to Afghanistan in complete disregard of the desire of the people of the US to end the wars abroad.[5] It has now[6] been reported that the US and its allies are planning to carry out attacks on Iran and Somalia. US has already established bases opposite Iran and has reportedly moved tactical weapons to its bases. Attacking Iran is a risk that can eventually lead to World War III. And while the US has not been able to subdue Afghanistan in nine years, its leadership is opening up a front against a nation that has survived the longest war fought in the twentieth century. By attacking Iran it might stir up the entire Afghanistan-Pakistan-Iran belt into an uncontrollable war. If it cannot win the Afghan war, how can it win this uncontrollable war? Therefore, use of nuclear bombs by the US and Israel cannot be ruled out.

It appears that the US elite wants total war, once and for all. It has stirred up tensions by holding a naval exercise with South Korea in the Yellow Sea. China protested very loudly and strongly against this exercise. As stated

---

[5]Data from the US Census Bureau suggests that more than 15 million American are unemployed and 38 million receive food stamps. A Rockefeller Foundation report *Economic Security at Risk*, counted approximately 46 million Americans as insecure in 2007. In 2005, this number was 28 million. More than one in every five Americans is faced with the possibility of becoming destitute. In June 2010, the Congress, that comprises of elected "representatives" of people, rejected a $33 billion medicare bill that would have provided relief to millions of poor Americans. However, it approved a supplementary war grant of $59 billion committing 30,000 more troops to the Afghan war.

[6]July, 2010.

by a Chinese general in *People's Daily*, "If the United States were in China's shoes would it allow China to stage military exercises near its western and eastern coasts?"[7] It has been viewed by observers as a threat to China - and the military general wrote the same in the *People's Daily* - "strategic reconnaissance and testing initial combat plans will pose a threat to China." No wonder while the US-South Korean naval exercise was in progress, the Chinese also staged a naval exercise which was overseen by Chinese military command at the highest level. This was a signal from China - "if the bottom line were to be crossed, then China would firmly react" said a Chinese analyst. The US has acquired a military base in Kyrgistan which has a several hundred mile border with China. How would the US feel if China, or Russia, were to set up a military base on the Canadian side of Niagra Falls?[8] This arrogant and provocative US-South Korea exercise was preceded by a joint US naval exercise with the Indian navy in the strategic Andaman and Nicobar islands in April-May 2010. This is close to the strategic Malacca Straits through which twenty five percent of the global oil

---

[7]The following is the response of a Pentagon spokesman to Chinese concerns regarding the fact that the US was too close to Chinese coastline for comfort: "Those determinations are made by us, and us alone...Where we exercise, when we exercise, with whom and how, using what assets and so forth are determinations that are made by the United States Navy, by the Department of Defense, by the the United States government". Rick Rozoff comments "There is no way such confrontational, arrogant and vulgar language was not understood at its proper value in Beijing".

[8]It is also important to note that subsequently the Russians also conducted a huge naval exercise in the Yellow Sea region.

transported by sea passes. This oil goes to China, Japan and Korea as well as Taiwan. In previous years also such exercises were conducted in this region forcing China to seek closer ties with Bangladesh and Burma with possible plans for off loading oil at a Burmese port and then transporting it to China through a pipeline.

The US is now busy exploiting Asian countries which may feel affected by China's rise. In the second quarter of 2010 the Chinese economy moved to number two position - China made a contribution of 1.335 trillion dollars to its GDP with Japan trailing at 1.285 trillion dollars of productivity. The inevitable rise of the Chinese economy cannot be stopped but the US and Japan wish to block its emergence. This is despite the fact that, on account of its huge population, China's per capita income is small - it stands at 98th position in the list of countries made on per capita basis. The US is trying to build an Asian NATO involving Japan, South Korea, Taiwan, Philippines, even Malaysia and others. It has engaged in military exercises involving all these countries and plans to hold more such exercises in the remaining part of 2010.

While provoking China, the US has also done its best to provoke Russia, by encircling it with military bases. Former East European, Central Asian and Balkan states are now full of US bases. The US agencies brought about regime changes in many former Soviet republics and acquired military facilities there. Former Warsaw Pact countries have, for all practical purposes, become US "military colonies." In the former Yugoslavian province of Kosovo the US has built one of the largest bases built in human history Camp Bondsteel. It plans to establish a missile shield communications center in the Czech Republic. It has recently involved Poland also in its plans to set up an anti-missile system. As reported by Global Research on August 3, 2010, "Central to the plan will be a fleet of 38 US navy Aegis class destroyers and cruisers with radar systems placed in Romania, Bulgaria, Turkey and Israel". Further, as Rick Rozoff points out, "The US has acquired four military bases in Romania and three in Bulgaria over the past four years and will soon activate a Patriot Advanced Capability-3 interceptor missile installation in the East of Poland, 35 miles from the Russian border. Longer range anti-ballistic interceptors are to follow according to Polish officials." At the same time the US is busy in Russia's backyard, in Azerbaijan, Kazakhstan, Uzbekistan and Turkmenistan in promoting bilateral military ties and also pursuing the the creation of "a Greater Central Asia extending from Afghanistan, through the Central Asian states, to the Middle East." Russia will then be bypassed and energy and other raw materials could be transported to the Black Sea, and thence onward easily. The scene for a great war involving China, Russia and the US is now set - it is a matter of time.

Unknown to the US authorities a sea change in the global perceptions about the US has taken place. There is a wind of defiance that is now blowing through Asia and elsewhere - people have now come to regard the US elite as the greatest threat to peace and to the freedom of nations. Time and again the US authorities have indulged in proven and documented deceptions, to take the good people of the US into wars abroad. Each time the elite has prevailed. But, as Catherine Austin Fitts wrote:

34. 120 years of US "Jihad"

"Those who win a rigged game get stupid". The world is witnessing this "Great Game" with disgust and knows very well that this stupidity will drown both, the US Empire and the rest of the world, in a sea of radioactive blood.

In 1979 a journalist, Syed Shabbir Hussian, wrote:

> The superpowers of today are not only ambitious, they are also ruthless. They examine situations from a different plane; they judge morality from a different angle. Break-up of countries, extinction of communities and races, and deaths of millions of human beings do not stir them. Their singlemindedness allows of no mellowness; fidelity is unknown to them.

The US military machine has evolved from killing a few scores, to hundreds, to thousands, to tens of thousands, to hundreds of thousands, to millions! It has kept up its proud record becoming the power that has probably killed, directly and indirectly, more human beings in 120 years, than have been killed in entire recorded history. The number of wounded and displaced, the number of cities and villages ravaged and destroyed, *collateral damage*, as it is callously and euphemistically called, is also more than that in the entire recorded history. This should weigh heavily on the conscience of any nation. But the nation has to know - it is its duty to know. The number of human beings killed, maimed, and rendered homeless by the US forces in service of its corporate masters, who deliberately remain out of public sight, is so staggering that humankind will stand up in revolt, when this knowledge becomes widespread.

Chapter 35

Letter to US Ambassador in Pakistan

June 7th, 2010

To The Ambassador of the
United States of America in Pakistan
Diplomatic Enclave, Islamabad

Excellency,

I would like to bring to your kind attention my experience at Logan International Airport, Boston, MA on the evening of May 22, 2010, and to place on record my protest at the treatment I received at the airport.

I was nominated for a conference on distance learning to be held from May 23-26, 2010, at the MIT. The Babar Ali Foundation had graciously offered to cover my traveling and other expenses. I applied for, and was issued, a B1/B2 visa by the US embassy on 22.02.2010. According to the visa stamp my security clearance was received on 18.02.2010.

This was to be my twelfth (12th) visit to the US since 1986, when I attended a conference at the University of Berkeley, California. I was a bit surprised when I noticed that I had been issued a one year visa only. It made me think but I took it in my stride.

When I landed at the Logan International Airport the immigration officer allowed me entry straightaway. However, once in the Customs area I was asked by a customs officer to go to one side where baggage of individuals was custom checked. The officer to whom I was directed told me that I had been marked for special registration. I was taken to a room where there were three or four other people like myself and about three to four officers at the desk.

I was first asked details about my deceased parents (names, dobs, addresses, etc.) and my address in Pakistan along with telephone numbers. While I answered the officer was apparently checking my answers on his computer. I was then asked to fill out these details in a form. Once this was done I was asked to place the right and left index fingers for finger printing for identification purposes and then the usual picture was taken. It appeared that the computer was able to "recognize" me and this phase was over in about 15 to 20 minutes. I was given a 28 page document titled "Special Registration Procedures for Visitors and Temporary Residents".

In the next phase I was brought back to the region

where baggage was checked for custom purposes. I was asked the usual questions as to whether I had the baggage with me all the time before boarding, did somebody give me a gift, what were the contents of my baggage. *Once my baggage was searched it was quite clear that the search was not custom related.* I was apparently a possible suspect involved in possible anti-US activity.

I was asked questions about my educational background, the institutions I went to, the places I had worked at, my addresses, details about my family members, their education, dates of births, professions, etc. I was also asked how many books had I written. Some of the answers were being noted down by one of the two officers.

The two officers asked me how much money I was carrying. I was asked to take out my money from a large wallet that I usually carry in my hand baggage while traveling - this wallet contained my expired credit cards, my US social security number that I had acquired while in the US as a Fulbright Fellow in 1988-89, my expired State of Georgia drivers license from those years and some other papers. Once the money was taken out this wallet was taken by one of the officers to a closed room where he kept it until the very end. Apparently he had rummaged through it and possibly checked my records since the cards inside the wallet were rearranged when it was returned to me.

This officer had told me that he wanted to check me on Wikipedia. I was surprised because I did not think I could be on Wikipedia. One of the two officers kept talking to me - most of it was normal talk about Pakistan but at one point this officer asked me if I was carrying a cell phone. When I gave it to him he switched it on (in the custom area the use of cell phones is forbidden) and apparently scrolled down. It appears that he was checking my list of contacts because, while scrolling, he asked me as to how many contacts I had on the phone. I told him I did not know to which he responded that I had many. So much for privacy.

Finally, the other officer emerged with my wallet and told me that he had checked me on Wikipedia and that I was OK. I mentioned my brother who had worked for NASA and was a US citizen and he asked for his name. After we had repacked my things, he asked me as to what my cell phone number was just in case they wanted to contact me. I gave it to him but I felt that if I had no cell phone then how they would have contacted me. It seemed to me they just wanted my cell number for their own reasons. I was also asked if I knew or would be seeing anyone in the Boston area to which I replied in the negative. I was then walked to the exit courteously by the officer who told me that sometimes they are asked to check individuals and it turned out that I was a "good guy" and "had done nothing wrong".

The entire process in the Customs area took about two hours. The officers were polite throughout their conversation with me. While I was sure that I had not done anything to warrant such questioning and that such questioning was a mere waste of time, it made me think.

I was asked to sit and wait for sometime during this period while the officers did whatever they were doing. I pondered over why was I being questioned and what could be the motive. I thought of the eruption of US militarism after 9/11, of certain laws passed by the Bush administration, of the ownership of 80% of US print and electronic media by only six large corporations, of Brzezinski's dictum that "democracy is inimical to the cause of imperial mobilization", of a statement by Gen. Tommy Franks that the people of the US will have to give up their constitutional liberties eventually, and of George Orwell, who discerned trends some of which have so clearly taken shape in post 9/11 USA. I also recalled what I had read in a report "Rebuilding America's Defenses" by the Project of New American Century (PNAC). I recalled the declassified documents reproduced in Robert Stinnett's book on Pearl Harbor. I also recalled certain statements by Mr. Dick Cheney and thought of the global "melee", dominated by the US, for oil and gas resources. I also recalled that it was believed that if 13% of US public became aware of serious wrongdoing on the part of the authorities, the authorities were likely to face serious consequences. But with 80% of media in the hands of the elite how could that happen? All these thoughts went through my mind as the officers were busy digging into records to determine whether or not I posed a danger to the US.

I did not report this to the Conference organizers. I felt that since the American people have a very high level of integrity and self respect, the Conference organizers might feel embarrassed at this treatment to a Vice Chancellor - I did not want to burden them with something which was not their doing. I did mention it to a fellow participant from Pakistan who had done his PhD from MIT. Apparently he, on his own, brought it to the notice of his personal friend, Professor Richard Larson of MIT, the soul and spirit behind the conference. I felt embarrassed and humble when Professor Larson said to me "I apologize on behalf of America". Why would the authorities of the US do things for which the decent people of the US have to apologize?

I had, in an interview with the US National Public Radio (NPR), recorded in my office on May 10th, stated that I considered the **people** of the US the greatest asset of mankind at this point in human evolution. The experience at Logan International Airport has not changed this perception. In fact the talks at the Conference by our American colleagues merely confirmed this assessment. Yet the treatment I received at the airport did not correspond with the stature of the US people. It indicates well thought out trends in the mindset and policies of the US establishment, trends that are unlikely to be checked. These trends will eventually transform the US, presumably by design, into a state of the type that USSR used to be, except that there will be a facade of two parties controlled by a single powerful elite. Today the US stands in the global arena in a position not dissimilar to that of Germany in the European arena a hundred years ago. Will this century become an American century? Or will the US miss the opportunity that Germany missed in the previous century? Only time will tell.

Yours sincerely

Professor Mujahid Kamran
cc: The Foreign Minister of Pakistan

Bibliography

[1] Abraham, Stephen E: *Testimony Before US Armed Services Committee* 2007 http://armedservices.house.gov/pdfs/ FC072607/Abraham_Testimony072607.pdf

[2] Ahmed, Nafeez Mosaddeq: *The War on Truth: Disinformation and the Anatomy of Terrorism* 2005, Arris

[3] Ahmed, Nafeez Mosaddeq: *The War on Freedom:* 2002, Progressive Press

[4] Ahmed, Nafeez Mosaddeq: *Bleeding the Gulf: The United Nations Sanctions on Iraq* 1998, Catholic Workers Magazine January / February 1998

[5] Anonymous: *Confessions of a Covert Agent Psychological Operations are m Speciality* November 27, 2007 http://artofmentalwarfare.com/pog/

[6] Anonymous: *Who Rules America? The Alien Grip on our News and Entertanment Media Must be Broken* 2001 www.natall.com/who-rules-america/

[7] Associated Press: *Body of Missing Air Force Captain Found* www.komotv.com/news/local/9679367.html

[8] Auken, Bill Van: *A new Pretext For American Militarism and Domestic Repression* 21 September 2007 www.wsws.org/articles/2007/sep2007/ rath-s21 prn.shtml

[9] Auken, Bill Van: *Dan Rather Sues CBS For Making Him a Scapegoat* 19 July 2007 www.wsws.org/articles/2007/jul2007/nie-j19 prn.shtml

[10] Auken, Bill Van: *Report: Strategic air Base Being Readied For War on Iran* 31 October 2007 www.wsws.org/articles/2007/oct2007/base-o31 prn.shtml

[11] Auken, Bill Van: *CIA Documents Point To Massive and Ongoing Government Criminality* 28 June 2007 www.wsws.org/articles/2007/jun2007/cga-j8 _prn.shtml

[12] Auken, Bill Van: *Congressional Report puts cost of US war at $ 1.6 trillion* 14 Nov 2007 www.wsws.org/articles/2007/nov2007/wars-n14_prn.shtml

[13] Auken, Bill Van: *New York Times public editor repudiates Moveon.org ad on General Petraeus* 25 Sep 2007 www.wsws.org/articles/2007/sep2007/move-s25_prn.shtml

[14] Auken, Bill Van: *Bush at the UN: a war criminal lectures the world on "human rights"* 26 Sep 2007 www.wsws.org/articles/2007/sep2007/move-s26 _prn.shtml

[15] Auken, Bill Van: *Social inequality in US hits new record* 16 Oct 2007 www.wsws.org/articles/2007/oct2007/usa-o16_prn.shtml

[16] Auken, Bill Van: *Congressional Democrtas to unveil new domestic spying bill* 9 Oct 2007 www.wsws.org/articles/2007/oct2007/usa-o09_prn.shtml

[17] Azul, Rafael: *Studios and striking writers to resume negotiations November 26* 19 Nov 2007 www.wsws.org/articles/2007/nov2007/writ-n19_prn.shtml

[18] Azul, Rafael and Lencho, D: *Striking workers protest in Hollywood* 22 Nov 2007 www.wsws.org/articles/2007/nov2007/writ-n22_prn.shtml

[19] b real: *Understanding AFRICOM: A Contextual Reading of Empire's New Combatant Command* Part I 21 Feb 2007 www.moonofalabama.org/2007/02/under standing a 1.shtml

[20] b real: *Understanding AFRICOM: A Contextual Reading of Empire's New Com-*

batant Command Part II 21 Feb 2007 www.moonofalabama.org/2007/02/under standing a 2.shtml

[21] b real: *Understanding AFRICOM: A Contextual Reading of Empire's New Combatant Command* Part III 22 Feb 2007 www.moonofalabama.org/2007/02/under standing a 3.shtml

[22] Baxter, Sarah: *US hits panic button as airforce "loses" nuclear missiles* 21 Feb 2007 www.timesonline.co.uk/tol/news/world/us and americas/article2702800.ece

[23] Benjamin, Mark: *For the CIA's eyes-only: was the destruction of two video recordings of harsh interrogations by the CIA a coverup?* 10 Dec 2007 www.globalresearch.ca/index.php?context =va&aid=7584

[24] Bhadrakumar, M K: *West traps Russia in its own backyard* www.worldsecuritynetwork.com/ showArticle3.cfm?article_id=17462

[25] Bhagwat, Niloufer J: *International Tribunal for Afghanistan at Tokyo; Final written opinion of Judge Niloufer Bhagawat: The People versus Goerge Walker Bush, President of the United States of America* www.ratical.org/radiation/DU/ICTforAaT. html

[26] Bidwai, Praful: *Nuclear clouds gather over Asia* Inter Press service News Agency

[27] Blumner, Robyn E: *From Tommy Franks, a dooms-day scenario* St Petersburg Times Online Tampa Bay 7 December 2003 www.sptimes.com/2003/12/07news pf/columns/From Tommy Franks a .shtml

[28] Boldin, Michael: *"Orwellian Legislation Stop the Unconstitutional "Protect America Act"* 21 September 2007 www.globalresearch.ca/index.phparticle id=6813

[29] Bollyn, Christopher: *America Pearl Harbored* 24 February 2002 America Free Press

[30] Brzezinski, Z: *Second Chance* 2007 Basic Books

[31] Brzezinski, Z: *The Grand Chessboard* 1997 Basic Books

[32] Buchanan, John: *Bush-Nazi Link Confirmed* October 19, 2003 The New Hampshire Gazzette

[33] Buchanan, John and Michael, Stacey: *Bush/Nazi Link Continued* November 7, 2003 The New Hampshire Gazzette

[34] Butler, Smedley D: *War Is A Racket* 1936, republished 2003 Feral Books USA

[35] Carmichael, William: *Re-open RFK Assassination* 22 November 2006 www.globlresearch.ca/index.php?context= va&aid3947

[36] Carter, Tom: *Massive US prison population continues to grow* 7 December 2006 www.wsws.org/articles/2006/dec2006/prisd07_prn.shtml

[37] Castillo III, Celerino and Harmon, Dave: *Powderburns - Coacaine, Contras and the Drug War* Sundial an imprint of Mosaic Press

[38] Chadda, Sudhir: *Iran may face naval blockade in Arabian Sea* 25 August 2007 India Daily

[39] Chan, John: *Central Asian exercises highlight risisng great-power tensions* 25 August 2007 www.wsws.org/articles/2007/aug2007/sco-a25 prn.shtml

[40] Chin, Larry: *Beyond Bobby: Exposing the continuing conspiracy and coverup of the RFK assassination* 27 November 2006 Online Journal

[41] Chossudovsky, M: *War and Globalization - the Truth Behind September 11* 2002 Global Outlook

[42] Chossudovsky, M: *Global Poverty in the late 20th century: Economic Depression and New World Order* www.a.ca/index.php?context= va&aid=365

[43] Chossudovsky, M: *The Spoils of War: Afganistan's Multibillion Heroin Trade* 5 April 2004 www.globalresearch.ca

[44] Chossudovsky, M: *The Pentagon's second 9/11 - another 9/11 could create botha*

justifiction and an opportunity to retaliate gainst some known targets 10 August 2006 www.globalresearch.ca/index.php?context=va&aid=2942

[45] Chossudovsky, M: *The Bush Directive for a Catastrophic Emergency: Building a Justification for waging war on Iran?* June 24, 2007 www.globalresearch.ca/index.php?context=va&aid=6134

[46] Chossudovsky, M: *The "Demonization" of Muslims and the battle for Oil* 11 April 2007 www.globalresearch.ca/index.php?context=va&aid=1

[47] Chossudovsky, M: *Low intensity nuclear war* www.ratical.org/radiation/DU/ LowIntensityNW.html

[48] Chossudovsky, M: *Impact of NATO's "Humanitarian" Bombings, the Balance Sheet of Destruction in Yugoslavia* Press Conference, Center for Global Research

[49] Chossudovsky, M: *Is the Annexation of Canada part of Military Agenda* www.globalresearch.ca/article/CHO411C .html

[50] Chossudovsky, M: *Canada's Sovereignty in Jeopardy: the Militarization of North America* www.globalresearch.ca/index.php?context=va&aid=6572

[51] Chossudovsky, M: *New Cold War. America Threatens Russia. War Games on Russia's Doorstep* August 4, 2010

[52] Chossudovsky, M: *Preparing for World W III, Targeting Iran PartI: Global Warfare* August 1, 2010 www.globalresearch.ca

[53] Cogan, James: *US army suicides at a 26 year high* 30 August 2007 www.wsws.org/articles/2007/aug2007/suic-a20 prn.shtml

[54] Cohn, Marjorie: *War and the New World Order* 27 September, 2007 www.globalresearch.ca/index.php?context= va&aid=6907

[55] Coll, Steve: *Ghost Wars - The Secret History of the CIA, Afghanistan and Bin Laden from the Soviet Invasion to September 10, 2001* 2004 Penguin Books

[56] Collier, Ellen C: *Instance of Use of United States Forces Abroad 1798-1993* Congressional Research Service October 7, 1993

[57] Congressional Research Service: *FACT SHEET: History of US Inlvovement in Africa* posted on www.africom.mil

[58] Corbett, James: *Bilderberg 2010 agenda leaked* 29 May 2010 http://admin.blacklistednews.com/ newspublish/home.print.php?news_id=8963

[59] Corbett, James: *Estulin: After G 20, Oligarchs moving on African Union, population reduction* 11 November 2009 http://www.corbettreport.com/articles/ 20091111_estulin_g20.htm

[60] Daniels, Peter: *US: Record numbers in US prison and parole* 3 Aug 2004 www.wsws.org/articles/2004/aug2004/pris-n05_prn.shtml

[61] Daniels, Peter: *US: Cheney sounds out Jordan, Egypt on US bombing of Iran* 27 Sep 2004 www.wsws.org/articles/ 2004/sep2004/pris-a03_prn.shtml

[62] Ellsberg, Daniel: *A coup has occured* 26 September, 2007 www.globalresearch.ca/index.php?context= va&aid=6897

[63] Engdahl, William: *A Century of War Anglo-American Oil Politics and the New World Order* 1992, 2004 Pluto Books

[64] Engdahl, William: *Seeds of Destruction - the Hidden Agenda of Genetic Manipulation* 2007 Global Research

[65] Everest, . Larry: *The US & Iran: A History of Imperialist Domination, Intrigue and Intervention* 22 August, 2007 www.globalresearch.ca/index.php?context= va&aid=6607

[66] Feldman, Bob: *Time for Ford Foundation & CFR to Divest* 8 October 2002 www.ratical.org/ratville/CAH/FordFand CIA.html

[67] Feldman, Bob: *Ford Foundation's Skull & Bones Link* 8 October 2002 www.questionsquestions.net/feld/ford sb.html

[68] Feldman, Bob: *Alternative Media Censorship: Sponsored by CIA's Ford Foundation* 8 October 2002 www.questionsquestions.net/gatekeepers .html

[69] Findley, Paul: *Deliberate Deceptions - Facing the facts about the US-Israeli relationship* 1993 Lawrence Hill Books

[70] Findley, Paul: *They dare to speakout - people and institutions confront Israel's lobby* 1985 Lawrence Hill and Co Publishers

[71] Fitts, Catherine Austin: *An Open Letter to Condoleezza Rice "You are a Liar"* April 9, 2004 www.fromthewilderness.com

[72] Fitts, Catherine Austin: *The Sory of Edgewood Technology Service* Part One www.scoop.co.nz/stories/HL0207/S00101 .htm

[73] Fitts, Catherine Austin: *The Sory of Edgewood Technology Service* Part Two www.scoop.co.nz/stories/HL0207/S00115 .htm

277

[74] Garcia, Michael J: *The War Crimes Act: Current Issues* January 22, 2009 Congressional Research Service 7-5700 www.crs.gov RL 33662

[75] Goff, Stan: *Full Spectrum Disorder - The Military in the New American Century* 2004 Soft Skull Press

[76] Gold, Matea: *Dan Rather files $ 70 million suit against CBS* Los Angeles Times 19 September 2007 www.latimes.com/entertainment/news /business/la-ex-rather20sep20,1,560381

[77] Green, Niall: *A new race for the North Pole* 20 Aug 2007 www.wsws.org/articles/2007/aug2007/pole-a20 prn.shtml

[78] Green, Niall: *Tensions mount between Georgia and Russia* 18 Aug 2007 www.wsws.org/articles/2007/aug2007/pole-a18 prn.shtml

[79] Greider, William: *Who Will Tell the People - The Betrayal of American Democracy* 1992 Touchstone Books

[80] Greider, William: *Secrets of the Temple - How the Federal Reserve runs the country* 1988 Simon and Schuster

[81] Grey, Barry: *CIA briefing memo exposes Bush lies on 9/11* 12 April 2004 www.wsws.org/articles/2004/apr2004/pdb-a12 prn.shtml

[82] Grey, Barry: *Rice testifies before 9/11 commission: more cover-up and lies* 9 April 2004 www.wsws.org/articles/2004/apr2004/pdb-a09 prn.shtml

[83] Griffin, Edward: *The Grand Deception* Part One www.freedom-force.org/granddeception.htm

[84] Griffin, Edward: *The Grand Deception* Part Two www.freedom-force.org/granddeception2.htm

[85] Griffin, Edward: *The Hidden Agenda* Part One www.freedom-force.org/hiddenagenda.htm

[86] Griffin, Edward: *The Hidden Agenda* Part Two www.freedom-force.org/hiddenagenda2.htm

[87] Grimmett, Richard F: *Instances of use of UNited States Armed Forces Abroad, 1798-2007* CRS Report for Congress, 14 January 2008

[88] Grosssman, Zoltan: *From Wounded Knee to Afghanistan A century of military interventions* revised October 8, 2001

[89] Grosssman, Zoltan: *Retaliation was a trap - Afghanistan: Roach Motel of Empires* 2 December 2009 www.counterpunch.org/grossman12022009.html

[90] Hamid, Z: *The new sinister US plan to wage war in Middle East* http://icssa.org

[91] Hartmann, Thom: *Repeal the Military Commissions Act and Restore the Most American Human Right* www.commondream.org

[92] Haass, Richard: *State sovereignty must be altered in global era* Tapei Times 21 February 2006, page 9 www.taipeitimes.com/News/editorials/archives/2006/02/21/2003294021

[93] Head, Mike: *Autralian government launches unprecedented attacks on lawyers as Haneef case falls apart* 25 July 2007 www.wsws.org/articles/2007/jul2007/hane-j25 prn.shtml

[94] Head, Mike: *Haneef terrorism charges dropped: a debacle for the Australian government* 28 July 2007 www.wsws.org/articles/2007/jul2007/hane-j28 prn.shtml

[95] Head, Mike: *Autralian government issues new "terrorist" smears against Haneef* 1 August 2007 www.wsws.org/articles/2007/aug2007/hane-a01 prn.shtml

[96] Heinberg, Richard: *The Party's Over - Oil wars and the fate of industrail societies* 2003 New Society Publishers

[97] Helms, Harry: *Inside the Shadow Government - National Emergencies and the cult of Secrecy* 2003 Feral House

[98] Hentoff, Nat: *History will not absolve us: leaked Red Cross report sets up Bush team for international war-crimes trial* 28 August, 2007 www.globalresearch.ca/index.php?articleid =6821

[99] Hui, Wang: *U.S.-China Tensions Continue to Escacalte US should stop meddling in Asian issues* July 30, 2010 www.globalresearch.ca

[100] Hutton, Will: *A battle for oil could set the world aflame* April 30, 2006 http://www.guardian.co.uk/ commentisfree/story/0,,1764620,00.html

[101] Jisi, Wang: *Strategic Conflict Inevitable Between China and US* August 6, 2010 www.globalresearch.ca

[102] Jones, Keith: *Canada's conservative government outlines agenda of social reaction and war* 19 October 2007 www.wsws.org/articles/2007/oct2007/cana-o19 prn.shtml

[103] Johnson, Chalmers: 737 U.S. Military Bases = Global Empire March 21, 2009 www.globalresearch.ca/PrintArticle.php? articleid=12824

[104] Kane, Michael *Crossing the Rubicon - simplifying the case against Dick Cheney* www.fromthewilderness.com/free/ww3/ 011805 simplify case .html

[105] Karbuz, Sohbet: *US military oil pains* 17 Feb 2007 www.energybulletin.net/16745.html

[106] Karlstrom, Eric: *The Bush "Dynasty of Death": Four Generations of Wall Street War-Making and War-Profiteering* February 2007 (available on web)

[107] KATU Web Staff: *Family asks for help finding missing USAF captain* www.komotv.com/home/related/9619217

[108] Kay, Joseph: *Report details abuse, torture of prisoners by US forces in Afghanistan* 10 March 2004 www.wsws.org/articles/2004/mar2004/afgh-m10 prn.shtml

[109] Kay, Joseph: *Democrats scuttle Cheney impeachment measure: fraud turns into farce* 9 Nov 2007 www.wsws.org/articles/2007/nov2007/impe-n09 prn.shtml

[110] Kay, Joseph: *Vast data mining programs behind 2004 dispute within Bush administration over domestic spying* 30 July 2007 www.wsws.org/articles/2007/jul2007/nsa-j30 prn.shtml

[111] Kay, Joseph: *Standoff between White House and Congress over attorney purge - domestic spying intensifies* 28 July 2007 www.wsws.org/articles/2007/jul2007/gonz-j28 prn.shtml

[112] Klare, Michael T: *Oil wars - transforming America's Military into a global oil protection ser-*

vice 8 October 2007 placed on TomDispatch.com www.countercurrents.org/peakoil-Klare091004.htm

[113] Klare, Michael T: *The global energy race and its consequences* Part I 14 January 2007 placed on TomDispatch.com www.zmag.org/contents/showarticle.cfm? Itemid=11862

[114] Klare, Michael T: *The global energy race and its consequences* Part II 20 January 2007 placed on TomDispatch.com www.alternet.org/authoors/3454/

[115] Lang, Ted: *The Hitler Project - Astonishing Revelations* (available on web)

[116] Lendman, Stephen: *Predatory Capitalism, Corruption and Militarism: What Lies Ahead in the Age of Neocon Rule?* 2007 (available on web)

[117] Lendman, Stephen: *The Miltarization and Annexation of North America* 2007 http: sjlendman.com/2007/07/militarization-and-annexation-of-north.html

[118] Lendman, Stephen: *Police State America - A Look Back and Ahead* December 17, 2007 www.globalresearch.ca/index.php? articleid=7622

[119] Lendman, Stephen: *Rulers and Rule in the US Empire - Review of James Petras's most recent book* www.globalresearch.ca/index.php?articleid =7037

[120] Lendman, Stephen: *The US Federal Reserve - Dirty Secrets of the Temple* www.globalresearch.ca/index.php?articleid =2712

[121] Lendman, Stephen: *The War on Working Americans* www.globalresearch.ca/index.php?articleid =6640

[122] Lendman, Stephen: *Greenspan's Dark Legacy Unmasked* October 1, 2007 www.globalresearch.ca/index.php?articleid =6946

[123] Lendman, Stephen: *Nobel Hypocrisy Peace Prize Awards to War Criminals* October 18, 2007 www.globalresearch.ca/index.php?articleid =7118

[124] Lendman, Stephen: *Torture, Paramiltarism, Occupation and Genocide - Torture as Policy Under George Bush* October 25, 2007 www.globalresearch.ca/index.php?articleid =7180

[125] Lindorff, Dave: *The Air Force Cover-Up of Minot-Barksdale Nuke Missile Flight* November 2, 2007 www.rense.com/general78/nuks.htm

[126] Loftus, John: *The Dutch Connection How a famous American family made its fortune from the Nazis* September 27, 2000 (available on web)

[127] Madsen, Wayne: *Another INsult From Bush and the Pentagon Neo-cons* November, 2004 www.fromthewildernes.com/free/ww3/112 404_kennedy_insult.shtml

[128] Maitra, Ramanatu: *US Scatters Bases to Control Central Asia* Asia Times 30 March 2005

[129] Martin, Patrick: *CIA 9/11 "accountability" report released: A whitewash that only raisdes more questions* August 7, 2007 www.wsws.org/articles/2007/aug2007/torta07_prn.shtml

[130] Martin, Patrick: *Red Cross confirms Bush administration, CIA used torture in interrogations* September 27, 2007 www.wsws.org/articles/2007/sep2007/raths27_prn.shtml

[131] Martin, Patrick: *Former CBS anchor Dan Rather, big corporations, government interfering in news* July 26, 2007 www.wsws.org/articles/2007/jul2007/galj26_prn.shtml

[132] Marsden, Chris and Hyland, Julie: *Britain: Anti-war MP George Galloway suspended from parliament* August 24, 2007 www.wsws.org/articles/2007/aug2007/ciaa24_prn.shtml

[133] Maul, Samuel: *Scapegoat Rather sues CBS over sacking for Bush military story* The Scotsman September 21, 2007 www.scotsman.com/international.cfm?id= 1511262007

[134] May, Eric H: *Next 9/11, Summer 2007*

[135] Millegan, R R Kris: *Skull and Bones Do the Illuminati really control the planet? Is George Bush connected to the most dangerous secret society in America? The answer may frighten you* June 14, 2006 www.hightimes.com/ht/news/content.php? bid=17&aid=3

[136] Minot Air Force Base Pubkic Affairs: *Minot Airman dies while on leave* September 12, 2007 www.minotaf.mil/news/story.asp?articleid =123067840

[137] Mitchell, Paul: *Britain: Guantanamo detainees detail years of torture* www.wsws.org/articles/2007/aug2007/guan-a15_prn.shtml

[138] Moore, Michael: *Stupid White Men* 2001 Regan Books

[139] Morales, Frank: *Bush moves towards martial law* http://towardfreedom.com

[140] Moret, Leuren: *Depleted Uranium is WMD* August 23, 2006 www.globalresearch.ca/index.php?articleid =3053

[141] Nazemroaya, Mahdi Darius: *Missing Nukes: Treason of the Highest Order* August 23, 2006 www.globalresearch.ca/index.php?articleid =7158

[142] Nazemroaya, Mahdi Darius: *Sino-Russian Alliance: Challenging America's*

ambitions in Eurasia September 23, 2007
www.globalresearch.ca/index.php?articleid =6688

[143] Nazemroaya, Mahdi Darius: *War and the New World Order* August 29, 2007 www.globalresearch.ca/index.php?articleid =6577

[144] Nazemroaya, Mahdi Darius: *The March to War: Detente and the Middle East or "Calm Before the Storm"* July 12, 2007 www.globalresearch.ca/index.php?articleid =6281

[145] Newsmax Staff: *Rather: Any Court Award to Journalist Causes* September 21, 2007 www.newsmax.com/insidecover/Dan_Rather _CBS_suit/2007/09/21/34557.html

[146] Oxfam International: *Signing away the future: how trade and investment agreements between rich and poor countries undermine development* www.oxfam.org/en/policy/briefingpapers /bp101_regional_trade_agreements_0703

[147] Oregon Truth Alliance: *Portland to Host Terrorism Drill "NOBLE RESOLVE 07-2" August 20-24,; Citizens Warn of Established Pattern for such Drills to go "live"* August 13, 2007 www.OregonTruthAlliance.org

[148] Palast, Greg: *The best democracy money can buy* 2003, A Plume Book

[149] Parsons, Lee: *Harper commits billions to build Canada an Arctic navy* July 19,

2007   www.wsws.org/articles/2007/jul2007/can-
j19_prn.shtml

[150] Parry, Robert: *Who is "Any Person" in Tribunal
Law* http://consortiumnews.com/2006/101906. html

[151] Petras, James: *The Ford Foundation and the
CIA - a documented case of philanthropic collaboration with the secret police* December 15, 2001
www.ratical.org/ratville/CAH/FordFand CIA.html

[152] Petras, James: *Rulers and the ruled in the US Empire - Bankers, Zionists, Militants* 2007 Clarity Press

[153] Pfeiffer, Dale Allen: *The end of the Age of Oil* 2004
Frustrated Artists Production

[154] Pfeiffer,   Dale   Allen: *Eating   Fossil   Fuels*   www.fromthewilderness.com/free/...
/100303_eating_oil.html

[155] Pfeiffer, Dale Allen: *China's Offshore Claims*
March 21, 2005 www.fromthewilderness.com

[156] Phinney, David: *A US Fortress Rises in Baghdad:
Asian Workers Trafficked to Build World's Largest
Embassy* October 16, 2006 www.corpwatch.org

[157] PNAC Project for the New American Century :
*Rebuilding America's Defenses: Strategy, Forces and
Resources for a New Century* by Donald Kagan, Gary
Schmitt and Thomas Donnelly

[158] POAC Project for Old American Century: *Bush Crime Family Tree* www.oldamericancentury.org/bushco/bush_ crime_family.htm

[159] Political Gateway: *Key US Air Force Official Found Dead* www.politicalgateway.com/news/read/ 108445

[160] Pravda: *Top US Air Force Official "Suicide" as Iran War Nears* October 16, 2007 http://english.pravda.ru/print/opinion /feedback/98912-us_air_force-0

[161] Randall, Kate: *Attorneys demand preservation of evidence of detainee toomestic spying* August 6, 2007 www.wsws.org/articles/2007/aug2007/spy-a06_prn.shtml

[162] Randall, Kate: *US mercenary firm denounced after civilian killings in Baghdad* Septmber 18, 2007 www.wsws.org/articles/2007/sep2007/blcks18_prn.shtml

[163] Randall, Kate: *Congress a* December 12, 2007uthorizes vast expansion of d www.wsws.org/articles/2007/dec2007/tortd12_prn.shtml

[164] Randall, Kate: *Bush calls for expansion of "Protect America" spy bill* September 22, 2007 www.wsws.org/articles/2007/sep2007/spy-s22_prn.shtml

[165] Ray, Ellen: *U.S. Military and Corporate Recolonization of Congo* . Covert Action Quarterly Spring /Summer 2000 http://www.thirdworldtraveler.com/Africa/ US_Recolonization_Congo.html

[166] Reuters (Hollywood Reporter): *Dan Rather making a stand with a lawsuit* September 21, 2007 www.reuters.com/article/industryNews /dUSN/19306286200700921

[167] Rogers, Tony: *Heir to Holocaust* Clamor Magazine www.wsws.org/articles/2007/dec2007/tort-d12_prn.shtml

[168] Rozoff, Rick: *Global Military Agenda: US Expands Asian NATO to Contain and Confront China* August 7, 2010 www.globalresearch.ca

[169] Rozoff, Rick: US tightens missile shield encirclement of China and Russia 22 February 2010 www.globalresearch.ca/index.php?context =va&aid=17948

[170] Rozoff, Rick: 2010: US to Wage War Throughout the World 31 December 2009 www.globalresearch.ca/index.php?context =va&aid=16720

[171] Rozoff, Rick: Thinking the Unthinkable: NATO's Global Military Map 3 October 2009 www.globalresearch.ca/index.php?context =va&aid=15506

[172] Rozoff, Rick: U.S. China Conflict, Moving From War of Words to Talk of War 15 August 2010 www.marketoracle.co.uk/Article21914.html

[173] Ruppert, Michael C: *Crossing the Rubicon The Decline of the American Empire at the end of the Age of Oil* 2004 New Society Publishers Canada

[174] Ruppert, Michael C: *My Dreams and the Color of Suffering* www.fromthewilderness.com

[175] Ruppert, Michael C: *Nowhere to Run Nowhere to Hide* www.fromthewilderness.com

[176] Ruppert, Michael C: *Condoleezza Rice Testifies: Lies a Sixth Grader Would Not Accept* www.fromthewilderness.com

[177] Ruppert, Michael C: *The POWs, CIA and Drugs Uglier Truths Behind the Sarin Gas Stories* 23 July 1998 www.copvcia.com

[178] Ruppert, Michael C: *Did John Singlaub Get His Clock Cleaned? Moorer Deposition in Tailwind Suits Confirms Allegations of Sarin Gas Use Against Vietnam Defectors, POWS - Incriminates CIA, Kissinger* www.copvcia.com

[179] Ruppert, Michael C: *The Kennedy's, Physical Evidence and 9/11* Nov 26, 2003 www.fromthewilderness.com

[180] Ruppert, Michael C: *The Lies About Taliban Heroin Russia and the Real Objective With Heroin as a Weapon of War* www.fromthewilderness.com

[181] Ruppert, Michael C and Kane, Michael: *The Markets react to Peak Oil Indutrial Society Rides and unstable Plateau Before the Cliff* October 5, 2006 www.fromthewilderness.com

[182] Ruppert, Michael C: *The End of the Grid New, Deadly Links between 9/11 and Peak Oil* Jan 5, 2006 www.fromthewilderness.com

[183] Scahill, Jeremy: *Blackwater The Rise of the World's Most Powerful Mercenary Army* 2007 Nation Books USA and Serpent's Tail UK

[184] Schwarz, Peter: *Tensions Between NATO And Russia Escalate* July 18, 2007 www.wsws.org/articles/2007/jul2007/russ-j18_prn.shtml

[185] Schwarz, Peter: *Why is the US press silent on US preparations for war against Iran?* September 19, 2007 www.wsws.org/articles/2007/jul2007/russgerm-s19_prn.shtml

[186] Scott, Peter Dale: *Deep Politics and the Death of JFK* 1993, 2006 University of California Press

[187] Scott, Peter Dale: *Tons of Cocaine: Caracas to Washington* September 29, 2006

[188] Scott, Peter Dale: *The Road to 9/11 - Wealth, Empire, and the Future of America* 2007 University of California Press

[189] Scott, Peter Dale: *Deep Politics II* 1995, 1996, 2003 Mary Ferrel Foundation Press

[190] Scott, Peter Dale: *The War Conspiracy - JFK, 9/11, and the Deep Politics of War* revised edition 2008 Mary Ferrel Foundation Press

[191] Scott, Peter Dale: *Drugs, Oil, and War* 2003 Rowman and Littlewood Published Inc

[192] Sieff, Martin: *Interview: US, Russia still face mutual destruction threat* May 18, 2005 http://www.wpherald.com/storieview.php? StoryID=20050518-072100-9737r

[193] Spencer, Naomi: *CIA Documents Point To Massive and Ongoing Government Criminality* 5 June 2006 www.fromthewilderness.com www.wsws.org/articles/2006/jun2006/pris-j05 prn.shtml

[194] Spencer, Naomi: *US prison population at all time high* 29 September 2007 www.wsws.org/articles/2007/sep2007/pris-s29 prn.shtml

[195] Steinberb, Jacques:*Dan Rather sues CBS for $70 million* The Times September 19, 2007 www.observer.com/articles/2007/dan-rather-sues-cbs-70-million

[196] Stinnett, Robert B: *Day of Deciet - The Truth about FDR and Pearl Harbor* 1999, Free Press

[197] Stinnett, Robert B: *December 7, 1941: A Setup from the Beginning* December 7, 2000 Honolulu Adevertiser

[198] Stinnett, Robert B: *The Pearl Harbor Deception* December 7, 2003 www.Antiwar.com

[199] Stormer, Robert:*Nuke transportation story has explosive implications* October 8, 2007 Forth-Worth-Star-Telegram www.wsws.org/articles/2007/jul2007/russ-j18_prn.shtml

[200] Sutton, Anthony C: *Wall Street and the Bolshevik Revolution* 1974 by Arlington House

[201] Sutton, Anthony C, Howard Altman, Kris Millegan and Ralph Bunch: *Fleshing Out Skull and Bones* 2003 Trineday, LLC

[202] Symonds, Peter:*Washington continues propaganda barrage against Iran* August 24, 2007 www.wsws.org/articles/2007/aug2007/iran-a24_prn.shtml

[203] Symonds, Peter:*Washington to brand Iranian forces as terrorist* August 16, 2007 www.wsws.org/articles/2007/aug2007/iran-a16_prn.shtml

[204] Symonds, Peter: *The US adopts belligerent posture in Baghdad talks with Iran* July 26, 2007 www.wsws.org/articles/2007/jul2007/iran-j26_prn.shtml

[205] Symonds, Peter: *US intensifies push for further US sanctions on Iran* November 2, 2007 www.wsws.org/articles/2007/nov2007/irann02_prn.shtml

[206] Symonds, Peter: *An insight into the White House debate over military action against Iran* July 18, 2007 www.wsws.org/articles/2007/jul2007/iran-j18_prn.shtml

[207] Tarpley, Webster G: *Cheney determined to strike in US with WMD this summer: only impeachment, removal or general strike can stop him* July 24, 2007 www.911truth.org/article

[208] The Progressive Review: *Skull and Bones* July 24, 2007 http://prorev.com/skull.htm

[209] Thomas, William: *Bringing the war home* 1998 Earth Pulse Press Inc

[210] Trausk, Arthur S: *The Conspiracies of the Empire* December 9, 2000

[211] Tucker Jr, James P: *Depleted uranium death toll among US war veterans tops 11,000* October 29, 2006 www.globalresearch.com

[212] Valle, Ramon: *Writers strike enters second week* 12 Nov 2007 www.wsws.org/articles/2007/nov2007/writ-n12_prn.shtml

[213] Valle, Ramon: *Ninety percent of voting Writers' Guild of America members authorize strike* 24 Oct 2007 www.wsws.org/articles/2007/oct2007/writ-o24_prn.shtml

[214] Walsh, David: *Increasing bitterness in film and television writers strike* 13 November 2007 www.wsws.org/articles/2007/nov2007/writ-n13_prn.shtml

[215] Walsh, David: *At mass rally Writers Guild leaders attempt to lull strikers to sleep* 10 November 2007 www.wsws.org/articles/2007/nov2007/wga-n06_prn.shtml

[216] Walsh, David: *US film and television writers launch their struggle* 6 Novemeber 2007 www.wsws.org/articles/2007/nov2007/writ-n06_prn.shtml

[217] Walsh, David: *Who is John Edwards?* 16 Nov 2007 www.wsws.org/articles/2007/nov2007/writ-n16_prn.shtml

[218] Walsh, David: *The Democratic Party candidates and the writers' strike* 8 November 2007 www.wsws.org/articles/2007/nov2007/writ-n08_prn.shtml

[219] Watson, Debra: *Record num-bers in US prisons* 5 Nov 2005 www.wsws.org/articles/2005/nov2005/pris-a03 prn.shtml

[220] Webb, Gary: *Dark Alliance* 1999 Seven Stories Press

[221] Weiner, Bernard: *How we got into this imperial pickle: A PNAC primer* 26 May 2003 www.crisispapers.org/editorials/PNAC-Primer.htm

[222] White, Jerry: *Rupert Murdoch takes over Wall Street Journal* 2 August 2007 www.wsws.org/articles/2007/aug2007/murd-a02_prn.shtml

[223] White, Jerry: *The motives behind the Bush administration's latest terror scare* 19 September 2007 www.wsws.org/articles/2007/sep2007/grees19_prn.shtml

[224] White, Jerry: *From the horse's mouth: Greenspan says Iraq war was for oil,* 27 July 2007 www.wsws.org/articles/2007/jul2007/terr-j27_prn.shtml

[225] Whitley, John *Seven Jewish Americans control most US media* November 21, 2003 www.rense.com/general44/ sevenjewishamericans.html

[226] Worthington, Andy *The Guantanamo Files - The Sories of 774 Detainess in America's Illegal Prison* Pluto Press 2007

[227] Worthington, Andy *An Interview with Guantanamo Whistleblower Stephen Abraham* December 2008, www.fff.org

[228] Worthington, Andy *Guantanamo Whistleblower: Lt. Col. Stephen Abraham is not the first insider to condemn the kangaroo courts* www.andyworthington.co.uk/2007/07/03/guantanamo-whistleblower-lt-col-stephen...

[229] WSWS Editorial Board: *Inteviews with striking workers and supporters* 6 November 2007 www.wsws.org/articles/2007/nov2007/wgan06_prn.shtml

[230] WSWS Editorial Board: *Broader issues facting US film and television writers* 2 November 2007 www.wsws.org/articles/2007/nov2007/wgan02_prn.shtml

Index

Forley, Michael, 50
Foundation, Babar Ali, 262
Foundation, Carnegie, 211
Foundation, Rockefeller, 256
Fox News, 82
Fox TV, 82
France, 229, 236
Franklin, Benjamin, 114
Franks, Tommy, 19
Freedom of Information Act, 2, 53, 168
Freetown, 252
Friedman, Milton, 179
From the Wilderness, 216
FTW, 135, 216
Fulbright, 246
Fulbright Fellow, 264
FX Channel, 82

Gabon, 232, 237, 252
Galbraith, John Kenneth, 181
Garang, J, 124
Garang, John, 123–125
Gaylon Sr, Robert, 208, 209
General Electric, 220
General Foods, 179
General Motors, 220
Geneva Convention, 98, 102, 107, 249
George Orwell, 94, 127

George, H Walker, 57–59, 61
Gerald, J B, 126
Germany, 3, 241
Ghana, 232
Gharib, Sayed, 148
Glasgow, 36
Globalization, 27
GNP, 30
Goebbels, Joseph, 161
Goering, H, 2
Goldensen, Leonard, 82
Goldwater, Barry, 214
Gore Vidal, 76
Gowen, William, 57
Great Dismal Swamp, 167
Greece, 236
Greenspan, A, 55, 174–180
Grenada, 248
Griffin. Edward, 209, 211
Grossman, Zoltan, 236, 243, 247
Guam, 239
Guantanamo, 115, 118, 131, 132, 156, 239
Guardian, 20, 166
Guatemala, 245, 246
Guggenheim Foundation, 208, 212
Guinea-Bissau, 252
Gulf War, 90, 93, 103

Swifts and Swallows

Mike Unwin

BLOOMSBURY WILDLIFE

LONDON · OXFORD · NEW YORK · NEW DELHI · SYDNEY

BLOOMSBURY WILDLIFE
Bloomsbury Publishing Plc
50 Bedford Square, London, WC1B 3DP, UK

BLOOMSBURY, BLOOMSBURY WILDLIFE and the Diana logo are trademarks of
Bloomsbury Publishing Plc

First published in Great Britain 2018

A catalogue record for this book is available from the British Library

Library of Congress Cataloguing-in-Publication data has been applied for

ISBN: PB: 978-1-4729-5011-6; ePub: 978-1-4729-5009-3; ePDF: 978-1-4729-5010-9

2 4 6 8 10 9 7 5 3 1

Design by Rod Teasdale
Printed in China

MIX
Paper from
responsible sources
FSC® C104723

To find out more about our authors and books visit www.bloomsbury.com
and sign up for our newsletters

giving
nature
a home

For all items sold, Bloomsbury Publishing will donate a minimum of 2% of the publisher's receipts
from sales of licensed titles to RSPB Sales Ltd, the trading subsidiary of the RSPB. Subsequent sellers
of this book are not commercial participators for the purpose of Part II of the Charities Act 1992.

Contents

Meet the Swift and the Swallow

Darting and gliding through the summer skies, few birds are more impressive in the air than the Swift and the Swallow. The two have much in common: both feed on flying insects and have bodies similarly adapted for this challenge; both breed on or around buildings, bringing them into close contact with people; and both are long-distance migrants, arriving in the UK every spring after spending winter in sub-Saharan Africa. Given these similarities, and the superficial resemblance of the two birds, it is hardly surprising that they have long been closely associated. Indeed, many people often mistake one for the other.

Appearances, however, can be deceptive. Swifts and swallows are not related. Swallows belong to the order Passeriformes – also known as passerines, or perching birds. This is the world's largest order of birds and comprises at least 110 families, including the likes of thrushes, finches and warblers. Within this order, the swallows make up the family Hirundinidae, known as hirundines, of which our UK Swallow – properly known as the Barn Swallow – is one of some 83 species.

Swifts, however apparently similar to swallows, belong to the Apodiformes, a completely different and much smaller order that comprises just three families. Our UK Swift is one of some 100 species in the family Apodidae. Its two sister families in this small order are the tree swifts (Hemiprocnidae) and, believe it or not, the hummingbirds (Trochilidae). Swifts are thus much more closely related to hummingbirds than they are to swallows, and swallows are more closely related to magpies and robins than they are to swifts.

These affinities may seem counter-intuitive. But the striking similarities between swifts and swallows are

Opposite: When a Swift is perched, its exceptionally long wings project well beyond the end of its tail.

Below: Unlike Swifts, Swallows habitually settle on fences, posts and other low perches.

due to a phenomenon known as 'convergent evolution', in which animals from unconnected evolutionary roots evolve to resemble one another by adapting in similar ways to a shared environmental challenge. In this case, the challenge is catching flying insects on the wing, one that demands a special skill set and a body customised to the job.

Left: Seen from side-on, a Swift reveals the aerodynamic lines of its body.

Growing together; moving apart

Unrelated species can evolve similar outward traits by adapting in similar ways to shared environmental challenges. This is called **convergent evolution**. The species in question have 'converged' from different backgrounds towards a similar point, which is usually reflected in their build or behaviour. Swifts and swallows, for instance, both have long, narrow wings,

forked tails, tiny feet, small bills, wide mouths and agile flight as adaptations for catching insects on the wing. Hummingbirds, on the other hand, which are related to swifts, have adapted to a very different lifestyle – one of hovering in front of flowers in order to extract their nectar – and so are quite different in appearance. This is an example of **divergent evolution**.

Above: Both the Swift (left) and Swallow (right) share a similar aerodynamic profile, with long wings and a short head.

Meet the Swift

The Swift – the one member of the Apodidae found in the UK – is properly known as the Common or Eurasian Swift, to distinguish it from other swift species around the world. For the purposes of this book, however, it is generally referred to as simply 'Swift', since this is the term most commonly used in the UK. Its scientific name *Apus apus* derives from the Greek word ἄπους, meaning 'without feet'. This refers to the ancient belief that swifts, whose tiny legs are barely visible to the casual observer, are simply legless swallows. The Common Swift was the first swift species to be scientifically described and has thus given its name to the Apodiformes order, embracing all swifts worldwide. We can only presume that the great Swedish naturalist Carl Linnaeus, who first described these birds in the tenth edition of his groundbreaking *Systema Naturae* (1758), would have known that swifts' legs, however diminutive, do exist.

Above: A close view of a Swift reveals the protective feathering that helps shield the eyes during high-speed flight.

Swifts in close-up

Whatever the science, the adjective 'swift' is the perfect name for this speediest of flyers. Indeed, few birds are swifter. The White-throated Needletail, a Himalayan relative of our Swift, has been clocked at an astonishing

169km/h (105mph), making it the fastest recorded bird in the world in level flight – a speed topped only by the Peregrine Falcon in a vertical dive. Our own Swift has been recorded at an impressive 111.6km/h (69.3mph) and, when hurtling above the rooftops, can appear much faster.

Size is hard to judge in flying birds. Seen dashing overhead, Swifts and Swallows may appear about the same. In fact, the Swift is appreciably bigger. Topping the scales at 35–56g (1.2–1.9oz), it is heavier than a House Sparrow and weighs nearly twice as much as a Swallow. Its wingspan of 38–40cm (15–16in) is also greater than a Swallow's, at 32–34.5cm (12.6–13.6in). Without a Swallow's long tail streamers however, its overall body length of 16–17cm (6.3–6.7in) is generally slightly less.

Size apart, you don't need binoculars to see that a Swift is quite different from a Swallow – and indeed any other bird. In colour, it is dark sooty brown, apart from a pale-ish patch on the chin, and appears black unless seen in good light. In its flight silhouette it resembles a crescent or boomerang, in which the two wings form one continuous swept-back curve that is unlike any other bird's. Other features all exhibit an aerodynamic unobtrusiveness: at the front, a rounded head with no visible neck and a short, barely visible bill; at the back, a short tail with a shallow fork that is often held closed. When perched – which is something you will seldom see – its exceptionally long wings extend well beyond the end of its tail.

This rakish shape and dark plumage, combined with distinctive stiff wingbeats, gives a flying Swift a very different character from any other bird. Combined with its screaming call and predilection for zooming around church towers at dusk, it helps explain how the Swift acquired its traditional name of 'devil bird'.

Where Swifts live

The Common Swift is the most widely distributed of all swift species. It occupies a total estimated breeding area of 39,800,000km² (15,367,000 square miles) across Europe and Asia, ranging from Spain in the west to Siberia in the east and, north to south, from Norway to Morocco. Birds from all these regions migrate south to spend winter in sub-Saharan Africa, from the equatorial centre south to northern South Africa.

Across this range, Swifts occupy many habitats and, during their wanderings, you can see them over almost any landscape. In effect their habitat is the air rather than the land, and they travel wherever they can find a steady supply of flying insects, from sea level to heights of over 4,000m (13,100ft) in the Himalayas. Before human times, their breeding sites comprised regions with crags and sea cliffs, which offered suitable crevices and caves for nests. But their adoption of buildings as nest sites means that today they also frequent urban habitats – indeed, in many areas they breed only in man-made structures.

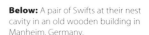

Above: On the map above the breeding range of the Common Swift is indicated in orange and its winter quarters in blue.

Below: A pair of Swifts at their nest cavity in an old wooden building in Manheim, Germany.

The worldwide population of the Common Swift is estimated at 25 million birds, which means that it is classified by the IUCN (International Union for Conservation of Nature) as Least Concern. In some regions, however, the species is in decline – including in the UK (see page 117), where the current estimated breeding population of 87,000 pairs represents a decline of 51 per cent since 1995, placing the Swift firmly on the Amber List of Birds of Conservation Concern.

How Swifts live

Swifts feed on the countless insects and other tiny invertebrates, known collectively as 'aerial plankton', that fill our summer skies, catching it in their gaping mouths. Their dependence upon this diet explains why Swifts are such masterful flyers, both fast and agile enough to catch their food and, because the supply is often very irregular, able to travel great distances to find it. In areas of plenty, Swifts may gather in large feeding parties, sometimes hundreds or even thousands strong.

Aerial plankton is long gone by winter, which explains why Swifts are summer visitors to UK skies. Indeed, they spend the shortest time here of all summer visitors, arriving in late April/early May and departing in late July/early August. This short sojourn is balanced by a similar length of time in Africa during winter, with the rest of their year spent travelling between the two.

When Swifts arrive in Britain in late spring they fly straight to their nest sites, usually clustered in loose colonies of several pairs. Pairs stay together for life and often reuse successful sites from previous years. Their nest is typically located in a crack or crevice in a building. It is fashioned from feathers, paper and other windblown material collected on the wing and glued together with saliva. The female lays on average two to three eggs – fewer than Swallows and most passerines – and both incubation (19–20 days) and fledging (6–8 weeks) last longer than in passerines.

Both adults share parenting duties, sometimes travelling great distances to find food, which they collect in food balls in their throat (see page 47) and bring back to feed their young. If the parents are away for more than a day or so, the young can survive by entering a state of torpor, in which their growth and metabolism slows down and they can reduce their energy requirements until food is available again. This is very unusual in birds.

Within days of leaving the nest, young Swifts set off for Africa on their first migration. So begins a life in which they spend more time on the wing than any other bird. They feed, drink, mate and even sleep on the wing (see page 37). Indeed, the only activity for which they

Below: Swifts often fly close together in 'screaming parties', calling loudly as they go.

Above: When drinking, as when feeding, a Swift has no need to land.

absolutely must touch down is breeding, simply because of the tiresome reality that eggs won't float in mid-air. Scientists monitoring Swifts have recorded individuals that go without landing at all for more than ten months (see page 32), and have estimated that an individual may fly more than 200,000km (124,000 miles) in a year. Such extreme flying feats may seem unimaginably demanding to us – yet Swifts are perfectly evolved for this lifestyle. And given that their lifespan of 20 years or more is much higher than that of Swallows and most other songbirds, it seems that evolution must be doing something right.

Left: Swift nestlings grow more slowly than Swallow nestlings: it takes 30 days before feathers start to replace their baby down.

Meet the Swallow

The swallow found in the UK is the most widespread of 83 swallow species worldwide, breeding right across the northern hemisphere and wintering in Africa and South America. Although here we tend to call it simply the Swallow, it is known elsewhere as the Barn Swallow to preclude confusion with other swallow species. The name comes, of course, from the bird's predilection for living around barns and other farm buildings, but it may not have originated in the UK: Gilbert White observed in his *Natural History of Selbourne* (1789) that the swallow was known colloquially as 'chimney swallow' in Britain

Below: The Swallow is invariably associated with farm buildings – including, of course, barns.

but in Sweden as *ladusvala*, which means 'barn swallow'. Either way, the bird's scientific name is *Hirundo rustica*, in which the first part refers to the swallow family (Hirundinidae) and the second means 'of the country'.

Swallows in close-up

The Swallow's aerial lifestyle has given it an aerodynamic shape that is broadly similar to a Swift's, with a streamlined body, short head, short bill and relatively long wings. Swallows are smaller, however: at 16–22g (0.56–0.78oz) they weigh roughly half as much, and their wingspan of 32–34.5cm (12.6–13.6in) is around 18 per cent shorter. Though Swallows just pip Swifts in terms of body length – 17–19cm (6.7–7.5in), compared with 16–17cm (6.3–6.7in) – this can be explained by their exceptionally long outer tail feathers, which in a male may measure up to 7cm (2.76in).

Above: A Swallow's red throat immediately distinguishes it from Swifts, House Martins and Sand Martins.

You will also notice, given a half-decent view, that Swallows are much more colourful than Swifts. Their glossy dark-blue upperparts contrast with whitish-beige underparts, and their red forehead and throat are neatly trimmed with a navy-blue breast band. The tail, also glossy blue above, has white 'window' spots at the base that are best seen when the tail feathers are spread. Fledglings are duller, with sooty upperparts, but still have the distinctive pale underparts and red throat combination that immediately precludes confusion with a Swift.

Left: Long tail streamers and blue upperparts immediately distinguish a Swift from a Swallow.

Below: Warm brown colouration and a habit of nesting in riverbank colonies are the hallmarks of a Sand Martin.

While Swallows may resemble Swifts at a glance, they have not adapted to life on the wing in quite such an extreme way. Their wings, while relatively longer than those of other songbirds, are not as disproportionately long as a Swift's. And their legs and feet are more developed, allowing them to perch on wires and branches and to land on the ground, where they can shuffle around. You will see a Swallow perched much more often than you will a Swift. A Swallow also has a warbling song and sharp flight calls, both of which are quite different from the high screaming voice of a Swift (see page 58).

Other than Swifts, the UK birds with which you might confuse a Swallow are its much closer relatives the House Martin (*Delichon urbicum*) and Sand Martin (*Riparia riparia*). Both belong to the swallow family and are also summer visitors, arriving and leaving at around the same times. Both also share similar open habitats, zooming around after aerial insects in a similar way. However, both are smaller, with shorter forked tails, and both have different markings: the House Martin is glossy blue-black above, like a Swallow, but has a bold white rump and is completely white below, with no breast band or red throat patch; the Sand Martin is warm brown above, with a brown breast band that contrasts with its otherwise white underparts.

Where Swallows live

The Barn Swallow has the widest range of any swallow species and is one of the most widely distributed birds in the world. It breeds right across Europe and Asia, from Ireland east to Japan, and right across North America, reaching its most northerly latitude at 68° north in Lapland. Those that breed in Europe and Asia migrate south to winter in Africa, Arabia and the Indian Subcontinent; those from North America winter in Central and South America.

This general picture of breeding in the northern hemisphere and wintering in the tropics, however, is complicated by a few breeding populations in the southern hemisphere, including in South Africa and northern Australia. Furthermore, vagrant Swallows – those that have wandered off course during migration – have turned up in many unlikely spots, from the Falkland Islands to Tristan de Cunha.

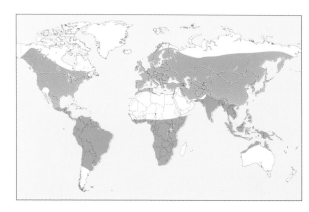

Worldwide, the Barn Swallow population is estimated at 190 million birds, which collectively range over some 51,700,000 km^2 (19.9 million square miles). The species is listed by the IUCN as Least Concern, although there are some localised areas of decline (see page 122). In the UK it is on the Green List of birds that are not threatened, with an estimated breeding population of 860,000 pairs.

Above: The map above illustrates the enormous global range of the Barn Swallow, breeding almost entirely in the northern hemisphere (orange) and migrating to spend winter in the southern hemisphere (blue).

Today scientists recognise up to six different geographical races, or subspecies, of Barn Swallow. These differ from one another in minor details of size and plumage. The UK race – referred to as the 'nominate' race as it was the first one scientifically described – bears the scientific name *Hirundo rustica rustica*. It occurs across Europe and northern Asia, east to the Yenisei River in central Asia. Among the others, the North American

Above: The North American race of the Barn Swallow, *Hirundo rustica erythrogaster*, has a narrower breast band than the European race.

Below: Swallows feed in open country, often flying fairly low to the ground.

race bears the name *Hirundo rustica erythrogaster*, and differs in its brighter red throat and incomplete breast band.

In the UK and everywhere else, the Swallow is a bird of open country with low vegetation: anywhere, in short, that offers both plentiful aerial insects and lots of space in which to catch them. It may occur from sea level to heights of up to 2,700m (8,900ft), but tends to avoid heavily forested or built-up areas and is absent from true deserts and polar regions. Historically, it has benefitted from forest clearance and other human activities that have expanded its ideal habitats.

Here in the UK, Swallows frequent suitable habitat the length and breadth of the land – even on remote islands, such as the Shetlands and Scillies. Their favourite habitats are meadows and farmland, preferably with nearby water and good nest sites, typically old farm buildings. On migration beyond our shores they may visit other landscapes, including sugar cane fields, desert oases and forest clearings.

How Swallows live

Swallows, like Swifts, depend on catching small flying insects on the wing for their survival. They generally feed at lower heights than Swifts and over a smaller area, not wandering as far from the nest site. As with Swifts, this diet explains why Swallows migrate south for winter. If they stuck around in cold, insect-free northern climes they would have nothing to eat.

Above: Swallows, like Swifts, feed almost exclusively on small, airborne invertebrates.

After their African winter, Swallows return north to Europe in spring. UK birds reach our shores from early April, sometimes even late March, arriving some three to four weeks earlier than Swifts. They head straight to their breeding colonies: usually long-established sites that have been occupied for generations. Although Swallows once nested in natural holes, today they are almost entirely dependent upon human structures, so gravitate to areas with barns, stables and other open buildings.

At the nest site the Swallows pair up, males performing twittering display flights to cement their bonds with females. The pair then build a nest – or, more usually, repair and spruce up last year's construction. The nest is made from mud, which both birds collect and plaster into a cup-like structure supported against a pillar or beam,

Below: A pair of Swallows work together to feed their growing brood, flying back and forth with new offerings hundreds of times a day.

Right: Swallows gather in a tree in South Africa prior to returning to their European breeding grounds.

Below: A young Swallow, newly fledged, continues to clamour for food.

lined with straw and feathers for insulation. The female lays a clutch of 3–8 (typically four or five) white eggs. Incubation lasts 14–19 days and the young fledge some three weeks later. The male and female stick together and share parenting duties, although males may also mate with other females in the colony – which means that the species, though socially monogamous, is genetically polygamous. With breeding starting early, a pair often has time for a second brood. Sometimes even a third (see page 76).

After fledging, young Swallows gather in large flocks – often near the coast or in wetlands – roosting together and feeding intensively in preparation for migration; they head south in September, occasionally as late as early October. Those from the UK head down through France and Spain, crossing the English Channel, the Mediterranean, the Sahara and the Congo Basin, before arriving in their African winter quarters some four to five weeks later. En route they gather at traditional pit-stops, sometimes in hundreds of thousands. At their destination they spread out, finding suitable habitats to sustain them until the following February, when it is time to head north again to breed.

Swallows do not generally live more than four or five years – typical for a songbird of their size – so the air miles clocked up in one individual's lifetime do not compete with those of the Swift. Nonetheless, the flying feats undertaken by this diminutive bird are impressive. Indeed, studies of Swallow journeys between Britain and South Africa have proved pivotal in our understanding of bird migration.

Swift, Swallow or martin?

Below is a quick ID guide showing the key features that help to distinguish between the Swift, Swallow, House Martin and Sand Martin.

	Swift	Swallow	House Martin	Sand Martin
Size	Largest of the four	Smaller than Swift; bigger than martins	Smaller than Swallow; same as Sand Martin	Same as House Martin
Shape	Long, narrow, sickle-shaped wings; medium-length forked tail, often closed	Long wings but shorter than Swift, long tail, deeply forked with long outer streamers	More compact than Swallow; shorter tail with shallower fork	Same as House Martin
Colour and markings	Dark sooty brown; appearing black at a distance; pale throat patch	Glossy blue-back above; beige-white below; red forehead and chin; dark blue breast band; white spots in tail	Glossy blue-back upperparts with striking white rump; white underparts	Brown upperparts; white underparts with brown collar around throat
Flight style	Long glides; stiff, deep wingbeats; tends to follow long trajectory; often very high	More fluttering than Swift; flapping and gliding; often changes direction; lower than Swift	Like Swallow	Like Swallow
Voice	High-pitched scream – often groups calling together	Twittering, babbling song; sharp 'kvik kvik' flight calls	Buzzing, twittering song; weak chirrup call	Chattering twitter
Perching and landing	Only perches at nest (clinging to wall); never on wires, branches or the ground	Perches on twigs, wires and the ground (when gathering mud)	Perches on twigs, wires and the ground (when gathering mud)	As House Martin; also on riverbank nest sites
Habitat	In the air over any landscape, including cities and old buildings; often high up	Open country, especially farmland with livestock; often near water	Around towns and villages; on edge of farmland	Along rivers and other water bodies
Nest	Cavity high in buildings; nest invisible	Inside outhouses and open buildings; cup nest made of mud, often on beam	Colonies under the eaves of houses; enclosed cup nest made of mud	Colonies of burrows in earth banks and cliffs, usually beside water; small entrance holes visible
Migration	May to Jul/Aug; latest visitor to arrive and earliest to leave	March/April to Sept/Oct	Mid-April to Oct	March to Aug/Sept; one of earliest UK summer visitors to arrive

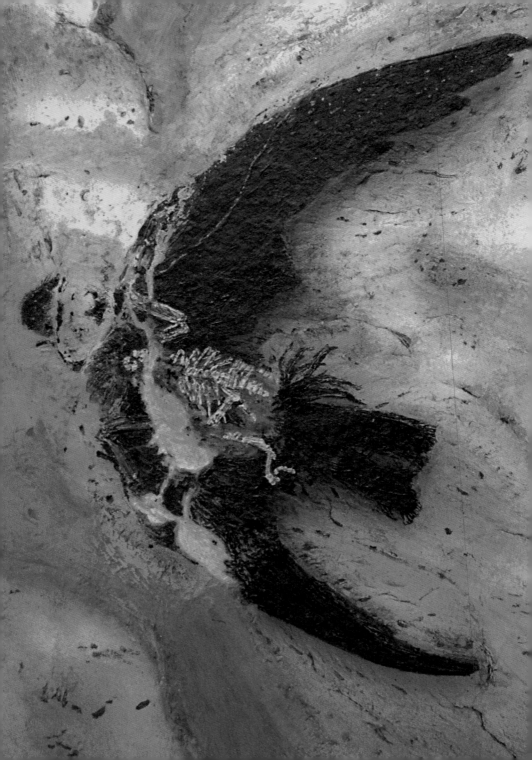

Ancestors and Relatives

Flipping through a field guide to the birds of Britain, it is tempting to assume that both the Swift and Swallow enjoy a unique status. The Swift is the only representative of its kind, after all, while the Swallow belongs to a family of just three – of which it is the only one to bear the name. But each bird forms part of a much wider grouping of very similar species found all around the world. And to appreciate 'our' two British birds – to understand their behaviour and how they came to be the birds that we know today – it is helpful to see them in the broader context of their relatives.

The swifts

Swifts, and their close relatives the hummingbirds, evolved during the Eocene Epoch, 56–33.9 million years ago, from a family of primitive birds known as the Jungornithidae. Fossils of this group found across Europe show features in the wing and pelvic bones that are characteristic of both hummingbirds and swifts today – in particular, a short humerus (upper arm bone) that can revolve in its socket.

Hummingbirds are thought to have split away from swifts in Europe about 42 million years ago, adapting to their own nectar-based diet. By 22 million years ago the ancestral species of today's hummingbirds was established in South America, and today there are some 338 species making up the family Trochilidae. To the casual observer these remarkable birds look nothing like swifts, with their brilliant iridescent colours and their long bills adapted for probing flowers for nectar. But look closely and you'll find clues to the shared ancestry. Both swifts and hummingbirds have tiny feet, with four toes generally pointing forward, and bare skin rather than the scales or

Opposite: Fossil of *Scaniacypselus*, preserved in shale deposits in Germany during the Middle Eocene, some 40 million years ago. The anatomy of this group of prehistoric birds shows clear ancestral links to present-day swifts.

Below: A Tourmaline Sunangel sips nectar from a flower in Ecuador. Like all hummingbirds, it is closely related to swifts.

Above: The long 'hands' of this Swift (left) and Ruby-throated Hummingbird (right) illustrate the similar structure of their wings, despite the great difference in the way the two birds fly.

scutes found on the feet of other birds. In both, these feet serve only for gripping and are no use for locomotion – other than a shuffle along a perch or inside a nest cavity. Furthermore, the birds' wings, while employed for very different kinds of flight, are strikingly similar in structure. Both have a reduced humerus bone that gives the wing a short 'arm' and very long 'hand'. This wing shape, and the revolution of the humerus bone in its socket, allows hummingbirds to hover and swifts to fly at great speed.

Today the swifts make up the family Apodidae, which comprises roughly 100 species around the world. They occur on every continent except Antarctica, with species that breed in northern and temperate areas tending to be migratory, while those that breed in the tropics – where aerial insects are on tap year-round – sticking closer to their breeding areas.

Taxonomists – the scientists of plant and animal classification – disagree about how exactly the family divides up. But most agree that it falls roughly into two subfamilies and four tribes, each of which in turn divides into a number of different genera. The Common Swift belongs to the Apodini tribe of 'typical swifts' and is one of 20 species in the genus *Apus*. Other groups of swifts

around the world include the needletails (Chaeturini tribe) and the swiftlets (Collocaliini tribe).

The treeswifts of southern Asia make up an entirely different family, called the Hemiprocnidae, of which there are just four species. They differ from true swifts in having softer, more decorative plumage, with crests and face markings, and a non-reversible hind toe that allows them, unlike true swifts, to perch on branches.

Above: Unlike swifts, the treeswifts of South East Asia – such as this Crested Treeswift – habitually alight on branches and other perches.

CLASS **Aves** 29 orders		
ORDER	**Apodiformes** 3 families 450 species	**Passeriformes** 110 families 5,000 species
FAMILY	**Apodidae** 100 species	**Hirundinidae** 83 species
SPECIES	**Common Swift**	**Barn Swallow**

Above: An Alpine Swift is much larger than a Common Swift and shows distinctive white underparts.

Above: The White-rumped Swift occurs in southern Spain and in addition to its white rump, has a distinctive white throat.

Above: The short tail and white rump of a Little Swift recall those of a House Martin.

Swifts around the world

Cross the Channel and you might meet one or two other swift species. The Alpine Swift (*Tachymarptis melba*) is the easiest to identify: much bigger than a Common Swift, with a wingspan of nearly 60cm (23.5in) and striking white underparts, you could even mistake it for a small falcon. Often seen zooming around mountainous areas, as the name suggests, it also occurs at sea level around the Mediterranean. The Pallid Swift (*Apus pallidus*), also found in Mediterranean regions and on the Canary Islands, is trickier to identify, being very similar in size and colour to the Common Swift, but is a little stockier and in good light appears slightly paler. In southern Spain you may also spot two smaller species that have colonised from North Africa: the Little Swift (*Apus affinis*) superficially resembles a House Martin, with its diminutive size, short forked tail and white rump; the similar White-rumped Swift (*Apus caffer*) is slightly larger, with a longer tail and a narrower white rump patch; and habitually parasitises the nests of the Red-rumped Swallow (see page 28).

Worldwide, there is a much greater variety. The most common North American species is the Chimney Swift (*Chaetura pelagica*), an all-brown swift that migrates north from South America in summer and may form huge roosts inside industrial chimneys. Most other New World species, such as the Chestnut-collared Swift (*Cypseloides rutilus*), occur in tropical South and Central America. South East Asia and its islands are home to numerous species

of swiftlet (*Aerodramus* genus), many of which breed in huge cave colonies. These include the Edible-nest Swiftlet (*Aerodramus fuciphagus*), whose nests – made entirely of hardened saliva – are harvested for bird's nest soup (see page 115). Spinetails are very small swifts with tiny spine-like projections at the end of their tail: the Mottled Spinetail (*Telecanthura ussheri*) is one of several African species that nests inside baobab trees. The needletails of South East Asia are larger, with longer tail spines and white undertail markings; at 25cm (10in), the Purple Needletail (*Hirundapus celebensis*), from Sulawesi and the Philippines, is the largest of all swifts. Palm swifts, such as the African Palm Swift (*Cypsiurus parvus*), have a long-tailed, skinny silhouette and glue their saliva nests to the underside of palm trees.

Above: The Chimney Swift is a common North American species, often found around industrial areas.

Above: The Edible-nest Swiftlet breeds in caves in huge colonies.

Left: The African Palm Swift has an unmistakable flight profile and is invariably seen around palm trees.

The swallows

Above: Swallows have a similar vocal apparatus to other members of the Passeriformes order, enabling them – unlike swifts – to sing.

Above: The Robin, like the Swallow, is one of more than 5,000 members of the Passeriformes order worldwide.

Swallows are thought to have evolved in Africa. The first swallows were probably hole-nesters, excavating their breeding burrows in the soft mud of riverbanks or other exposed substrates. The family subsequently spread around the globe, including to North America, where fossils of a species resembling today's Swallow have been found dating back 3.5–3.3 million years. Not surprisingly, fossils of such delicate little creatures are very seldom found.

Today swallows make up the family Hirundinidae – one of more than 110 families in the order Passeriformes, also known as passerines, perching birds or songbirds. This is by far the largest order of birds and accounts for more than 5,000 of the world's 10,000 or so species, from wrens to ravens. All share certain anatomical features, notably the structure of the vocal muscles, or syrinx, which distinguish them from other bird orders. The passerine families most closely related to swallows include tits, chickadees, babblers and *Sylvia* warblers such as the Blackcap.

The Hirundinidae family embraces some 83 species across 19 different genera worldwide. Some – generally those with shorter, squarer tails – are known as 'martins'; others – generally longer-tailed ones – are known as 'swallows'; however, there is no scientific distinction between swallow and martin, and the word 'hirundine' is often used to describe any species in this family.

All hirundines share the same basic anatomy. This includes a short neck and round head; a short bill with strong jaws and a wide gape; long, pointed wings; and a slender, streamlined body. Most have forked tails and many have long tail streamers. These features have all evolved as adaptations for flight, enabling hirundines both to zoom about after insects and also to undertake long-distance migrations. All hirundines also have short legs and small feet with, like other passerines, three toes pointing forward and one back. They use these for perching but they can also walk – for instance, when collecting nest material on the ground – in a slightly

clumsy shuffle. Many species have glossy upperparts and pale or reddish underparts, sometimes striped or streaked. Species that inhabit dry or mountainous areas tend to be browner. Most species show very little difference between the sexes.

Above: The Barn Swallow is one of many swallow species that collect mud as a nest-building material.

Hirundines also all share a similar lifestyle to our own Swallow's, living in open habitats where they feed primarily on flying insects, using their excellent flying skills to catch prey on the wing. Some make mud nests; others live in natural holes or excavate burrows in earth banks. Species from northern, temperate regions are long-distance migrants while those from the tropics tend to be more sedentary. Some, such as the Swallow, have withstood the world's heavy human footprint, adapting to feed in modified landscapes and using man-made structures as nest sites. Others, however, have struggled to cope with the damage we have done to their habitats and a few species are now very rare.

Right and below:
The Red-rumped
Swallow is a
Mediterranean
species that
constructs a
tunnel entrance
to its mud nest.

Above: Eurasian Crag Martins build their mud nests
on cliffs and crags, as their name suggests.

Swallows around the world

Today hirundines are found on every
continent except Antarctica. They vary in
weight from the 10g (0.4oz) White-thighed
Swallow to the 55g (1.9oz) Purple Martin.
Africa is home to the greatest diversity, with
some 33 species breeding on the continent.

For the UK birdwatcher, a hop across
the Channel introduces a couple of new
hirundines. In Mediterranean regions,
including Spain, Portugal and Greece,
you might come across the Red-rumped
Swallow (*Cecropis daurica*), which has
blue upperparts, striped underparts, an
orange face and rump, and often nests
under bridges. The Eurasian Crag Martin
(*Ptyonoprogne rupestris*) also inhabits
southern Europe, primarily in mountainous
areas, where it makes its mud nest on cliffs
and rock overhangs. It has a short, square
tail and is brown above and pale below,
without the throat band and forked tail of
the similar Sand Martin.

Travelling further afield introduces
greater variety. Across the Atlantic, the
Purple Martin (*Progne subis*) is one of the
best-known North American species. This
large, glossy blue-back hirundine has lost
many traditional nest sites to invasive
European starlings but has taken readily
to nest boxes, and in many areas is now
almost entirely dependent upon artificial
housing (see page 118). In Australia, the
Welcome Swallow (*Hirundo neoxena*) has
enjoyed better fortunes, managing off its
own bat to colonise New Zealand, where it
started breeding in the 1950s. This species
closely resembles our Barn Swallow, but
without the blue breast band. Among
numerous African swallows are the common

Wire-tailed Swallow (*Hirundo smithii*), a non-migratory species found along slow-flowing rivers, and the elegant Blue Swallow (*Hirundo atrocaerulea*), a rare species with exceptionally long tail streamers that may nest in disused aardvark burrows. The African River Martin (*Pseudochelidon eurystomina*), which breeds along the Congo River, belongs to a subfamily within the Hirundinidae, of which the only other species – the White-eyed River Martin (*Pseudochelidon sirintarae*), found only in Thailand – may now be extinct. Both differ from other swallows by having more robust legs. A few hirundines are restricted to small islands or island groups, where they have evolved unique forms distinct from their mainland relatives. These include the rare Bahama Swallow (*Tachycineta cyaneoviridis*) of the Bahamas and the Mascarene Martin (*Phedina borbonica*) of Madagascar and its neighbouring Indian Ocean islands.

Above: The Purple Martin of North America is a large hirundine that has taken readily to purpose-built nest boxes.

Above: The African River Martin of Equatorial Africa belongs to a separate subfamily of hirundines, characterised by their more robust feet.

Right: The Wire-tailed Swallow is a common African species associated with lowland rivers.

Built for Flight

Swifts and Swallows are both among the most impressive flyers in the bird world. And they have to be: their survival depends upon catching flying insects and migrating halfway across the globe twice a year, so only complete mastery of the air will do. It is these powers of flight, and the similar ways in which the two birds' bodies have adapted to meet the challenge, that has long linked them so closely in our imagination. Indeed, flying is responsible for many of their similarities, both of structure and behaviour. But there are still significant differences in the way each bird goes about it.

Swifts: always airborne

Swifts, more than any other birds, appear born to fly. Just a glimpse of them gliding, wheeling and accelerating through open airspace demonstrates that the sky is their element. Indeed, almost all their basic physiological processes take place on the wing, including feeding, drinking, mating and sleeping. You might even speculate whether, were it not for the inescapable reality that eggs cannot be laid in mid-air, a swift would ever bother to land.

These avian flying aces are capable of extraordinary airborne feats. One Asian species, the White-throated Needletail, is the fastest known bird in level flight, having been recorded at speeds of 169km/h (105mph). Our Swift is no slouch either and can reach a cruising speed of 111.6km/h (70mph), though 40km/h (25mph) is a more usual speed when hunting. An individual may travel more than 200,000km (124,000 miles) in a year, covering up to 900km (560 miles) a day during the breeding season. During its lifetime of 20 years, a long-lived bird will have flown the equivalent of five return trips to the moon. And altitude is no obstacle: Swifts have been recorded at 5,700m (18,700ft) over the Himalayas in Ladakh, India.

Opposite: Swifts passing at speed through urban air space.

Below: A Swift's mastery of flight allows it to both bathe and drink without having to land.

Above: Swifts may cross the highest mountain ranges during migration, reaching altitudes of over 5,700m (18,700ft).

Below: With a wingspan of more than two metres, the Magnificent Frigatebird dwarfs any swift, but has a similar capacity to remain airborne for long periods of time.

Of all these impressive statistics, surely the most mind-boggling relates to the amount of time Swifts spend in continuous non-stop flight. Scientists have long speculated about how often, if at all, these birds touch down between breeding seasons – especially in their early years. A 2010 experiment, in which 19 Swifts were tagged at their British breeding sites (see page 85) and then monitored during their migratory travels in Africa, found that three of the birds tagged did not touch down once. Never! The others all spent at least 99.5 per cent of their time in the air, making only occasional emergency landings when forced down by turbulent weather. Ten months is the longest proven continuous flight of any bird. The Swift's only rivals in this respect are frigatebirds (Fregatidae), lightweight tropical seabirds that stay airborne for weeks at a time. It is quite possible that some Swifts spend even longer airborne: possibly even years – not touching down after fledging until they return to breed during their fourth summer.

Wonder wings

A Swift's unique flying prowess comes down to the way in which it is built. To appreciate this, we should first remind ourselves of the anatomy of more typical flying birds. In all birds, wings are simply modified front legs. No longer required to support the body on terra firma, their structure has adapted to provide the power, lift and manoeuvrability essential to flight. Thus the upper arm (humerus) in birds is proportionally much shorter than in most mammals and held close to the body in order to generate power in the wing beat. The forearm (ulna and radius) and 'hand' (metacarpus and phalanges) are, by contrast, proportionally much longer than in mammals; these make up the visible part of the wing in flight and, with flight feathers attached, provide the bird with lift, speed and direction.

Left: This Wandering Albatross illustrates how a bird's wings are modified front limbs, comprising an upper arm (humerus), forearm (ulna and radius), wrist (carpus) and hand (metacarpus and phalanges), just like our own arms.

A Swift's wings, however, are unlike those of any other birds – except their close relatives, the hummingbirds. The hand is proportionally much longer, with longer carpus bones and very long primary feathers. Indeed, a Swift's ten primary feathers are proportionally the longest of any bird, measuring three times the length of its much shorter secondary feathers (of which there are 8–11). In passerines, including Swallows, the primaries are only twice the length of the secondaries.

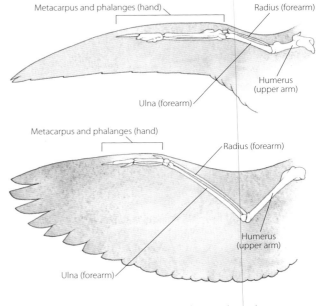

Metacarpus and phalanges (hand)

Radius (forearm)

Humerus (upper arm)

Ulna (forearm)

Metacarpus and phalanges (hand)

Radius (forearm)

Humerus (upper arm)

Ulna (forearm)

Right: The skeleton of a Swift (above) shows how the structure of its wing differs from that of most other birds, such as this Blackbird (below). It shows a proportionally shorter forearm (ulna and radius) and upper arm (humerus).

Below: The wings of a flying Swift form a single, crescent-like curve, with the carpal (wrist) joints held close to the body and barely visible.

It is these long hands that give the Swift its distinctive sickle or boomerang shape in flight, with the rest of the wing barely visible. The primary feathers are held close together to form a distinct backward-curving blade, providing a strong downward and forward force that powers this bird along faster than almost any other. Like hummingbirds (but unlike other birds), swifts can rotate their wings from the base. This allows the wing to remain rigid and fully extended, enabling it to generate power on both upstroke and downstroke. It is a design that leaves the Swift suited both to rapid flight and gliding. Indeed, Swifts spend a lot of time gliding – much more than passerines do – and their relatively small pectoral muscles illustrate the importance of this technique relative to flapping, which requires more muscular power.

The rest of the Swift's body presents a supremely aerodynamic shape. With its short, conical head mounted on a tapering cylindrical torso that ends in a tail held closed to a point – except when opened for slowing or manoeuvring – it is essentially a missile on wings. To avoid any extra drag, neither bill nor feet project from the body. A spray of feathers in front of the eyes reduces glare, working like a pilot's aviator goggles.

Flying, landing and taking off

Kitted out with such specialised flying gear, a Swift flies
in a highly distinctive manner, its wingbeats coming in
brief rapid bursts, interspersed with long, raking glides.
Flying together, a party appears to scythe through the sky,
each pursuing long, sweeping flight paths quite unlike the
more fluttery, irregular trajectories of Swallows (see
page 43). Alive to every nuance of the air, Swifts gain
height using thermals – columns of warm air rising from
the sun-heated ground – and coast on the deflective air
currents that rise from hills and cliff faces. They are even
thought to navigate using the wind, adapting their
orientation in response to clues from air currents rather
than by following ground-level landmarks.

To slow down, land and change direction, a Swift
adjusts the angle of its wings and spreads or twists its
forked tail. However, it is built for a broad aerial canvas
and does not have the close-range manoeuvrability of a
Swallow, which can stall, reverse and adjust direction
with much greater precision (see page 41). Indeed,
in more enclosed surroundings, a Swift's flight is less
efficient: it often needs to make several circuits before
entering its nest site.

Above: A Swift applies the brakes
by spreading its tail as it prepares
to enter the nest and land.

Above: Swifts take off by simply dropping into the air from the entrance to their nest.

And it is here, at the nest, that the Swift reveals the downside of a body adapted entirely for flight. Its tiny legs, equipped with four sharp-clawed toes, are little more than landing gear. They can cling like tiny grappling hooks to vertical surfaces and support the Swift's body just enough for it to shuffle about within the confinement of its nest cavity, but they cannot grip a horizontal perch or provide locomotion on the ground. To reinforce its grip on a vertical perch – for example, the side of a building – a Swift uses its specially stiffened tail feathers (of which there are ten) as a brace. Spinetails and several other swift species have evolved sharp, bare spines at the ends of their tail feathers for extra grip.

It is sometimes said that a grounded Swift cannot get airborne without assistance. It's true that a Swift does not have legs that can launch it into the air and that when taking off from its nest it simply freefalls into space and opens its wings. In fact, an adult Swift is capable of taking off from the ground or similar flat surface, but youngsters, recently fledged, may struggle. Should you come across a grounded Swift unable to take off, you should follow expert advice (see page 121).

Doing it on the wing

A Swift's aerial prowess allows it to perform many tasks in the air that other birds must perform on the ground. Foremost among these is feeding (see Chapter Four): it is, of course, the Swift's aerial diet that has driven its evolution into the flying machine we see today. Swifts also drink on the wing, by capturing rain droplets in mid-air or by swooping down to scoop water with their bill from a lake; take a bath, by flying slowly through a rainstorm; and gather nest material, plucking feathers, grass, paper and other lightweight items from the breeze.

In matters of love, Swifts also have no need to land. Though copulation also takes place at the nest (see page 57), the urge often strikes – uniquely for swifts – in mid-air. There is no evidence to prove which is the more effective approach. Mid-air copulation is usually preceded by a high-speed aerial chase, before the male lands on the female's back and the pair descend in a shallow glide – appearing to the observer like a single four-winged bird. The act itself takes just a couple of seconds, with the two birds twisting their tails to allow the transfer of sperm from cloaca to cloaca.

Above: A male Swift mounts a female during mid-air copulation, using his claws to cling on briefly.

Below: A bathing Swift flies low and fast over the water, ducking its body briefly beneath the surface but taking care not to waterlog its wings.

Perhaps the most impressive of a Swift's aerial accomplishments is its capacity to sleep on the wing. Swifts are among very few birds known to do this; the others include such high-altitude gliders as frigatebirds and vultures. They ascend to a great height, often 3,000m (10,000ft) or more, then descend slowly, maintaining altitude as long as possible by gliding into the wind, with occasional flaps. Descending at a rate of 300m (1,000ft) every five minutes allows them to roost for about half an hour in this way, doing so in a series of power naps. Like other birds, Swifts practise unihemispheric slow-wave sleep (USWS). This means they can switch off one side of their brain at a time, alternating regularly between the two. While dozing, they leave one eye open – the opposite one to the sleeping side of the brain – to keep watch.

Below: Vultures, such as this Eurasian Griffon Vulture, may also – like Swifts – sleep on the wing, taking advantage of their low wing loading to circle slowly at high altitudes.

Roosting usually takes place in the evening when the air is still and there are fewer predators around. During the breeding season, flocks from several colonies may combine in larger roosting parties, which climb high over the colony as darkness approaches. One of the first suggestions that Swifts are able to sleep in this way came from the account of a French World War I pilot who cut his engine at altitude and, while gliding silently towards the ground, found himself passing motionless birds. Once back on terra firma he discovered the body of a Swift trapped in the fuselage of his aircraft.

How birds fly

Above: A Sparrowhawk (left) uses its short, broad wings to manoeuvre at speed in confined spaces, whereas a Peregrine Falcon (right) uses its longer, more pointed wings for high-speed flight over distance.

Though flight may seem miraculous, the mechanics are quite straightforward. A flying bird must overcome gravity with an upward force, known as lift, and must counter drag by producing a forward force, known as thrust. It does this by flapping its wings. On the down stroke, the wing forces air backwards and propels the bird forward. On the up stroke, the wing folds up in order to minimise drag.

Once aloft, the aerofoil shape of the bird's wings – like an aircraft wing in cross section – continues to generate lift, with the air flowing faster over the curved upper surface and thus increasing the air pressure below. Manoeuvring is then a matter of making adjustments, such as tilting one wing or beating the other faster, to make a turn. To land, birds first flap more slowly to allow gravity to take effect then use their tail as a brake and drop their feet into position.

Flight technique depends on wing shape. Birds with short, rounded wings can accelerate quickly and manoeuvre skilfully but can't flap for long. Those with longer, narrower wings can sustain higher speeds for more extended periods. The short, broad wings of a Sparrowhawk (*Accipiter nisus*), for instance, enable it to twist and turn after prey in a short pursuit through dense woodland, while the longer, pointed wings of a Peregrine Falcon (*Falco peregrinus*) allow it to pursue prey over distance.

Many large birds save energy by soaring or gliding. Those with long, broad wings, such as vultures, can use air currents to stay aloft for hours and manoeuvre at low speeds without stalling. To gain height they hitch a ride on thermals – the columns of warm air that spiral up from the sun-heated ground. The ratio of weight to wing area is known as wing loading. Birds with a low wing loading are the more efficient flyers: they can remain airborne and continue manoeuvring at low speeds. Birds with a high wing loading must flap much more quickly, fly faster and have a much wider turning circle. Wing loading is calculated by dividing a bird's mass by the total surface area of its wings. The lower this figure, the less energy a bird need expend in order to fly. Small birds can get away with a lower wing loading as their bodies can store proportionally more energy for flapping, than can those of large birds.

Swallows: agility and aerobatics

Above: A Swallow makes final adjustments of its wings and tail in order to turn, brake and manoeuvre with exceptional control and agility.

A Swallow's life is not as exclusively aerial as a Swift's. It does not sleep or mate while airborne, and it spends much more time perched – able to alight on twigs, wires and other horizontal surfaces, land on the ground, and generally move around with greater competence. Nonetheless, it is a highly accomplished flyer, possessing both the agility to capture its prey on the wing and the efficiency to make transcontinental migrations of many thousands of kilometres.

A close look at a Swallow shows a bird more thoroughly adapted to an aerial lifestyle than other passerines and one that does, indeed, share several features with a Swift. These include long, pointed wings, in which the ten primary feathers are generally held closed, as well as a streamlined body, with a small bill, short neck and conical head. This shape, as with a Swift's, helps reduce the energy cost of flight. The long wings and low wing loading reduce the amount of power required to support the bird's weight in the air, while the

Above: The long wingspan of a Swallow helps reduce drag in flight.

Left: A perched Swallow reveals primary feathers that are proportionally much longer than those of most other passerines.

high aspect ratio – a long wingspan in relation to wing area – reduces drag in flight. In flight, Swallows have been shown to expend 40 per cent less energy than other passerines of a similar size.

A Swallow also has a deeply forked tail with long streamers, giving it the most attenuated shape of UK hirundines. This offers additional aerodynamic advantages, providing lift to further increase the bird's buoyancy. Held closed to reduce drag in level flight, it can also be spread, raised, lowered or twisted to help the bird slow or turn – a vital skill when it comes to pursuing the larger, faster insects that Swallows prefer. In experiments, scientists attached long tail streamers to shorter-tailed House Martins and found that this improved their ability to fly through a maze. Swifts do not possess the stalling and turning skill of Swallows: they generally pursue weaker insect prey at greater speeds and so do not have the same need for close-range manoeuvrability.

Above: When there is plentiful food in the air, Swallows may feed close together, manoeuvring around each other skilfully.

Agility over speed

To the human eye, a flying Swallow might appear to be dashing around at high speed. In fact, it is significantly slower than a Swift. Measurements using stopwatches, wind tunnels and film footage have concluded that a Swallow moves at 14–68km/h (8.6–42mph) while foraging and at a steadier 41–46km/h (25–28mph) while on migration. Speed is not the point: the Swallow's need is for low-energy, manoeuvrable flight with quick direction changes.

Right: A young Swallow hovers briefly, low above the ground, in search of insects.

A Swallow's flight action is very distinctive. It comprises bursts of easy wingbeats, interspersed with curves, swoops, jinking manoeuvres and short glides. Studies have shown that gliding takes up about 20 per cent of a Swallow's foraging time. Flapping is faster and so helps in catching more powerful insects (such as bluebottles and horseflies) but consumes more energy. Slower flight, with more gliding, serves for easier prey such as aphids and midges. Thus, researchers have found that the percentage of gliding is high early in the season but falls later in the year once Swallows start having to work harder to feed their brood.

The distinctive flickering action of a Swallow's wings reflects an unusual flight technique. In level flight, most other passerines alternate between regular wingbeats and short periods of gliding on extended or semi-folded wings. Hirundines such as Swallows, however, have a more flexible style, varying how often they flap their wings and the length of each downstroke. They deploy something called the 'interrupted upstroke', in which they flex the primaries while only partially spreading the wing, in order to maintain more lift. The apparently erratic nature of this flight gives Swallows a signature on radar that is different from that of any other bird.

Above: A Swallow pursues midges rising from the surface of the water.

Below: By spreading its tail, a Swallow provides lift to increase its buoyancy in the air.

An Airborne Menu

You are what you eat – or so dieticians would have us believe. Both the Swift and Swallow are living advertisements for that maxim. Their diet is 'aerial plankton': the innumerable insects, spiders and other airborne invertebrates that fill our summer skies. And it does indeed dictate everything about them, from their anatomy and powers of flight to the long seasonal journeys they must make in order to keep the food on tap. But feeding is not simply a matter of hoovering up the food indiscriminately, as whales do with ocean plankton. A diet of airborne invertebrates presents unique challenges, not least tackling the vagaries of weather and season. Swifts and Swallows both meet these challenges in their own way.

Swifts: sweeping up

Swifts, even more so than Swallows, depend upon capturing airborne invertebrates in flight. They know no other way of feeding. Happily, this presents them with multiple options. Indeed, the Swift takes the greatest known diversity of prey of any European bird, with over 500 different species recorded.

This enormous menu includes the following: aphids and other bugs (Hemiptera); ants, bees and their relatives (Hymenoptera); spiders – taken when dispersing aerially on their silk parachutes (Arachnida); beetles (Coleoptera); moths and butterflies (Lepidoptera) and a variety of lacewings, termites and other airborne minibeasts that commute through the summer skies. But there are exceptions: Swifts feeding around beehives in the Democratic Republic of Congo were seen to avoid stinging female workers and take only the stingless drones. Indeed, Swifts will always avoid stinging insects – although their appetite for hoverflies, whose markings mimic those of wasps, suggests that they can see beyond warning colours when distinguishing the edible from the inedible.

Opposite: Swifts do not gulp down everything in their path but target individual flying insects with unerring accuracy.

Below: Aphids occur in vast numbers during summer. Their young, winged offspring are an important food source for Swifts and Swallows.

Above: Newly hatched baby spiders disperse through the air on silken threads, and are a major component of the aerial plankton that sustains both Swifts and Swallows.

Above right: Mosquitoes take to the wing early on a summer's evening, offering an enticing target for Swifts and Swallows alike.

Below: Ladybirds and other small, flying beetles are captured individually by Swifts and, especially, Swallows.

Swifts are opportunists and will seek out concentrations of food, such as swarms of midges and aphids. Where possible, however, they target larger items – anything they can fit within their gaping bill and food pouch. Prey size varies with season and conditions: early in the season Swifts will rely on smaller species, such as aphids and spiders, which hatch and swarm in great abundance; by August, however, this supply has dwindled and they tend to target larger prey such as flying beetles. Choice also reflects weather conditions: in good weather average prey size is 5–8mm (0.2–0.3in); in poorer weather, when larger insects lie low, this falls to 2–5mm (0.1–0.2in).

Having a ball

Thankfully, our knowledge of what Swifts eat is not reliant upon watching them feed, which would be beyond the powers of human eyesight. The prey that they ingest gathers into balls at the back of their throat, bound together with saliva produced from their specially enlarged salivary glands. Also known as boluses, these food balls are biggest – and most important – during the breeding season, when the Swifts are feeding their young. This is when they can be collected at the nest and their contents analysed. Research into UK Swifts found the average food ball to weigh 1.5–2.5g (0.05–0.09oz) and to contain anything from 300–1,000 individual items.

The composition of a food ball varies with location and season: one may contain predominantly ants; another predominantly hoverflies. One food ball analysed in Oxford, during a plague of aphids in July, was found to comprise 898 items; of which 726 were aphids, 48 leafhoppers, 22 spittle bugs, 23 craneflies, 18 dung flies, 13 ladybirds and 10 ants. Studies of a different population in Gibraltar found a lower average of 300 items per food ball. From this, scientists calculated that each nest would receive roughly 3,000 items per day, and that with roughly 3,000 nesting pairs in Gibraltar, some 9 million insects would be captured in the area as a whole every 24 hours. Such figures give some indication of the major impact that Swifts can have on the invertebrate life of an area – and thus their great ecological significance.

Above: A Swift returns to the nest with a food ball in its throat.

Below: Some of the many invertebrates extracted from the food ball of a Swift.

Above: A storm front sweeps up large clouds of flying invertebrates, providing ideal feeding conditions for Swifts.

Feeding strategies

Swifts do not simply chase around the sky gulping down anything that flies into their open bill. Typically, they feed in a zone about 50–100m (164–328ft) above the ground, a little higher than Swallows and other hirundines (though height depends upon conditions). In rainy conditions they may swoop down low, foraging just a metre or so above the ground. In turbulent weather, food may be swept up high and Swifts will follow, foraging at up to 1,000m (3,280ft). Rough weather also directs Swifts towards water, where aquatic insects become active while terrestrial ones are lying low, and large numbers may gather over lakes during approaching storms. In general, however, Swifts tend to avoid low pressure centres and other areas of bad weather. They fly into the wind in search of better weather and will divert around an area of rain, covering up to 800km (500 miles) a day, in their search for food.

This capacity to eat up distance quickly allows Swifts not only to avoid bad weather but also to exploit food bonanzas far from their breeding sites. Gatherings of 2,000 or more have been observed over insect-rich wetlands and gravel pits, drawing individuals from as much as a 100km (62 mile) radius. Swifts tied down by bad weather along the south coast of England think nothing of nipping across the Channel to feed in northern France; populations from Western Scotland will commute to Lough Neagh in Northern Ireland to feed on the great swarms of flies that gather there.

When foraging, Swifts tend to pursue long, sweeping trajectories, though they will swerve off their line in pursuit of individual items. At big swarms of midges, aphids or other weak-flying prey that hangs in the air, they will make pass after pass, gorging on the bonanza in the manner of tuna corralling and attacking a bait ball of sardines. However, they tend to whittle away at the swarm by picking off individuals on the periphery rather than ploughing straight through the middle.

During the breeding season Swifts prefer to feed closer to the colony, in order to keep their young well provisioned with food balls – although the capacity of the youngsters to enter a state of torpor during hard weather (see page 62), allows their parents to forage further afield if required. On their wintering grounds in Africa, however, they may wander great distances, often following storm fronts for hundreds of kilometres to regions where fresh rainfall produces abundant flying ants, termites and other tropical insects. Indeed, termites and ants (Hemiptera) make up a significant proportion of their food from August to February. In Africa, Swifts often fly higher than the local species they encounter – just as back home they tend to fly above hirundines. This phenomenon, known as ecological separation, helps reduce competition between species foraging in the same area.

Below: A Swift opens its gape to grab an airborne insect.

Swallows: cherry picking

Above: Larger prey items, such as this dragonfly, are taken back individually to the nest.

Below: Hoverflies are favourite prey for Swallows on their summer breeding grounds.

The Swallow's menu, like that of the Swift, comprises a large spread of airborne invertebrates, including ants, bees and their relatives (Hymenoptera); beetles (Coleoptera); and moths and butterflies (Lepidoptera). In Europe, some 80 different insect families have been recorded on their menu, with mayflies, damselflies and stoneflies being particular favourites.

Nonetheless, Swallows show subtle differences from Swifts in the composition of their diet and the way in which they go about obtaining it. In general, they take prey of a larger average size, such as large flies and beetles, and rely less on small, weak-flying insects such as aphids. Studies around some breeding sites have shown that large flies, such as bluebottles and horseflies, make up around 70 per cent of the Swallow diet.

That is not to say that Swallows overlook the little stuff. Like Swifts, they are drawn to seasonal swarms of midges and mayflies – and will also visit lights at dusk to capture gathering moths. Also like Swifts, their diet varies with the season. One study in the USA found that flies made up 82 per cent of the Swallow diet during March, but only 18 per cent in September. Weather is critical to choice of prey, as it determines the type and quantity of insects available. Large flies become much more active at high temperatures; when the weather is cool Swallows generally have to fly further.

On their wintering grounds, Hymenoptera – such as flying ants – become more important, along with termites, half-grown grasshoppers and butterflies and moths. One study in Malaysia found that 46 per cent of the Swallow's prey there comprised flying ants – and more than 1,000 ants were found in the stomach of a single bird.

Flying closer to the ground than Swifts, and with the ability to forage among vegetation or even on the ground, Swallows will also branch out into items that seldom or never feature on the Swift menu. These include caterpillars and other non-flying invertebrates, and even some plant matter – including berries in the USA and, in South Africa, the seeds of the *Acacia cyclops* bush, from which they digest the fleshy outer part and regurgitate the hard kernel. To gain extra calcium for egg-laying, Swallows will also ingest small pieces of snail shell or eggshell. They have been observed feeding this to their chicks – along with small fragments of chalk that have crumbled from the walls of their nest site.

Above: A Swallow returns to its nest with another beakful for its brood.

Below left: Swallows may ingest small pieces of snail shell for extra calcium.

Below right: Swarms of winged termites are an important food source for Swallows at their winter quarters in Africa.

Catching a meal

Swallows forage within a much smaller area than Swifts. Studies of breeding birds in Scotland showed that they caught their prey at an average distance of 170m (558ft) from the nest and a maximum distance of 600m (1,969ft); similar studies in Italy and the USA showed that they journeyed no further than 400m (1,312ft) from the colony. A good nest site must be close to reliable food sources. Typically, these comprise a mixture of ponds, rivers or other water bodies; livestock pasture with plentiful animal dung; and hedgerows, which are especially valuable during poor weather when flying insects look for cover.

A Swallow's general foraging technique involves sweeping the area, usually at heights of 7–8m (23–26ft), where insects tend to concentrate in normal conditions. Swallows are much more erratic than Swifts in their flight path, constantly slowing, accelerating and changing direction as they track the more unpredictable movements of their larger prey. Like Swifts, however, they will be drawn to any concentrations, such as midges in a mating swarm or mayflies emerging from the water's surface.

Swallows are also adept at taking advantage of any animals that disturb insects as they work over the ground, including cattle and even flocks of starlings. In their African wintering quarters, they often accompany herds of wild game (such as elephants or buffalo) and are drawn to grass fires, which flush out a mass exodus of fugitive minibeasts. On the same principle, they will also follow farm machinery and even lawnmowers, snapping up anything put to flight.

During the early breeding season Swallows tend to forage in pairs. Once they have a brood to feed they will

Below: Swallows feed around impala on their African winter quarters, helping themselves to insects stirred up by the grazers.

gather prey in food balls – like a Swift's, though much smaller, with an average of around 15–18 items per ball. Outside the breeding season, on their wintering grounds, they often forage in large flocks, sometimes thousands strong. Such flocks also form over reedbeds, where Swallows roost before setting off on migration, feeding frenetically to fuel up before the long flight ahead.

When aerial options run out, Swallows are versatile enough to find food in other locations. They can hover to pick caterpillars off leaves or remove insects from spider webs; will perch on thistle heads or even the back of a pig; and at the beach will alight on seaweed to feast on the sandhoppers that swarm there. Using the same flying skills that enable them to scoop a drink from the water's surface, they will also snap up small floating prey from a pond, and have even been seen to snatch a stickleback.

Above: Swallows settle in a reedbed after feeding over the surrounding water.

Below: A Swallow feeding over a crop of oilseed rape. Fields of cereal crops offer less insect variety than does cattle pasture.

Born in a Tower

For Swifts, as with all birds, spring means breeding. Indeed, siring the next generation is the very reason they return to British shores from Africa. With little more than three months to spend here there is no time to lose if they are to raise a brood. Their arrival in early May triggers a frenzy of activity, starting with finding a nest site and pairing up. By late July, with luck, each pair will have added a clutch of its own offspring to the great Swift exodus about to depart for Africa. Success in this endeavour presents numerous challenges – to which Swifts rise with some unique strategies of their own.

Pairing up and prospecting

Swifts pair for life – or at least for as long as both partners remain alive. These pair bonds may form when the birds are just one year old. But Swifts mature more slowly than Swallows and will not produce their first young until year four, when they have reached breeding maturity. Some first-year birds do not return from Africa. The rest might show up in July to check out the colony, but don't stay long and never start building. In their second year, things progress a little further: the birds arrive in mid-May, pair up and make a first attempt at nest building. But it is only when three years old, in their fourth summer since hatching, that the birds arrive in early May and breed for the first time.

During winter in Africa, an established pair of Swifts go their separate ways. All being well, however, the two birds reunite on their breeding grounds – ideally, occupying the same nest from the previous year. If both partners survive and the nest site remains undisturbed, they may breed together in the same spot for many years in succession. If one bird does not return from Africa, however, the other will immediately pair up with a new partner.

Opposite: Church towers and other old buildings provide vital breeding sites for the Swift across much of its range.

Below: A party of Swifts zooms around the skyline of Uzes, France, where the ancient towers provide perfect nest sites.

Above: A newly arrived Swift peers out from the entrance to its nest.

The first challenge for a newly arrived male is to reclaim his old nest site – or, if he is a first-time breeder, grab a new one. Without a nest site he will never keep a partner. Swifts generally breed in colonies of up to 40 pairs so there is healthy competition for sites. Newly arrived birds zoom around the breeding site, prospecting for vacant nest holes. They fly close by the hole entrances, brushing or banging them with their wings. If a pair is already in residence they will drive away the interloper with a shrill screaming duet – and sometimes, if

Right: A Swift inspects its nest site from the year before, preparing to make a few home improvements.

he doesn't get the message, a physical attack. But if there is no response, then the hole is probably empty, in which case the prospector will claim it. Females also join these fly-pasts, checking holes in search of their partner – or, if unpaired, a newly eligible bachelor.

An experienced pair is generally able to reclaim its nest site from the previous year. Once the two birds have arrived, they re-establish their pair bond with a ritual display. This renewal of vows starts with hostility and suspicion, the two birds advancing towards one another with wings raised and screaming, but softens as they become reacquainted, offering each other their white throats as a signal of submission and soon settling down, wings quivering, to preen one another tenderly. These greeting displays continue through the breeding season, whenever one partner appears at the nest.

With the pair bonded, things become more intimate. Mating mostly takes place inside the nest hole, the female raising her tail and twisting her body towards the male who, with a short copulation scream, mounts her. This manoeuvre may take him several attempts, gripping her back with his claws and her nape with his bill until he is securely in position. After copulation, which may occur three or four times in quick succession, the two return to their tender mutual preening.

Above: A pair of Swifts rest side by side in their nest box in Cambridge.

Mating can also take place in flight (see page 37). In this case, the female flies in front of the male with her wings held vertically to attract his attention. Once he catches her up she slows down, wings quivering, and allows him to mount her in mid-air. The two birds then fly slowly together on a horizontal trajectory, the male's wings held high and the female's extended horizontally, tails twitching until after a few seconds, the act is completed.

Coming to blows

Competition between Swifts for nest sites is intense and can lead to serious conflicts. If a stranger enters an occupied nest hole, the occupier raises his body as high as his short legs will allow, lowers his head and moves forward, screaming aggressively. If the intruder fails to take the hint, the occupier will turn his body slightly to one side, flicking one wing towards his opponent and exposing his sharp-clawed feet. If this threat display still fails to do the trick then the two birds may fight, grappling with claws, cuffing with wings and pecking violently – all the time uttering their piercing screams.

Above: A Swift drives off an intruder outside the entrance to its nest.

Swift fights may last for more than five hours, with interludes of calm as the two catch their breath between bouts. The victor is often the one that manages to get onto its back beneath his antagonist, thus gaining a better upward purchase. The loser will utter a piping call in retreat. Sometimes the two combatants tumble from the nest to the ground, where they have been found locked together for up to 25 minutes. Such fights may prove fatal to one or both birds. They generally only take place before egg-laying starts and when only one of the occupying pair is present.

The scream

Swifts are no songbirds, but their drawn-out scream is one of the sounds of summer, and in its own way as evocative as any nightingale melody. This piercing call – often written as '*sreeee*' – comes in two different pitches, of which the higher is the female's. With slight variations, more obvious to a Swift's ear than a human's, it serves several purposes, including greeting, courtship, contact and threat. Other calls include a softer clucking used by pairs when preening each other, a plaintive piping given by the defeated antagonist in a fight, and a drier, more Swallow-like '*chiroo*' given by groups mobbing a bird of prey. Youngsters also utter a range of whistles and hisses at the nest, to threaten intruders or beg food from parents.

Swifts often form 'screaming parties', gathering in groups of up to 20 or more to zoom around their breeding sites, calling out and being answered in turn by nesting Swifts. Larger screaming parties form at higher altitudes, especially late in the breeding season, when they spiral up to great heights to roost on the wing. Large flocks foraging together also keep up a chorus of screaming. This is likely to encourage other Swifts to join the group, with the benefit that a larger number of birds will seek out the best feeding areas, thus benefiting every individual. Like many migrant birds, Swifts tend to be quieter on their wintering grounds.

Nesting

Long ago, before human times, Swifts bred only in natural cavities such as caves or tree hollows. Today a few colonies can still be found in such locations, including one in Scotland that has adopted woodpecker holes and tree nest boxes on the RSPB's Abernethy reserve. In general, however, Swifts now breed almost entirely at man-made sites. These are typically in crevices high up on buildings, including holes in walls, gaps beneath windowsills and free spaces under eaves and within gables. As Swifts usually enter their nesting holes in direct flight and leave by free fall, they choose a site with a clear flight path below the nest hole.

Above: A Swift at its nest site in the abandoned hole of a Great Spotted Woodpecker in Abernethy Forest, Scottish Highlands.

Swifts are gregarious birds and, at suitable nesting locations, they generally form colonies – although a few pairs manage to set up homes by themselves. The size of a colony depends largely on the number of available nest sites, with at least a metre's separation needed between them. Typically, a well-established colony will comprise 30 to 40 pairs.

Not any old building will do, however. And although Swifts have nested alongside humans in Britain since Roman times, unfortunately modern building designs – and the techniques and materials used in renovating older buildings – no longer provide them with the nest sites they need. Today Swifts nest almost exclusively in pre-1944 buildings. Studies have shown that while ten per cent of houses built before 1919 can offer suitable homes, the figure for inter-war housing is seven per cent and for post-1944 housing only 1.4 per cent (see page 99). Swifts will take readily to nest boxes, however, provided they are installed in the right places to the right specifications (see page 118).

Above: Gaps and crevices in a traditional pitched roof provide suitable nest sites for Swifts.

The nest

Once a pair of Swifts has settled on a suitable site they go about building their nest, sharing the work between them. This is a simple cup-like structure, made from feathers, paper, straw, hay and other lightweight, windblown material that the birds collect on the wing then bind together using glutinous saliva from their specially enlarged salivary glands. The nest measures on average 12.5 x 11cm (4.9 x 4.3in), and has an inner cup diameter of about 4.5cm (1.8in).

A pair will use the same nest year after year, renovating it each breeding season to repair any damage or deterioration suffered during their 40-week migratory absence. As the nest is mostly organic, insects such as clothes moths, carpet and larder beetles may tuck in, consuming all but the most indigestible elements such as old feather shafts.

Below: A newly hatched Swift beside the still unhatched egg of its sibling.

From eggs to fledglings

With the nest built, the female is ready to lay. She produces from one to five white, pear-shaped eggs, two or three being the norm in UK birds. These measure around 25 x 16mm (1 x 0.6in) and weigh about 3.6g (0.1oz). They are laid at two- or three-day intervals, and incubation starts with the last – or sometimes the second in a clutch of three. Parents continue to incubate for an average of 19.5 days, though they may stay on the eggs a little longer if bad weather slows their development. The two adults share the work, putting in shifts that may last from a few minutes to several hours, and change over regularly. The sitting bird spends a lot of time rearranging the nest material and gathering it closer together.

Young Swifts hatch at 24-hour intervals, so for the first week they are different sizes. This is unusual among small birds and works as an insurance measure: in times of plenty the younger birds soon catch up but if food is scarce the older one will get the largest share, which means at least one will survive. At hatching the chicks are blind and naked, and weigh around 2.75g (0.09oz).

Growing up

Swifts grow more slowly than Swallows. Down starts to appear by day 13 and covers their whole body by day 17. After 30 days this fluffy baby coat is fully replaced by feathers. At four weeks the nestlings generally reach their maximum weight – an average of 56g (1.97oz) – but they then slim down again while their body directs its resources towards growing adult plumage. Weather, as in all aspects of Swifts' lives, has an important influence on growth, with inclement conditions slowing things considerably. In one study, conducted during a warm period in Switzerland, the youngsters reached 50g (1.7oz) just ten days after hatching. In another study, during a cold spell in Oxford, they reached only 5g (0.17oz) in exactly the same time.

From two to three weeks, the youngsters become increasingly restless, shuffling around their nest chamber and sometimes even crawling between their own nest and their neighbours'. They stand up on their tiny legs, start to preen one another and exercise their rapidly growing new wings by performing press-ups on their wing tips – raising themselves for up to ten seconds at a time.

Above: A clutch of three recently hatched Swift chicks, their down just starting to appear.

Below: These two young Swifts at their nest in a building in Sussex are ready to fledge.

Above: An adult Swift crams a food ball into the gape of one of its hungry brood.

The parents brood their young continuously during the first week and for about half of each day during week two. Thereafter both birds devote their time to providing the daily insect diet that fuels their offspring's rapid growth, flying up to 900km (560 miles) each day as they comb the skies. The meals arrive as food balls, formed and stored in the adult's throat, each containing hundreds of tiny flying invertebrates (see page 47). At first the parents break up these balls to share between their brood, but after about two weeks each youngster gets its own food balls regurgitated directly into its gaping bill.

By day 14 the adults are bringing back up to ten food balls a day. The chicks' demands for food becomes increasingly vociferous, the noise of the adult's return prompting a chorus of screaming and begging. Once they have grown larger, they will flap their wings and chase their parents around the nest cavity. At the appearance of danger – including a researcher taking a peek into the nest – they may perform a threat display, opening their wings and lunging forward. If captured by a human handler they may even feign death.

Closing down

Young Swifts have a survival strategy that is almost unique among birds. During sustained poor weather, the supply of aerial plankton may dry up, obliging parents to fly far and wide in search of enough food to feed both their chicks and themselves. Sometimes they are obliged to abandon their brood for up to 48 hours. Remarkably, the youngsters can survive such lean periods by entering a state of torpor, a coma-like condition in which their temperature falls and metabolism slows to almost nothing. During this time (in which they rely upon fat reserves) they may lose half their weight, slowing their development and delaying their fledging. But the process still allows them to survive conditions in which most baby birds would simply perish from starvation. A similar capacity even extends to Swifts' eggs, which can survive levels of chilling – if the parents have to spend more time away from the nest foraging – that would kill the embryos of any other bird. Development simply slows down until a parent returns, with incubation extended for a few days.

Good to go

In a good year, young Swifts fledge at about six weeks old. The precise time varies from 37 to 56 days, according to weather conditions, but in the UK the birds are ready to leave after an average 42.5 days in the nest – generally towards the end of July. This is a relatively long fledging time compared with other birds of roughly the same size, however the fledglings must be completely self-reliant from the moment they set out.

The youngsters usually leave in the early morning or straight after sunset, the first hatched chick setting off first. For several days beforehand they will have spent long periods at the entrance peering out. Once in the air, they rarely return to the nest and from this point on they receive no more food from the adults. There is no time now for flying lessons or further exercises: their wings and flying skills must be good enough for them to feed themselves immediately. After all, within a few days they will be flying to Africa. A few birds may fledge prematurely, especially during poor summers. Such individuals may struggle to remain airborne and sometimes crash-land. They are doomed – unless they are found, reared and given a second chance. This is a job for experts (see page 121).

Above: A fledgling Swift performs wing exercises while its sibling looks on.

Below: Swifts fly around their breeding colony at Fakenham, Norfolk.

Parents generally leave the nest a few days after the last of their young, males usually before females. By the start of August they, like their offspring, will be on their way to Africa. Breeding success in UK Swifts is calculated at 58–65 per cent, which means that a pair can expect in an average year to raise 1.3–1.7 chicks to maturity. Those that survive will return to breed in four years' time and then, all being well, continue to do so for years to come. Indeed, for such a small bird, the Swift can live for a remarkably long time. The oldest ringed individual lived for at least 21 years, and it is quite possible that some do even better.

Born in a Barn

It is the necessity to breed that brings Swallows back to our shores every spring. They waste no time, pairing up within days of arrival before building their nest, raising their youngsters and, if time allows, going straight on to produce a second brood. The birds eke out every last second of summer, exploiting the abundant food and fine weather until the nights start to draw in and they must head south again – along with their new generation of youngsters. This round-the-clock dedication has long established the Swallow as a model of selfless parenting. Nonetheless, breeding also involves some more brutal strategies that, while making perfect reproductive sense for the birds, are rather less palatable for us humans.

Pairing up

Courtship often starts before Swallows even reach our shores, with some males singing and displaying on their wintering grounds and during their migration flights. Males generally show up before females, with older, more experienced individuals arriving first. They immediately lay claim to a breeding site, which consists of a few square metres that either has an existing nest or offers the potential to build a new one. They sing vigorously from nearby perches and chase off any rivals that attempt to muscle in. Late-arriving males may find all the prime spots already taken.

Once the females arrive, males display to compete for their attention. They glide showily overhead, sing vigorously and flutter around the object of their desire, fanning their tails. A prime breeding location may see numerous males all performing in this way simultaneously. If a female

Opposite: A pair of Swallows is seldom far apart during the breeding season. The male (foreground) can be distinguished from the female by his longer tail streamers.

Below: Swallow display flights consist of gliding passes, calculated to show the male's plumage and flying skills to best effect.

appears interested, her suitor will fly back and forth to the nest or nest site, using sharp enticement calls to encourage her to follow. If she lands nearby, he will lower his head and peck in the direction of his proposed site, attempting to seduce her with his house-hunting discernment. It is the female, however, who calls the shots. If she is unimpressed by her first suitor, she quickly moves on to another. Most females find a partner within three days of arriving. Males, however, will often court two or three females before they get to mate.

A cheerful twitter

Swallows have a twittering voice that is invariably described as 'cheerful'. The male's song is a jumbled, warbling stream of short phrases that may continue for up to 15 seconds, usually with a rattling trill at, or near, the end. He usually sings in the vicinity of the nest, either perched or in circling song flights overhead. Both sexes also give sharp 'wit-wit' contact calls, sometimes run together into a longer stream, while the alarm call is a louder, disyllabic 'zi-witt'. Other calls – more recognisable to a swallow's ear than a human's – include a 'wi-wi-wi' enticement call, used by males to lure females, or by parents to entice young back to the nest for roosting, and a 'chirr-chirr' alarm, given when a predator is spotted at a distance. Youngsters in the nest also make a range of begging calls. Check the RSPB website under 'Swallow' to hear a short audio clip.

Once paired up, a pair quickly gets down to business. Copulation takes place at the nest site and on roofs, trees, wires and other nearby perches. The male sings to solicit the female's assent and hovers in front of her, tail spread. If she accepts, he mounts her with wings fluttering and, as both twist their tails, transfers sperm from his cloaca to hers. The act takes just a few seconds and is followed by preening.

A female is fertile for a short period – on average from five days before the laying of her first egg until the day before her last. During this time, copulation continues non-stop, especially in the early morning – up to 1.5 times per hour, and perhaps 50 times in total for a clutch. It comes to an end by the time the female is incubating her clutch. Females may store sperm in their reproductive tract for up to five days.

Below: Copulation in Swallows takes just a few seconds.

Led by the tail

Extensive studies of Swallow courtship behaviour reveal just which of a male's qualities most impresses a female. Number one is his tail. Females prefer males with long and symmetrical tails, both features being indicative of health and strength and therefore of likely breeding success. Big white tail spots also seem to demonstrate the same thing.

Above: Prominent white spots in the tail of a male Swallow serve, like the length of the streamers, as an indication of breeding potential.

Experiments in which the spots on some males' tail were reduced or obscured using black ink showed that these individuals were less likely to have a second brood, and so would produce fewer fledglings in a season.

The desirable qualities in a male are passed down genetically. In choosing long-tailed males, therefore, females know that their partners are likely to produce long-tailed male chicks. These will in turn be strong and healthy, most likely to withstand threats and disease, to arrive on breeding grounds early, to find the best nest sites and to produce the most broods in a year. But there are downsides. Long-tailed males, it seems, make worse parents, devoting less time to feeding their chicks than do lower-status short-tailed males and being more likely to pursue other females on the side (see page 70).

Other factors influencing a female's choice of mate include his song, with long, vigorous refrains also indicating health and thus breeding potential. Studies in the USA suggest that colourful plumage can also play a role in the North American race *Hirundo rustica erythrogaster* with brighter reds on the face and underparts making a male more attractive.

To have and to hold?

Swallows are socially monogamous birds: pairs stay
together for successive years and raise several broods
together. But this does not tell the whole story. Few
partnerships keep all their eggs in one basket, so to speak,
and other breeding strategies – what scientists call 'extra-
pair copulations' and others might label 'playing away' –
are very much the norm.

Putting aside human value judgements, this makes
perfect sense. In evolutionary terms, success for a male
Swallow means fathering as many chicks as possible,
while for females it means producing chicks of the
highest quality. Birds of both sexes will do whatever it
takes to achieve these ends. Spend any time watching a
Swallow breeding colony and you will see (whether you
realise it or not) females being pursued by males that are
not their partners. Their own mates will drive away these
chancers where possible – but should they be absent, and
the interloper be particularly persistent or attractive, the
female will be tempted.

Extra-pair copulations are most common in large
colonies, where around one-third of broods will usually

Above: A pair of Swallows in a
farm building in Norfolk put the
finishing touches to their nest.

Above: A Swallow peeks out from its nest under a wooden roof.

Below: A male Swallow uses a convenient signpost to display to a female.

contain at least one extra-pair chick. The sneaking around usually happens among immediate neighbours and is most frequent during a female's first fertile period (before her first brood). This strategy can prove especially important for late arriving females, who missed the best males and may now improve the quality of their chicks by mating with males superior to their own partners. The most promiscuous males are, conversely, usually the strong birds that arrived early and paired up quickly. Indeed, females prefer their extra-pair liaisons to be with mated males; especially ones with impressive tails.

Males, while always checking out neighbouring females, still devote much of their time to 'mate guarding' – doing all they can to prevent themselves from being cuckolded behind their back. The oldest, largest males are the most successful in this respect. Most will stay within 5m (15ft) of their mate, from three weeks before she starts laying until the start of incubation, spending some three-quarters of their time in her presence. They will see off any rival males that come too close, sometimes even disrupting an attempt at copulation with an alarm call that scatters all the birds in the colony. By continuing to copulate frequently with their mate, they also ensure that – even if she has been secretly entertaining other suitors – it is their sperm that is most likely to fertilise her egg.

Regardless of how many other birds they mate with, a pair of Swallows generally stays together throughout the breeding season. Many will reunite again the following year – though mortality rates are high over the winter and many birds find themselves widowed between seasons. In one study in Scotland of 150 pairs, 15 per cent remained together for two years and just two pairs lasted for three years. One pair in Germany even managed four years. Regardless of death, however, pairs may split up if breeding is failing, either party initiating the divorce in order to try again elsewhere.

Darker arts

Male Swallows that arrive too late to pair up, or that lose their mates, must quickly seek out alternatives. Widowed females – those who have lost their mate, perhaps to a predator – offer one such opportunity, but a newcomer must replace the widow's brood with one he has sired himself. He may thus resort to infanticide: killing her offspring by pecking them in the head and dropping them out of the nest. This usually only happens during the chicks' first four days. It may seem brutal but it is a breeding strategy pursued by many animals, from lions to meerkats. It allows a male to maximise his own genetic legacy and increases the chances of breeding success for the widowed female, who would have struggled to raise her original brood alone.

A female may also resort to laying eggs covertly in the unattended nests of neighbours and leaving them to raise her chicks. This is known as egg dumping and is a form of the 'brood parasitism' routinely practised by birds such as cuckoos, which outsource their childcare to other parents. Eggs dumped in an empty nest are rejected, but if smuggled into an existing clutch they are usually accepted.

Above: A female Swallow repels the advances of a neighbouring male. Such advances, however, are not always unwelcome.

Nesting

Above: A traditional dairy farm, with its insect-rich pasture and old outhouses, provides the perfect breeding environment for Swallows.

Below: Swallows will make use of many human props when building their nest, such as this security camera in China.

As with most birds, 'location, location, location' is the mantra for Swallows intent on nesting. The bird was once largely a cave nester – there is evidence of Swallows in caves at Creswell Crags, Derbyshire, from 15,000 years ago – but today it is invariably tied to human landscapes. In Europe this generally means farmland – especially grazed pasture. Cattle farms are best, as cows leave the largest piles of insect-attracting dung, churn up ample mud for nest-building and don't crop the grass too low, thus allowing invertebrate life to flourish. One study in Italy showed that Swallows bred on 91 per cent of farms with livestock but only 44 per cent of farms without; and that, in Denmark, the decline of dairy farming in some areas has led to the decline of Swallows.

Whatever the habitat, it is human structures that most often provide the nest sites. Indeed, Swallows have been nesting on human artefacts since at least the time of the Ancient Egyptians, and the availability of such structures has allowed them to colonise areas they might not otherwise usually inhabit – for example, by breeding in log cabins in the far northern tundra.

Most pairs choose a spot inside an accessible outbuilding, such as a barn or stable. Sheds, garages, mine shafts and wells will also do – and, in Asia, houses and shop fronts. Inside, Swallows use beams and other horizontal projections as a support – or build the nest into cracks and corners. In one study of 192 nests in Scotland, 41 per cent were on beams and 38 per cent in a roof apex. A rough substrate is important to give the structure traction, wood thus being better than cement, metal or plastic. But if the basic criteria are satisfied, Swallows can improvise around almost anything. Nests have been found built on picture frames, hats, lampshades, brackets, electrical wires, masonry bolts, chains, gear wheels, a sunflower seed head nailed to a beam and even the corpse of an owl. And motion is no deterrent, with nests recorded on oil pumps and, in Denmark, passenger ferries. Swallows will also happily make use of nest sites provided for them, including pieces of wood nailed in a suitable place and the artificial cup nests now available commercially (see page 124).

Above: Swallows typically build their nest on a beam or similar horizontal support, and near the roof.

Wherever a nest is placed, it should satisfy the birds' key needs: a nearby source of building materials, predator-proof perches and a clear flight path for easy access. Successful nests are usually built at a height of 2–4m (6.5–13ft), out of the reach of predators and close to a ceiling where they receive protection from the elements and can maintain a more constant temperature – keeping eggs and chicks snug in cold weather and cool when it turns hotter. And darkness is not a problem, Swallows need very little light, and dimly lit nests are safer from predators.

Mud, glorious mud

Once a pair has settled on a site, the construction work begins. The nest is a neat open cup made of mud, mixed with variable amounts of coarser material, such as dry grass or horsehair. If mud is scarce they may supplement it with other materials including dung, seaweed and moss. A newly built nest is about 20 x 10cm (7.8 x 3.9in), with a cup some 4–8cm (1.5–3.1in) deep. It weighs on average 255g (9oz), including the lining.

Building a nest from scratch takes 5–12 days, the process taking longer when dry weather makes fresh mud harder to find. Both males and females contribute to building, though males seldom contribute more than 25 per cent. Between them, they may collect 750–1,400 pellets of mud. Its source may be anything from a stream edge to a cow's hoof print, and requires the Swallow briefly to land – usually spending a few seconds on the ground while it fills its bill. Each pellet means a separate trip so a new nest may require more than 1,000 trips in total, with most work done early in the morning to allow the mud time to dry by nightfall. Studies have shown that an average pair may fly more than 220km (137 miles) in the process of completing their nest-building.

Below: A pair of Swallows visit the edge of a puddle to collect the mud pellets with which they build their nest.

Construction

The construction starts with a ledge, or base, from which the walls are built upwards and outwards. Each mud pellet is manipulated into position with tongue and bill. The bird vibrates its head to tamp down the mud, thus eliminating any air spaces that might cause the nest to dry out and crack. The nest quickly takes shape: either a flat-bottomed half sphere on a horizontal support, or a deeper quarter sphere on a vertical one. So sturdy are Swallow nests that they have been known to last 48 years, though 12–15 years is more usual.

Above: With the base of its nest in place, the Swallows build upwards and outwards to fashion a cup structure that will hold the eggs and brood.

Lining

Next comes the lining: first a fresh layer of dry grass then an insulating covering of feathers. The latter helps reduce the rate at which the eggs cool when the female isn't sitting. White chicken feathers are most popular, with an average of 33.5 used per nest, though fur, cotton wool or other soft material may serve just as well. The female gradually removes this layer as the chicks grow bigger, to ensure that they don't overheat.

Below: The female Swallow is largely responsible for incubating the eggs.

Recycling

A less laborious strategy is reusing an old nest. This generally involves just a little extra mud to plaster over cracks and strengthen crumbling edges, and adding a new feather lining. It takes far less time and energy than starting from scratch and for first broods it is generally the favoured option – one study in Scotland showed that 76 per cent of pairs stuck to this approach for their first brood. Reusing a nest allows birds to start laying up to four days earlier than when building from scratch. But there are drawbacks: old nests can become unstable and harbour more parasites as the season draws on. This explains why, in the same study, only 21 per cent of pairs used an old nest for their second brood.

From egg to fledgling

With a male and female mated, and their nest ready and waiting, the main event is about to begin. The date on which a female lays her first egg varies with climate and geography. In the UK, laying starts for most southern birds in late April or early May – on average 16 days after they arrive – and is about a week later in the north. Second broods generally follow in July. Thus, first broods fledge in June and second broods in late July and August. After that the weather usually becomes too dicey and most birds are preparing to leave – although fledging continues into September, and even October has been recorded.

A female lays her eggs one at a time, once a day and usually early in the morning. She will usually keep going until she has laid five or six, though may continue until seven or eight. Clutches of ten, occasionally recorded, probably involve more than one female. Second clutches are generally smaller than first ones: studies in Scotland recorded an average first clutch size of 4.89 eggs and an average second clutch size of 4.41. There are many variables, including weather, food supply and health. Old females tend to lay earlier and have larger clutches. As with many birds, clutches are larger in more northerly latitudes.

Below: A typical Swallow clutch will contain five to six eggs. Feathers may also be collected to provide nest insulation.

The eggs are white, with variable amounts of blotchy red, and speckled in lilac and grey. In UK Swallows, they average from 19.6 x 13.7mm (0.7 x 0.5in) in size and weigh 2g (0.07oz). Incubation usually starts when the last or penultimate egg of the clutch is laid. This ensures that all hatch at roughly the same time. In European Barn Swallows only females are known to incubate, but in the North American race, males sometimes help out a little. The eggs are incubated for some 60–80 per cent of daylight hours, usually in 20-minute bursts. The female's body keeps the clutch at an average temperature of around 35°C (95°F), with this dropping to as low as 25°C (77°F) when she pops away from the nest for a feed. In the UK, incubation usually lasts from 13–15 days. In poor weather it may be longer – reducing the time available for a second brood.

A clutch usually hatches over a period of 24–36 hours, with the first eggs laid being the first to hatch. The female immediately removes the egg shells, which are a giveaway to predators, and drops them a few metres away. The hatchlings are blind and naked, and weigh just 1.5–1.9g (0.05–0.06oz). The first to hatch tend to weigh the most – and in hard times smaller chicks die, leaving more food for others.

For the first few days the female broods her hatchlings to keep them warm. From day five,

Above: The bright gapes of young Swallows begging for food stimulate the parents to keep providing it.

when they are able to regulate their body temperatures, she spends less time with them. The youngsters grow fast, with the first pin feathers appearing by days four and five. At nine days they can flap their wings and at 12 days they can preen. By days 13–15 they are well feathered and have reached a peak of 22–25g (0.7–0.8oz) – heavier than their parents. By now they are clambering around on the edge of their nest.

After this peak they lose weight as their body tissues lose water. However, their pectoral muscles continue to develop and their wings and outer tail feathers keep growing until days 28–30: aerial insectivores must be able to fly efficiently as soon as they fledge, whereas ground-feeders, such as blackbirds, can continue to grow after they have left the nest. At fledging, a young Swallow's average wing length is 80 per cent of an adult's, its tail length 50 per cent and its head and body length 96 per cent.

Begging and feeding

With a hungry brood in the nest, the parents face their most exhausting challenge. Both birds spend most of the day in flight, feeding both their offspring and themselves. Studies suggest a pair must catch 150,000 insects to rear a brood. The weather and food supply are critical factors: chicks rarely starve, but poor conditions can compromise their health and, ultimately, their survival.

The chicks don't let their parents forget their responsibility, begging ever more vociferously for food as they grow. At first they don't respond until the adult has landed, but soon they start to anticipate a delivery, reacting to the adults' contact calls and shadows. They stretch out their necks and gape wide, revealing a bright orange/red gape with pale yellow flanges (flaps of skin) that stand out in the gloom and stimulates the parents to stuff food down their gullets.

Nest health and safety

As the chicks continue to grow, the parents take great care to keep the nest clean and defend their brood from danger. To maintain hygiene in the first few days they remove the faecal sacs in which the youngsters produce their droppings, either eating them or dropping them several metres from the nest. By five to six days, the chicks have learned to defecate over the rim. Newly hatched chicks will gape at anything, including predators, but older chicks soon learn to flatten themselves low in the nest when they hear the adult's alarm call. Meanwhile, the parents conduct a spirited defence of the nest, diving at and even striking predators while giving an alarm call that alerts their neighbours to do the same. It's a risky business: both cats and sparrowhawks may capture Swallows that mob them. The aggression intensifies as the chicks get older, however, with parents even diving at human intruders.

Left: A Swallow flies away to dispose of a faecal sac from the nest.

This food comes in the form of food balls or boluses (see page 53), with the parents feeding one chick on each visit. Over the course of a day, all chicks in a clutch receive similar amounts of food. Males do most of the feeding for the first few days, while the female is still brooding; thereafter both parents share the burden. Feeding rates tend to peak from late morning to early afternoon, falling off towards the beginning and end of the day when most insects are less active. The age and size of the brood determine how long parents spend on foraging: one study in Scotland found that, at one day after hatching, they made six food deliveries an hour; at six days they made 17 an hour, and at ten days they made 29 or more an hour.

Off, up and away

Young Swallows leave the nest at anything from 18–23 days. The average fledging date in the UK is 21.1 days, compared with, for example, 20.7 days in Virginia and 21.2 days in Spain. Sometimes an entire clutch fledges on the same day; at other times their emergence is more staggered. Once out of the nest, the youngsters hang around the immediate vicinity for a week or so, perching quietly in a secluded spot as they continue to await their parents' food deliveries. They flutter and call when the adults arrive, sometimes flying up to beg on the wing. This behaviour usually continues for five to seven days but gradually the youngsters become less reliant on their parents as they learn to catch insects for themselves.

Above: A Swallow fledgling stretches its wings, preparing for flight.

After two weeks, the family groups break down as young Swallows begin to roost with other birds of the same age. Slow starters may still be around when their parents are on their second brood, but at this point the male may chase them off; it is time to cut the apron strings. After all, for their next challenge – migrating to Africa – they will be on their own, and life will not be easy. Although 70–90 per cent of Swallow hatchlings survive to fledging, some 70–80 per cent of birds fail to survive their first year. As adults, most will survive less than four years – although one record of 11 years proves that a few hardy individuals are made of sterner stuff.

Globetrotters

The migration of Swifts and Swallows continues to defy the imagination. How can these tiny feathered birds – one weighing no more than a tennis ball; the other just half that – fly from Britain to Africa and back every year? And why? It is only in the last 100 years that we have come to understand the simple truth behind migration: that however perilous these journeys might be, staying put would be worse. Birds migrate to stay alive. For Swifts and Swallows, enduring our northern winter would mean starvation. By heading off to warmer lands, where insects fill the skies, they are at least increasing the chances that we will enjoy them for another summer.

Swifts: constant wanderings

Of all the UK's summer visitors, the Swift pays us the most fleeting visit. It is, on average, the last species to arrive and the first to leave, spending less than three months on our shores. From early May until early August, Swifts are racing around our skies. Then suddenly they are gone again. We know they go to Africa, but beyond that, many questions remain unanswered.

Opposite: A mixed party of adult and juvenile Swifts circles the ruins of Castillo de Turegano in Segovia, Spain. Soon they will depart for Africa.

Below: Seed-eaters such as this Goldfinch survive cold northern winters by feeding on seeds and berries. Swifts and Swallows have no such option.

Winter quarters

The Swift is migratory right across its range. British Swifts belong to the nominate race *Apus apus apus*, which breeds from the UK east to Siberia. All birds of this race winter in sub-Saharan Africa, mostly in a broad central band that extends across equatorial Africa, notably the Congo Basin, and south to Zimbabwe and Mozambique. The majority winter south of the equator, but recent records have revealed scattered wintering populations

in West Africa and small numbers north of the Sahara, including in Egypt and in the Arab Gulf states.

A second race of the Swift, *Apus apus pekinensis*, whose breeding range extends from Iran to China, winters in the arid south-west of Africa, particularly Namibia and Botswana. Swifts wander huge distances on their African wintering grounds, following weather systems to where the food is most plentiful, so it is likely that the paths of the two races sometimes cross and that both may enter regions where they are not usually found. Elsewhere around the world, a few also turn up as 'accidentals' – individuals blown off their usual migration path – in places as far-flung as Svalbard, Iceland, the Azores and even Bermuda.

Right: The arrow on this map shows the principal migration flyway followed by UK Swifts travelling to and from Africa. However, there are many variations: some birds will travel more directly across the Sahara; some will continue further south; and some may make more direct sea crossings for a quicker return journey.

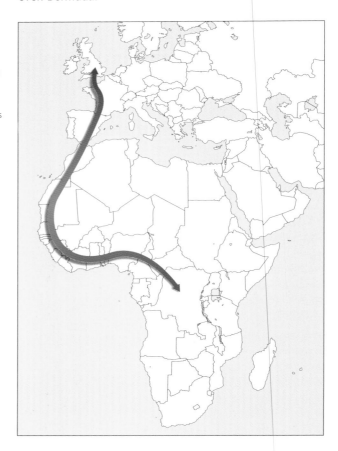

Heading south

Southbound migration for Swifts starts from late July, as soon as the young have fledged, and continues into early August. Swifts have only one brood so there are no late departures like those of Swallows, many of which don't leave until late September. Being able to feed on the wing, Swifts have less need to build up the fat reserves that most migrating songbirds depend upon for their journey, and can thus set out almost immediately after breeding.

The first to depart are the new fledglings, along with the unsuccessful breeders and immature yearlings. Breeding males are next, followed by breeding females. Departure is thought to be triggered by changes in day length. Thus, Swifts that breed in the far north, for instance Finland, leave later – around the second half of August. The dwindling of the aerial insect supply probably also helps spur the migrants into action. Either way, they don't hang around: one young Swift that left its UK nest on 31 July was found in Madrid on 3 August, just four days later.

Above: A migrating Swift flying low over the sea in Northumberland, UK, as it approaches the coast.

Above: Many UK Swifts find winter quarters in the insect-filled skies over the vast Congo Basin of Equatorial Africa.

Above: A Swift chick is ringed at its nest box in Worlington, Suffolk. If it is caught again elsewhere, this ring will reveal more about its migration journeys.

The travellers head on a broad front across Europe, skirting the Alps in a roughly south to south-westerly direction. Those from western and central Europe, including UK Swifts, cross the Iberian Peninsula and the western Mediterranean into north-western Africa, most likely heading south around the Atlantic coast to the west of the Sahara. Those from Russia and south-eastern Europe cross over the eastern Mediterranean and skirt the Sahara to the east. Some birds may cross the Sahara more directly, though the absence of records from Libya suggests that relatively few make the longer sea crossing over the central Mediterranean.

Having rounded, or crossed, the Sahara, our UK Swifts reach the humid savannah of the Sahel region, arriving from mid-August. From here they turn roughly south-east and continue towards central and southern Africa. By September they are zooming around their winter quarters in skies thick with insects. They do not settle at a single destination, however, but keep wandering, following weather fronts towards fresh rainfall and the promise of more food. It is hard to keep track of them at this time, but some regular localised movements are known: in East Africa, for instance, large numbers head south during December, though it is still unclear exactly where.

Returning north

As the northern spring arrives, a few Swifts remain in Africa – notably the sexually immature one-year-olds that fledged the previous summer. However, the majority head back north, with the southernmost starting their journeys from as early as late January and early February. By April the spring passage through North Africa is at its peak and towards the end of the month most are moving up through central Europe, reaching their UK breeding grounds from early to mid-May. In more northerly regions they may not arrive until June.

The weather along the journey determines the arrival date. Swifts may travel hundreds of kilometres to skirt low-pressure systems – especially in the Baltic, Scandinavia and North Sea regions. Occasionally they are even obliged to turn back: in early November 1984, following very warm southerly winds, Swifts reappeared along the Norfolk coast, their surprise appearance accompanied by deposits of Sahara dust. Spring migration is thought generally to be faster than autumn, with the Swifts racing to beat the competition and secure a good nest site.

Above: The Sahara represents a formidable barrier to Swifts flying to and from Equatorial Africa. Most skirt the desert by following a more westerly route rather than crossing it directly.

On the trail of Swift A322

Technology is helping scientists discover what Swifts get up to once they enter Africa. In 2010, as part of an ongoing project covering countries from Sweden to Israel, scientists at the British Trust for Ornithology (BTO) fitted tiny geolocators to 15 Swifts at their UK nests, hoping to retrieve them the following summer when they returned to breed. The geolocators, which weigh just 0.5g (0.02oz), record light intensity. When fed into a computer programme, the data they collect reveals when and where the birds travelled, within an accuracy range of 128km (80 miles).

In the summer of 2011 geolocators were recovered from nine of the birds. The data was startling. Their southward routes followed roughly what had been expected, down through Spain and West Africa then inland from Senegal and east to the rainforests of the Democratic Republic of Congo, where they spent much of the winter. However, their movements from there were far more wide-ranging than

expected, extending as far as Mozambique in the east, Angola in the west and South Africa in the south. What's more, the birds didn't take the expected direct route back northwards but headed out across the Atlantic near the mouth of the Congo in an arc up to Liberia. Here they paused for around ten days, presumably to fatten up for the final leg of their journey back to Britain. Both this route and the layover surprised researchers, who had previously thought Swifts made their way north more directly, feeding on the wing as they travelled.

From Liberia, however, the final leg was extremely rapid. One bird, numbered A322, covered the last 5,000km (3,100 miles) in just five days, maintaining an average speed of around 40km/h (25mph) as it crossed the Sahara Desert, and dashed up through Europe to its nest site in Fowlmere, Cambridgeshire. In total, A322's migration took it 19,950km (12,400 miles). Others went even further, covering more than 27,350km (17,000 miles).

Swallows: ringing is believing

Think Swallow and you think migration. This species has long been emblematic of the astonishing journeys that many bird species make around the world – perhaps because its confiding and conspicuous life alongside our own has long made its arrival the most celebrated and its departure the most lamented. When Swallows arrive, it seems, they bring the summer. When they leave, they take it away.

It is thus not surprising that this bird has proved central to our understanding of bird migration. Many of the earliest myths surrounding birds' winter disappearance centred upon it. Writers from Aristotle to the great 18th-century naturalist Gilbert White perpetuated the idea that Swallows hibernated – in crevices, or even in the mud at the bottom of ponds, the latter perhaps explained by the discovery of their corpses below reedbed roosts.

By the late 18th century, however, the idea of migration was gaining credence. Thomas Bewick's *A History of British Birds* (1797) cites reports of the birds flying north

Below: Each of these metal rings will be fitted on the leg of a different Swallow. Each has a unique number that will identify the bird if recaptured elsewhere and will reveal where it started its journey.

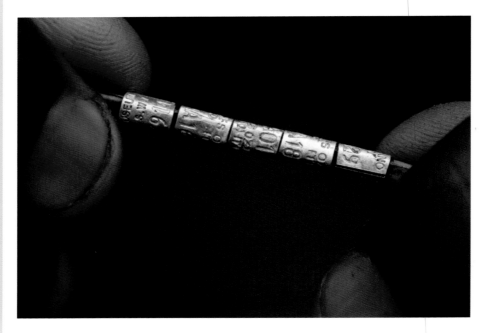

in great numbers between the islands of Menorca and Majorca. He rejects the idea that they 'retire into water', suggesting instead that: 'they leave us when this country can no longer furnish them with a supply of their proper and natural food'. By the early 19th century, there were credible reports of the birds seen at sea on the English Channel, the Mediterranean and the coast of West Africa, all of which lent weight to the idea that Swallows and other species made long seasonal journeys.

Only in the twentieth century, however, did ringing (the fitting of a small metal band to a bird's leg which, if recovered elsewhere, reveals the bird's journey) provide the evidence. This arrived in 1912, when a Swallow ringed the previous year in Staffordshire was retrieved in Natal, South Africa (see page 95). Since then, millions of Swallows have been ringed across many countries. Technology has gone on to produce the likes of satellite imagery and geolocators, gradually painting an ever clearer picture of the epic journeys these tiny birds make.

Above: Swallows gather together on a beach on the east coast of South Africa.

Below: A Swallow completes the spring return flight to its breeding quarters faster than the autumn departure to its winter quarters.

Winter quarters

Each of the different races of the Swallow around the world (see page 28) occupies different winter quarters. In all cases, these are south of their breeding grounds. The UK race, *Hirundo rustica rustica*, which breeds across Europe and northern Asia, winters mostly in sub-Saharan Africa, with a few in the Indian subcontinent.

Above: A flock of wintering Swallows gather at their overnight roost in the elephant grass at Ebakken, Nigeria.

The bulk of the African population winters south of the equator. They spread out from east to west across the continent according to their breeding quarters: those from Eastern Europe and Asia winter in eastern regions, as far south as South Africa's KwaZulu-Natal; those from Western Europe winter in western regions, as far south as South Africa's Cape Peninsula. Swallows from the UK and Ireland fetch up largely in Botswana, Namibia and South Africa's Western Cape. Swallows from Italy and Spain, by contrast, are recorded wintering in Ghana and Nigeria. In some places populations mix: one roost studied in Ghana was found to have breeding birds from Belgium, France, Germany and southern Europe. Across much of Africa this species is the most abundant hirundine during the northern winter, with some 80–90 million birds entering the continent every year from Europe alone.

Other races of the Swallow travel elsewhere. Those from Asia, other than *rustica*, winter in southern and South East Asia, from the Indian subcontinent through Indonesia to northern Australia. The North American race *Hirundo rustica erythrogaster* winters in South America as far south as northern Argentina. Across all races, a few of the most southerly breeding populations stay put, including those in southern Spain, southern Japan and southern California: there is not enough of a seasonal change at those latitudes to justify their journeys.

Swallows utilise many habitats in their winter quarters, including swampy wetlands, forest clearings and cultivated areas, so long as these provide the insect food they need. They are highly gregarious, feeding in loose flocks of hundreds or even thousands, and returning from wide foraging areas to a crowded roost. Individuals tend to be faithful to their winter quarters and, unless conditions change, return to the same roost from one year to the next.

African mega-roosts

Migrating Swallows gather in some parts of their winter quarters in enormous roosts. South-east Nigeria has some of the best known: peak numbers at one roost in the foothills of the Mbe Mountains, Cross River State, have been estimated at over two million. It makes for an extraordinary spectacle at dawn and dusk, as countless individual flocks, each many thousands strong, fly in and out of the long elephant grass. This roost has only been known to western scientists since 1987, but in recent years numbers have been falling, due both to the encroachment of agriculture and also to the mass trapping of the birds (using sticks smeared with a palm-resin adhesive) for local food and income. At one stage, over 200,000 birds were harvested annually. Conservation schemes now work with the local community to protect the birds and provide alternative sources of income.

Below: An African sky filled with Swallows before they gather at their evening roost.

Heading south

Most UK Swallows start heading south during September. Departure is an extended affair, however: birds that raised just a single brood may leave as early as late July; those that managed a second or even a third brood may not leave until October. Some years see a few exceptional hangers on: one bird was recorded at St Andrews, Scotland, on Christmas Day, and several have been seen foraging on beaches in Cornwall during January. These, however, are very much exceptions to the rule and most individuals lingering beyond October are unlikely to survive.

As with Swifts, the triggers for Swallows to leave are thought to be shortening day length and dwindling food

Right: The arrow on this map shows the principal migration flyway followed by UK Swallows travelling to and from Africa. Swallows from further east in Europe take a more easterly route down the Nile Valley and end up in eastern parts of South Africa.

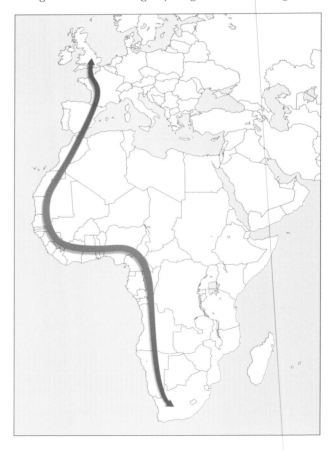

supply. During the days before departure, they gather in large numbers, often around wetlands, which offer the richest source of food at this late season and safe roosts among reedbeds. Hundreds line up on overhead wires. They feed energetically, building up fat reserves for the long journey ahead and waiting for the right weather conditions – ideally a northerly or north-easterly tailwind – to fire the starting gun.

UK Swallows start their migration within the British Isles, those from eastern regions travelling down the east side of the country and those from western regions down the west side. After leaving our shores via the south and south-west coast, they cross the Channel then follow the Biscay coast of France before traversing the Iberian Peninsula down to the Mediterranean. Here they join up with fellow southbound travellers from as far afield as Sweden and Norway.

These western Swallows now cross the Mediterranean at its narrow western end, over the Straits of Gibraltar and into Morocco. Others cross elsewhere: Italian birds head straight over the central Mediterranean, while those from Eastern Europe cross via the eastern Mediterranean and the Middle East. The first UK birds are in Africa by late July and early August, with numbers peaking from mid-September to late October. From here, they head across the 1,500km (930 miles) of Sahara on a broad front to reach the richer feeding grounds of the Sahel, where they refuel – making mass pit stops at wetlands and oases, before continuing south over the Congo Basin and down into southern Africa. The majority have reached their winter quarters by late October or early November.

Above: Swallows may gather in large flocks on telegraph wires prior to their southbound migration.

Returning north

The return journey is triggered by changes in day length and food supply on the Swallow's winter quarters. High rainfall means good feeding, allowing the Swallows to complete their moult (see page 94) and depart earlier – with the outriders setting off from southern Africa as early as late January. Spring migration is quicker and more direct than in autumn, with the birds in a hurry to reach their breeding grounds and get started; more Swallows are recorded passing through Algeria and Tunisia and the Balearic Islands at this time of year. By late February the main movement is under way, with most birds

Above: Swallows gather in the branches of a dead acacia tree before their departure from the African savannah.

reaching Mediterranean shores by March. Large numbers continue to pass through Gibraltar during May and even June. These are mostly birds from the previous summer, however, which may have left it too late for breeding.

After crossing the Mediterranean, UK Swallows travel up the east coast of Spain and the western coast of France, usually entering Britain via the south-west as they follow the areas of warmest weather. The first arrive as early as late February but the main wave takes place during late March and early April, reaching northern England and Scotland by May. Males tend to arrive before females, with the earliest generally being the oldest and those in best condition. By arriving early, they can steal a march on the competition and bag the best nest sites – although they risk encountering a late flurry of winter weather, which can prove disastrous.

Climate has a significant effect on Swallows' average arrival dates in the UK. Since 1959, these dates have shown a consistent correlation with average temperatures over the February–April period, the birds arriving earlier when it is warmer, both in Britain and along their route north through Spain. The pattern of warm springs since the late twentieth century, attributed by most scientists to global warming (see page 123), has seen consistently earlier average arrival dates.

Migration strategies

There is still much that we don't fully understand about Swallow migration, including exactly how the birds navigate. It is likely that, as with other migrating birds, they orientate themselves using the position of the sun and polarised light. Experiments have also shown that they can make use of an internal magnetic compass, which is especially important on overcast days. Unlike many small birds that navigate by night, Swallows travel mostly by day. This allows them to take advantage of their ability to feed while flying. It is thus likely that they take more visual directions from rivers, coastlines and other topographical features. They may also pick up on olfactory cues when nearing their breeding or wintering grounds.

Swallows also tend to migrate at lower altitudes than most small birds – often just a few metres above the ground. This allows them to hunt for insects along the way. For this reason, they often fly into a headwind or crosswind, which makes insects easier to catch. Hunting is harder in a tailwind because of turbulence close to the ground; Swallows may take a break if they find the wind blowing in their direction of travel. Strong tailwinds can be particularly dangerous over water, blowing the travellers off course without any visual landmarks by which to reorientate themselves. Swallows sometimes turn up on ships or oil rigs far out to sea: one was recovered 320km (200 miles) off the south-west coast of Ireland.

Above: A migrating Swallow takes a breather on the deck rail of a ship.

Swallows tend to migrate in small, loose groups – tens rather than hundreds – allowing space for each individual to hunt. But they may come together to form large streams of hundreds of thousands, both in flight and at roosts. Along the way, they may mingle with other migrants, including other hirundines, swifts and bee-eaters.

Below: A Sedge Warbler almost doubles its body weight when laying down fat reserves in preparation for its autumn migration.

Bottom: This fledgling Swallow is still in its juvenile plumage. Once it has grown its adult plumage, it will replace it once a year through moulting.

Speed varies according to conditions. Birds may travel less than 50km (30 miles) per day or more than 400km (250 miles). Ringing records illustrate this: one Swallow made it from Paris to Ghana in 27 days, thus covering an average 188km (116 miles) per day; another travelled 3,028km (1,881 miles) from Italy to Niger in just seven days, at an impressive average of 433km (269 miles) per day. Adults travel faster than juveniles. And, driven by the imperative of breeding, all birds travel faster during their spring migration than their autumn one, sometimes making the journey from southern Africa to the UK in as little as five weeks. It is on this journey north that Swallows generally make the most direct flights across the Sahara; indeed, desert mortality is reported more for this species than any other migrant.

Fit to travel

Most small, migrating songbirds build up a thick layer of fat before setting off, in order to provide the energy to fuel their largely non-stop journey. Indeed, some, such as the Sedge Warbler, almost double their body weight. Because Swallows can feed in flight along the way, they don't need such substantial fat reserves. But they do need some, which is why they make pit-stops for a few days before flying over places where insects are unavailable – for example, stopping in southern Europe before crossing the Sahara. The extra fat is deposited under their skin, around their internal organs and within their muscles and liver. The heaviest birds are the strongest fliers: scientists have calculated that those weighing 24g (8.4oz) or more can cross the Sahara in a single endurance flight without refuelling.

Moulting is also critical. Once a year, after breeding, Swallows replace their plumage by shedding the old feathers and growing new ones. This takes place mainly in their winter quarters. It is a slow process, starting from mid-September to mid-November and ending from late January to late March. It has to be slow, as the birds must be able to keep flying to catch food and must not be disadvantaged by having incomplete plumage during migration. The body feathers are the first to be replaced.

Next come the wings, with the primaries moulted from the inner to the outer, and finally the tail, which is replaced outwards from the centre. Moult requires energy and is thus completed more speedily when food and rainfall are abundant, breeding males being fastest. During moult, the glossy blue-back feathers become duller and flecked.

With this ring...

One particular Swallow proved pivotal in our understanding of bird migration. On 6 May 1911, a solicitor and keen birdwatcher named John Masefield slipped a tiny aluminium ring, numbered B830, onto the leg of a Swallow chick in its nest in Cheadle, Staffordshire. Bird-ringing was then in its infancy, and though people had an inkling about migration – they knew that many birds appeared in the spring then, after raising their chicks, disappeared southwards in the autumn, presumably somewhere warmer for winter – nobody had any idea of how far they went, let alone that they might reach southern Africa. Imagine the astonishment when news arrived of B830 18 months after Masefield had ringed it. This news came in a letter dated 27 December 1912 sent to Harry Witherby, a publisher who had founded the journal *British Birds* and was a leading proponent of ringing. It was from Mr C H Ruddock, proprietor of the

Grand Hotel, Utrecht, Natal, South Africa. 'Dear Sir', it read. 'On December 23, a Swallow was caught in the farmhouse of the farm Roodeyand, 18 miles from this town, with a metal label round its leg, with the words Witherby, High Holborn, London, and on the other side B830. The farmer, Mr J Mayer, took the label off and has it in his possession. As I am interested in birds of any sort and the migration of same, I shall be glad to know if you received this letter safely.'

From this letter we learned that Swallows breeding in the British Isles migrated to winter in South Africa, travelling more than 8,000km (5,000 miles) and crossing the Sahara Desert in the process. Such a journey had until then seemed inconceivable. Ringing has since produced countless revelations, from the distance flown by the Arctic Tern to the longevity of the Manx Shearwater. But none has been greater than that provided by John Masefield's Swallow number B830.

Left: Swallows caught in a mist net at their roost in France. The researchers will tag, weigh and measure the birds before releasing them.

Life and Death

Life for Swifts and Swallows is a relentless battle for survival. These birds may appear to have mastered the air, but a battery of dangers lies in wait, from hungry predators to wild weather. The early days are the toughest: in both species, a high proportion of casualties come within the first year. But age brings strength and experience and as the birds grow, the odds tilt in their favour. There are some things, however, for which experience offers no help. Historically, both birds have benefitted from the way in which humankind has modified their environment. But today our destructive impact on the places where they breed, feed and migrate presents the biggest threat.

Swift survival

Swifts are relatively long-lived. If they can get through their first year, they may live upwards of another ten – at least twice as long as Swallows and other passerines. One study in the Czech Republic found that the level of mortality among first year birds was 29 per cent, but by their fourth year it had dropped to 12 per cent. The oldest recorded Swift was a bird ringed in Sweden that reached the ripe old age of 21. Others, unrecorded, may live even longer.

Opposite: The Hobby is one of very few predators that regularly targets Swifts.

Below: Eleonora's Falcon is a specialist predator of small birds migrating over the Mediterranean, and sometimes captures Swifts and Swallows.

Natural threats

Few predators can capture an adult Swift. This bird's great speed and agility allow it to out-fly all but the most specialised of aerial hunters. The only UK raptor that presents a serious threat is the Hobby (*Falco subbuteo*). This dashing falcon, which itself appears almost Swift-like in flight, is a specialist predator of hirundines and occasionally snatches the odd Swift. Elsewhere, the Eleonora's Falcon (*Falco eleonorae*), which specialises in capturing migrating birds over the Mediterranean, occasionally takes Swifts, as does – very rarely – the Peregrine Falcon (*Falco peregrinus*). It is generally only young, inexperienced individuals that fall prey.

On its African wintering grounds, the Swift must dodge a greater range of predators. Surprisingly, perhaps, it even features on the human menu in some parts of Africa. This can only happen when the birds feed low down and thus come within the range of nets – for example around beehives. Otherwise, terrestrial predators pose no threat to a bird that never lands. Even at the nest, Swifts are relatively safe from attack. They breed high, out of the reach of cats, rats and most other mammals, and their tameness when approached by researchers suggests that they generally have little to fear.

The elements are more dangerous. Swifts' lives revolve around the weather and they are highly attuned to reading the forecast, which means they can generally dodge or ride out rough conditions. But casualties are sometime recorded: many Swifts were found dead after one severe thunderstorm in Zambia, for instance. Sustained cold can also pose a threat to nesting birds as it reduces the availability of their insect food. But Swifts can withstand lean times, with a slow metabolism to prevent excessive energy use and, in chicks, the capacity to enter a state of torpor (see page 62).

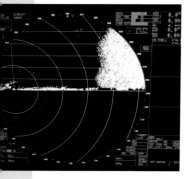

Below: This radar image from the Camargue, France, illustrates how Swifts (small yellow points on the screen) move away from a heavy downpour (large white area, top right of the screen).

Blood suckers

At the nest, Swifts are prey to various parasites that feast on their blood. One particular species, the Swift Lousefly (*Crataerina pallida*), is found only on Swifts. About 7mm (0.3in) long, with a flattened triangular body and very small wings, this biting fly spends its entire life cycle around Swifts. In late summer, the adult produces larvae, which pupate and lie dormant over winter inside the vacated nest. In spring, when the first Swift eggs are laid, they hatch and feed on the blood of the nestlings and the adults, sucking about 25mg of blood every five days. Louseflies may appear alarming to anybody who handles a Swift, and one might assume that they compromise the birds' health. However, research suggests that they do little serious damage; after all, the parasites' own success depends upon Swifts also reproducing successfully. Scientists have found no relationship between the number of louseflies a Swift's nest harbours and key factors in the Swift's breeding success, such as clutch size, brood size, time of fledging and weight of fledglings.

Above: A Swift Lousefly clings to the plumage of its host.

The human factor

Over history, Swifts have benefitted from many of the things people have done to their environment. By clearing forests we have created open habitats in which insects are easier to hunt, and by erecting buildings we have created a new range of nest sites. This means Swifts are no longer dependent upon crevices and tree hollows and thus, in many areas, they have expanded their range.

Over the last century, however, our impact has been less helpful. Modern agriculture, with its replacement of insect-rich habitats with sterile monocultures and the spraying of the land with insecticides, has dramatically reduced the food available to all insect-eating birds, Swifts included. Other forms of pollution also take their toll on swifts around the world: there are even records of African Palm Swifts (*Cypsiurus parvus*) dying after drinking from a chlorinated swimming pool.

In the UK and over much of Europe, however, the greatest threat to Swifts has come over the last few decades with the loss of traditional nest sites to modern building techniques and materials. The demolition or refurbishment of old warehouses, factories and social housing, especially buildings constructed before World War II, has left Swifts without the vital eaves, crevices and cavities on which they once depended. This is thought to be the main cause behind the dramatic decline in the UK Swift population, which fell by 51 per cent between 1995 and 2015. There are, however, things that can be done (see page 117).

Below: The destruction of pre-WWII social housing has deprived Swifts of many prime breeding sites.

Swallow survival

Above: Traffic poses a serious hazard to Swallows as they pursue insects low over roads.

Below: House Sparrows can take over the nests of Swallows and other hirundines, such as these House Martin nest boxes.

Swallows do not live as long as Swifts. Life expectancy in the UK is 1.68 years for females and 1.59 for males. However, this reflects the high number of birds that fail to survive their first year. Those that get through and return to breed in their second summer may live for up to another four. The UK longevity record is 11 years, for a bird from Hampshire, but anything over five can be considered exceptional.

Threats at the nest

Danger starts in the nest. Bad weather – if conditions are too hot, cold or wet – makes feeding more difficult. Few chicks starve to death, but parents may delay breeding and so are unable to raise a second brood. This affects breeding productivity: a pair raises more fledglings when weather conditions are favourable.

Swallows must also deal with competitors for their nest sites. They defend their patch vigorously and will drive away most interlopers, such as House Martins. But House Sparrows can be a menace. In the USA they are blamed for the loss of Swallows from parts of New England during the

1800s, when they first appeared as an invasive species. The damage they do ranges from stealing feathers to more severe crimes, including removing eggs and chicks.

Predators that may raid Swallows' nests in the UK include cats, rats and various predatory birds. Elsewhere they range from snakes to raccoons. Unusual records from the USA include that of a bobcat destroying 34 Swallow nests at a single site and, in one Texas breeding colony, up to a quarter of nesting pairs losing chicks and/or eggs to fire ants. Predators are thought to cause less than ten per cent of losses, however. More are caused by other Swallows: in large colonies, up to 25 per cent of chicks may fall victim to their neighbours (see page 71).

Various parasites prey on nesting Swallows, as they do on Swifts (see page 98). The Tropical Fowl Mite (*Ornithonyssus bursa*) is a particular problem: this bloodsucker overwinters in nests, waiting for the birds to return in spring – some nests may contain more than 10,000. The health of the chicks can suffer and, in severe cases, they may even die of blood loss. Research has shown that a heavy infestation makes it harder for adults to rear a first brood and thus reduces the likelihood of their raising a second one.

Staying alive

Adult Swallows must dodge a range of predators aiming to make a meal of them. They are more vulnerable than Swifts, flying more slowly and generally closer to the ground, nesting in more accessible places and spending more time perched. Recent fledglings, not yet wise to the ways of the world, are most at risk. Cats take their toll, as do a number of raptor species, of which the Sparrowhawk and Hobby are the most significant, the latter being an agile aerial predator that is specially adapted to catching hirundines. Elsewhere in the world, birds recorded as preying on Swallows include gulls, grackles and goshawks. Huge roosts on wintering grounds attract numerous predators. Studies of one roost in Nigeria, comprising 1.5 million Swallows, found that African Hobbys (*Falco cuvierii*) took 5,000 birds in a season at an average of 14 per day. A lot, yes, but hardly a dent in the vast population.

Above: Swallows in North America must contend with a variety of nest raiders, including raccoons.

Below: Domestic cats are estimated to kill up to 55 million birds in the UK every year, including Swallows.

The predators don't have it all their own way, though. Swallows are spirited in their defence, mobbing raptors vigorously and issuing alarm calls that prompt others to do the same. A Sparrowhawk, for instance, may attract a retinue of Swallows that dive-bomb it repeatedly, sometimes even striking it, until they have driven the danger from their breeding site.

Severe weather, such as torrential rain or unseasonal cold, can also prove fatal – largely because it turns off the supply of insects. Mass Swallow casualties were recorded in central Europe in the autumns of 1931, 1936 and 1974, when thousands of migrating birds perished in severe weather on their way south. Problems also arise on the birds' wintering grounds: prolonged droughts in South Africa, for example, have dried up important wetland roost sites. When spring turns cold, Swallows that arrive early may huddle together to minimise energy loss. This has been recorded in buildings in Norway and southern Russia, and such incidents may have contributed to the hibernation myth (see page 86).

Below: This adult female Hobby feeds a captured Swallow to her young brood.

The human factor

For Swallows, as with Swifts, it is we humans who today pose the greatest threat. There are many hazards that we place in the way of these birds from road traffic, which in one study was found responsible for 40 per cent of deaths among recent fledglings, to obstacles such as wires and windows.

In some parts of the world people are also significant predators of Swallows, from the Ebbaken-Boje area of Nigeria – where in 1995, one village alone trapped over 200,000 Swallows by means of glue on palm twigs – to northern Laos, where an estimated 100,000 birds are caught annually for sale at market. For impoverished communities in developing countries, wild birds can be a significant source of protein. There is less of an excuse for the slaughter in the Mediterranean, however, where at its peak hunting once claimed an estimated 160,000–430,000 Swallows every year in Malta alone.

Alarming as these statistics may sound, they do not compare with the wholesale population declines that

Above: A Swallow mobs a Kestrel. This raptor does not generally pose a threat to Swallows but they will drive it out of their breeding territory nonetheless.

Above: This ghostly print, left by feather dust, shows where a pigeon collided with a window. Such collisions are a deadly hazard for fast-flying birds such as Swallows that live and feed around buildings.

Above: Swallows captured from their reedbed roost in Nigeria are cooked over an open fire for local consumption.

come with damage to the Swallow's environment. Like Swifts and other insect-eating and farmland birds, Swallows have suffered from modern farming techniques, which in large areas have replaced the traditional farmland that once offered such a rich variety of insect prey. Agricultural intensification during the 1970s and 80s is thought to be a large factor behind population declines of 20–50 per cent in many European countries, including Spain, Italy, Denmark and the Baltic States, with local extinctions in some areas.

Pollution also plays its part. Insecticides sprayed on crops not only reduce the Swallow's food supply but also, when the birds snap up poisoned insects, accumulate as harmful chemical residues inside them. In the USA, pollutants known to have damaged Swallows include selenium in a Texas lake that was recorded at high levels in the birds' kidneys, and lead along Maryland highways that impaired feather growth and immune functions in populations that nested by the road.

Our relationship with the Swallow and its environment has a complex history, however. We should not forget that over the centuries human activities have been very beneficial to the bird. Around 10,000 years ago, when humans discovered farming, we began a process of clearing forests and opening up habitat that allowed the Swallow to colonise new lands – and even to live alongside us. But in Europe the shift from mixed to arable farming in the early 19th century changed all this. Horses were no longer needed for labour, livestock was increasingly reared indoors, land was drained, ponds lost and fewer outbuildings suitable for nest sites were constructed. Farms were no longer the insect-rich havens that had lured the birds in the first place.

All is not lost. In Britain, the Swallow is not faring so badly; in some regions, including north-west Scotland and the Western Isles, populations are even on the increase. This is a resourceful and versatile species, able to survive some of the most severe threats and dangers that nature can contrive. How it will adapt to the inevitable changes of the coming century remain to be seen.

Below: More intensive agriculture does not support the biodiversity that Swallows need in order to flourish and thrive.

Icons of Summer

Swifts and Swallows are deeply woven into our lives, having acquired, over the ages, a cultural value that far transcends their status as simply birds. Both have worked their way into our language, imagery and mythologies, embodying qualities that range from freedom and fidelity to health and prosperity. Art, literature and religion are alive with both birds. But the connotations of the two are quite distinct: the Swallow's image is all about cheerful, welcoming familiarity; the Swift's, by contrast, is one of wild and elusive mystery.

Swallows: making summer

'One swallow doesn't make a summer.' This proverb, popular in numerous forms and languages around the world, encapsulates the cultural value of the Swallow and dates back at least as far as Aristotle's *Nicomachean Ethics* ('For as one swallow or one day does not make a spring, so one day or a short time does not make a fortunate or happy man'). Although it sounds a cautionary note, warning us not to base conclusions on a single piece of evidence, it is a perfect expression of how this bird is seen as the harbinger of our favourite season. The Czech language employs a similar expression, describing anything new – for instance, the first song by a new singer – as a 'first swallow'. In Argentina, seasonal labourers are known as *trabajadores golondrinas* ('swallow workers').

It is easy to see how this small bird has acquired such emblematic status. First, swallows are everywhere – found on six continents – so everybody knows them. Second, they disappear at the gloomiest time of year, when autumn signals a closing down for winter, then reappear in spring, a time of hope and reawakening. Third, they live alongside us, appearing to enjoy a special collective bond of trust as they build their homes and raise their families alongside ours, part of the fabric of village and rural life. Fourth, their presence is almost

Opposite: In the fairy tale *Thumbelina*, the miniature heroine escapes marriage by fleeing to a far away land on the back of a swallow she nurses to health during winter. (From *Hans Christian Andersen's Fairy Tales*, Constable, London, 1913.)

Below: This Swift tower at Logan's Meadow Local Nature Reserve, Cambridge, comprises nest boxes for up to 100 pairs of Swifts. It is designed as a public artwork to look like a setting sun with Swifts flying overhead.

Above: The Swallow is the national bird of Estonia and appears here on a signpost outside a souvenir shop on Toompea Hill, Tallinn.

Right: Egyptian papyrus depicting a perched swallow – a detail from the papyrus of Ani, 13th century BC (British Museum).

wholly beneficial (messy droppings notwithstanding): they don't plunder crops, like pigeons or crows, but instead provide the perfect natural insecticide service, ridding us of bluebottles and other pesky insects. And finally, they are things of beauty: their dazzling iridescent plumage flashing in and out of our lives with effortless, swooping grace.

Small wonder, then, that few birds are as cherished as Swallows. The Swallow is the national bird in both Estonia and Austria, and in Australia, the name of a similar species, the Welcome Swallow, suggests that swallows are just as popular Down Under. Today, with our increasingly urban lifestyles detaching us from our rural roots, the link may not be as strong as it once was. Nonetheless the bird continues to inspire great affection – not only among country folk, but also scientists and bird ringers, for whom it remains a flag-bearer of the entire bird migration phenomenon and is the subject of a disproportionate number of studies.

Belief and superstition

In ancient times, Swallows were seen as emissaries of the gods and were associated with the souls of the departed. Various deities from Greek and Roman mythology were able to transform into a Swallow, and grieving mothers considered the bird to be sacred as it carried the souls of their dead children. The Egyptian god Isis was said to change into a Swallow at night. And during the hajj, the annual Islamic pilgrimage to Mecca, the Swallow was considered to be a symbol of faith and, in myth, would help drop stones onto the heads of enemies.

Around the world, this association with hope and renewal is still woven into many traditional beliefs. In Tanzania, a Swallow's nest built on a property is seen as a blessing, with the bird's chicks being a good omen for the birth of children, while in Croatia, where one proverb states that a Swallow 'transforms a house into a home', the bird's presence is traditionally held to protect a dwelling from lightning strikes. Such beliefs have worked in the Swallow's favour. Across much of rural England, for example, the destruction of a Swallow's nest was once thought to produce bloody milk in cows or prevent hens from laying.

Above: An Ancient Egyptian pendant depicting the goddess Isis taking the form of a Swallow, from the Egyptian Museum, Cairo.

Art and literature

The Swallow's graceful lines lend themselves easily to artistic interpretation. Indeed, the bird features on some of the earliest known artworks, including a painting at least 3,600 years old uncovered on the Greek Island of Santorini, buried by the eruption that devastated the Minoan civilization. In classical Chinese paintings, the Swallow, which represented happiness and the arrival of spring, was often depicted upon a flowering peach branch. In western heraldry, where the Swallow is known as a 'martlet' or 'merlette', it is held to represent younger sons with no lands.

Below: Swallow tattoos arose as a nautical tradition celebrating a sailor's wanderings. Today they are as popular as ever and take many forms.

The emblematic use of Swallows continues to this day. In Portugal, ceramic Swallows, known as *andorinhas*, are still exchanged between lovers and suspended outside homes as symbols of harmony, happiness and prosperity. And the sailor's Swallow tattoo – which developed as a symbol of safe return – remains as popular as ever. Tradition holds that a mariner received a tattoo of this fellow wanderer after having completed 5,000 nautical miles (9,300km) at sea; adding a second after 10,000 nautical miles (19,000km). The Swallow even provided a convenient logo for Britain's InterCity trains, although some jaded commuters might suspect that the bird itself arrived faster than the locomotive ever managed.

Literature around the world is liberally sprinkled with Swallows. One of the bird's earliest appearances is in Aesop's fable *The Spendthrift and the Swallow*. This recounts how a young man, on seeing a Swallow, decides that summer has arrived and thus sells his last coat to raise money. Soon after, the weather changes and he finds the bird's frozen body. Now shivering himself, he blames the Swallow for his ill fortune. The moral, of course, is that one Swallow doesn't make a summer.

Above: Two decorative ceramic Swallows, known as *andorinhas*, affixed to the wall of a house in Portugal.

In *The Waste Land*, T S Eliot quotes from a Latin poem *'Quando fiam uti chelidon [ut tacere desinam]?'* ('When will I be like the swallow, so that I can stop being silent?'). John Keats ends his *Ode to Autumn* looking forward to spring, when 'gathering swallows twitter in the skies'. And Shakespeare doesn't miss out, citing the Swallow in several plays for its speedy flight, from 'True hope is swift, and flies with swallow's wings' (*Richard III*, Act 5), to 'I have horse will follow where the game / Makes way, and run like swallows o'er the plain' (*Titus Andronicus*, Act 2). Another reference, in *The Winter's Tale* (Act 4), shows that the bard, ever ahead of his time, seems to have grasped migration long before any scientist: 'Daffodils, That come before the swallow dares, and take / The winds of March with beauty'.

The Swallow in Chinese culture

In traditional Chinese culture, the Swallow is the harbinger of spring and symbolises everything from happiness and prosperity to children and affection between brothers. The birds' conspicuous pair bonds have also made them representative of love and fidelity. Traditionally, families did not disturb Swallows nesting in their roof, believing that the birds brought them luck. As a symbol of good fortune, the bird acquired a distinct pictographic character 'yan' (燕), the form and structure of which conveyed its spreading wings, open mouth and extended tail. The bird is also symbolic of feminine grace and beauty, with its twittering call likened in poetry to a woman's voice. Zhào fēiyàn (飞燕), literally 'flying swallow Zhao', was an empress of the Han dynasty famed for her slender beauty, and *yan* is still frequently used in girls' names. Swallows were once much more numerous in China than today, with Beijing known as the 'capital city of Swallows' (燕京 yàn jīng).

Swifts: devil birds

The Swift's popular image is rather different from that of the Swallow. Its mysterious nature – racing around at breakneck speed, never touching the ground, nesting among us but remaining somehow aloof, and disappearing upward into the heavens – has inspired more awe than affection. Mystery can breed suspicion: the old British folk name of 'devil bird' has sinister connotations. But Swifts have never incited fear in the same way that, for instance, owls have in many parts of the world. And they have never been persecuted. The prevailing feeling is more a sense of otherness; that the Swift belongs to another realm entirely. Its traditional Persian name, *Bad Khorak*, which translates to 'wind-eater', expresses this perfectly.

Below: This depiction of a Swift flying over a hotel in Flims, Switzerland, conveys the sense of mystery often associated with the bird.

That is not to say, however, that the Swift is not just as strongly associated with summer as is the Swallow. Indeed, given that its brief visit is confined almost entirely to summer, rather than bleeding into spring and autumn, the association is that much more intense. 'Swifts seem a more realistic statement about our short season of plenty', writes Mark Cocker in *Birds and People*. He suggests that our recent shift in focus from rural to urban lifestyles has placed the Swift more at the centre of our consciousness, and that it is gaining ground on the Swallow as a symbol of summer – certainly for city dwellers. The bird has certainly experienced a surge in popularity over recent times, with legions of dedicated Swift fans and conservation groups.

Swifts in culture

It can be difficult to pin down the representation of Swifts in culture, because the bird is so often confused with the Swallow. This is evident even in the Old Testament: 'Yea the stork in the heavens knoweth her appointed time; and the turtle and the crane and the swallow observe the time of their coming', says the oft-quoted passage from Jeremiah. But the Hebrew word *Sis*, translated as 'Swallow' in the *King James Bible*, is still today the name for Swift.

Of all the arts, it is surely architecture with which Swifts are most closely associated. Their habit of nesting in human structures is thought to date back to the Sumerian civilization, 7,000 years ago, and ever since then they have shown a fondness for monumental architecture and ecclesiastical buildings – places that evoke powerful feelings among us. These associations run worldwide. One of the earliest recorded Swift colonies inhabits the Western Wall in Jerusalem, where even today the birds can be seen whizzing around above worshippers. Hao Xinru, ornithologist at Beijing University, recalls watching flocks of Swifts flying near the Forbidden City.

Above: A stamp from the republic of Belarus featuring a Swift.

Below: Jerusalem Mayor, Nir Barket, addressing guests at a welcoming ceremony for thousands of Swifts returning from South Africa to nest in the Western Wall. Jerusalem, Israel, 12 March 2012.

Right: Swifts in a painting by Bruno Liljefors (1886). The great Swedish artist was one of the first to draw and paint birds in the wild, rather than from museum specimens, and thus to capture their movement.

'Chinese royal gardens were created to embody the theory of harmony between human beings and nature', he explains. 'If there are no birds in them, does it not devalue the cultural basis of traditional buildings?'

In scientific literature, Swifts form the subject of several classic studies. The best known is that of David and Elizabeth Lack, launched in 1947. Their unwavering scrutiny of the birds that nested in the central spire of the Oxford Museum of Natural History on Park's Road, central Oxford, taught us much of what we know today about the bird – from the capacity of the chicks to enter a state of torpor (see page 62) to the ability of feeding adults to navigate around atmospheric depressions. The study continues to this day at the same location, based on the descendants of the original birds.

The appeal of Swifts – their elusive otherness, and ability to drag the wilderness into the heart of the city – has also stirred many a creative pen. In his poem *Haymaking*, English poet Edward Thomas describes the form of the swift as being: 'As if the bow had flown off with the arrow'. And in *Swifts*, one of the most powerful literary celebrations of any wild animal, Ted Hughes uses such language as 'shrapnel-scatter terror', 'charred scream' and 'arrow-thwack into the eaves' to capture with stunning originality the essence of a bird that he describes as 'not ours any more'.

Nest on the menu

Another important role played by swifts in human culture is a culinary one. The birds' predilection for nesting in human structures means that such structures can be built to attract them – and indeed young swifts were once harvested in Italy from purpose-built swift towers. A much larger market exists in South East Asia, however: not for the birds themselves, but for their nests. This does not concern the Common Swift, but two species of swiftlet: the aptly named Edible-nest Swiftlet (*Aerodramus fuciphagus*) and its relative the Black-nest Swiftlet (*Aerodramus maximus*). Both are cave dwellers that nest in colonies and glue their saliva nests to cave walls. In the past, some colonies were enormous – one cave in Sarawak held up to 4.5 million swiftlets. Since at least the 17th century, and probably long before, humans have harvested these nests to eat. The saliva, made of a mucin-like glycoprotein, hardens into colourless layers that are thought to contain various health-enhancing properties, from aphrodisiac to alleviating gastric trouble. It was once thought to be an algal foam gathered from the sea (*fuciphagus* means 'seaweed eating').

The swift nest industry is highly lucrative. Key caves are closely guarded, with local collectors acquiring concessions over particular sections. Gathering the nests from the cave roof is dangerous work, and the scaffolding is dismantled at the end of each season so as to deny access to poachers. Today the huge economic value of the industry – and the consequent decline of wild swiftlet populations – means that harvesting from wild caves is unsustainable. Special towers have thus been constructed in many areas to entice the swiftlets to breed. The conditions inside replicate those of a cave, with low light, a water-based cooling system and the constant recorded playback of twittering birds. Once collected, the nests need very little processing. Black-nest Swiftlet nests have more inedible items to remove. But the more highly prized 'white nests' of the Edible-nest Swiftlet may sell for upwards of £1,790 per kg.

Below: The extensive limestone caves in Krabi, Thailand (left), support breeding colonies of the Edible-nest Swiftlet, which builds its nest of saliva on the cave walls (top right). These are harvested and prepared for consumption as bird's nest soup (bottom right) for the lucrative Chinese market.

Protecting Swifts and Swallows

A British summer would be unthinkable without Swifts and Swallows racing around our skies. Yet we can never take them for granted. Both birds face threats, largely from human development. Swallows, at present, are doing reasonably well: a healthy population shows no imminent sign of serious decline. Sadly, the same is not true of Swifts, whose UK population has fallen steeply in recent decades. If both birds are to continue to delight us for generations to come, and to play their roles in a healthy environment, then we must learn to look after them and the places where they live.

Swift: skydiver in free fall

The IUCN classifies the Swift's status as Least Concern. With an estimated global population of 95.5–162.5 million pairs, including 19.1–32.5 million in Europe, scientists do not currently consider the species to be under serious threat on a worldwide basis.

In some parts of the Swift's range, however, things are not so rosy. The UK is one of these: at the time of writing, our breeding population is estimated at 87,000 pairs. But this is currently falling by an average of three per cent per year. Indeed, the population as a whole fell by 51 per cent between 1995 and 2015. Today the Swift is on the UK Amber List of Birds of Conservation Concern. If this decline continues, it will soon make the Red List of birds that require urgent conservation action.

The causes of the Swift's decline are complex and include changes to its food supply both in the UK and Africa. But one critical factor is undoubtedly the loss of nest sites. Swifts' exclusion from the places where they have for so long lived among us, due to modern building and renovation techniques (see page 99), is leaving

Opposite: A Swift drops from its nest in the eaves.

Below: A Swift exits a nest box attached to the eaves of a cottage near Trowbridge, Wiltshire.

them with nowhere to breed. With a little thought and planning, this problem is easily solved.

Helping Swifts at home

Anyone lucky enough to share a home or neighbourhood with Swifts can make a difference. Small, inexpensive alterations and additions to the buildings in which we live and work can give them just what they need to breed, without compromising the buildings. And Swifts make delightful tenants: neat and unobtrusive, they leave no mess and thrill us with their dashing comings and goings.

All Swifts need is a suitably sized, enclosed living space with a small entrance hole. This is easily provided on both existing and new structures. Open eaves can be left as is, boxed eaves can be converted by drilling holes at the front or side. Each hole should be approximately 5cm (2in) in diameter. Inside the box you can install plywood partitions to separate individual nest sites and reduce conflict: each pair needs a minimum space of 20–30cm (8–12in) wide and 15cm (6in) high.

You can also fit nest boxes – either within the eaves or on the wall under the eaves. A box should be at least 5m (16.4ft) above the ground and well clear of any

Below: A Swift in Sweden flies to its nest box bearing a food ball for its young.

obstructions, such as trees and creepers, that might provide access for cats, rats and other potential nest raiders. It should not be in direct sunlight and the hole must be directed to the open air, so the bird can take flight by dropping down directly from the nest. To keep out other birds while Swifts are away, block the opening until they return.

Another option is nest bricks. These are hollow blocks with a customised entrance hole, designed to attract a pair of Swifts and hold a nest. They can be installed in the top course of brickwork below the roof and, once *in situ*, need no maintenance.

A range of nest boxes, nest bricks and other products tailor-made for Swifts are now commercially available. You can even fit a webcam to watch the action live. However you choose to accommodate your Swifts, remember two golden rules: first, do all your work between September and April, when the birds are absent. Second, never install just one nest site: Swifts are sociable birds and need neighbours. Any house should have room for at least two; larger buildings may have room for 20 or more.

Above: Nest boxes attached beneath the eaves provide nest sites for Swifts where no natural cavity is available.

Several organisations (see page 126) offer excellent advice for those planning Swift-friendly renovation work or aiming to attract Swifts to their property. These include Swift Conservation, which provides practical instructions and guidelines, and the Swifts Local Network, which embraces more than 30 local groups around the country.

Cities for Swifts

National planning policy guidance in the UK states that councils should enhance biodiversity when building developments enter the planning stage. Responsible authorities that care about wildlife can thus lend Swifts a helping hand. Town planners and construction companies are working with conservationists to ensure any new build is Swift-friendly, encouraging measures such as the installation of Swift bricks and nest boxes.

Right: Nest bricks for Swifts built into a new apartment building.

In 2013, Belfast was launched as Britain's first 'Swift City'. Northern Ireland's capital has a large Swift population and a lot of reconstruction work. Conservationists are working with developers to ensure that breeding sites are retained or introduced for Swifts as the city's skyline continues to evolve. Other Swift Cities include Exeter and Cardiff and, from May 2017, Oxford, which launched a competition to design a Swift-friendly tower. In all these places, volunteer groups are looking out for Swifts, conducting population surveys in summer, putting up Swift boxes in public buildings and trawling through planning applications to ensure that developers are all onside.

Below: A Swift peeks out from its nest brick.

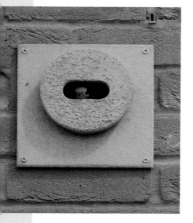

Spreading the word

You can also help Swifts by keeping an eye out for local building and development projects in your area. If you know of a colony under threat, or see renovation work starting on a known nest site, try a friendly approach to the householder or building contractor to alert them. Remember, many people simply don't know about Swifts: much of the damage is done unwittingly. If the work is taking place during the breeding season and poses an immediate threat, inform the contractor that nesting Swifts are present and that they are legally protected. Check the RSPB website for guidance on what to do in such circumstances (see page 126).

You may also know friends and neighbours who have nesting Swifts. If they are planning work that may affect nest sites you can explain measures they might take to safeguard the birds. Direct them to the Swift Conservation website where they can find all the information and advice they need.

Every year the RSPB collects data on where Swifts are breeding and, just as importantly, where they have stopped. They share this with the National Biodiversity Network, to help local authorities and developers protect existing Swift nest sites and plan for Swifts elsewhere. The British Trust for Ornithology (BTO) also collects data through its Nest Record Scheme. Your observations could be vital. If you have Swifts nesting on or near your property, you can send details to the RSPB Species Recovery Unit via an online questionnaire (see page 126). Or if you have a nest box camera, you could share your data with the BTO. Encourage friends and neighbours to report their observations, too. All this data helps conservationists build up a picture of where Swifts are breeding. They can then work to protect them.

Above: A Swift flies over a party of birdwatchers at RSPB Titchwell Marsh nature reserve, Norfolk. Observations from members of the public play an important part in Swift conservation.

Crash-landings

You may sometimes find a Swift on the ground. This is most likely to be a young bird that has fledged prematurely. An inexperienced flyer, it has crash-landed and now can't get airborne again. Such birds have little chance of survival in the wild, but an expert can sometimes rear them to allow a second chance. Healthy adults are quite capable of taking off from level ground, so any grounded adult is likely to be sick or injured in some way. Don't simply launch a Swift from a high building, as some may advise. Gently pick it up, place it in a suitable box on a warm lining, and consult a professional Swift carer, who can suggest what to do and may be able to take care of the casualty.

Above: A grounded Swift needs careful and expert handling.

Swallow: fluctuating fortunes

The Swallow is one of the most widely distributed birds in the world, with an estimated global population of 290–487 million individuals. Europe, which takes up approximately 20 per cent of its global range, has an estimated population of 58–97.4 million individuals. With these numbers, it is hardly surprising that the species is listed on the IUCN Red List as Least Concern.

In the UK, the Swallow has a healthy population. Its numbers rose at the start of this century, increasing by 18 per cent from 1995 to 2015. The latest population estimate is of 860,000 pairs – around ten times more than that of Swifts. Recent BTO Breeding Bird Surveys recorded increases of four per cent and six per cent in 2013–14 and 2014–15 respectively, but then a decline of 19 per cent in 2015–16. Despite this recent drop, the Swallow maintains its Green List status within the UK.

Below: Swallows leave their reed bed roost at sunrise in Aude, France.

A glance at the Swallow's recent fortunes in neighbouring Europe tell a different story. The 1970s and 80s saw population declines of 20–50 per cent across much of north-west and central Europe, including in Scandinavia, Denmark, Spain, Italy, the Baltic, Romania, Croatia and Ukraine. Elsewhere it has suffered range reductions, including in Albania, Moldova, Austria, Romania and parts of the Arabian Peninsula.

Swallow populations have always fluctuated. In North America, for example, serious declines along the Eastern seaboard were recorded as early as the 1800s, attributed to competition from the newly arrived and invasive House Sparrow. But in recent years, the species has expanded significantly across that continent, west into California, north to northern Alberta and south to Mississippi. Europe has also seen recent expansions into the western and northern limits of the bird's range, including into such remote outposts as Iceland, the Faeroes, the Shetlands and the Orkneys.

Above: Swallow chicks beg from their nest in a horse stall. The availability of traditional open farm buildings is an important factor in the breeding success of Swallows.

The Swallow's fluctuating fortunes are tied to two critical variables: the weather and farming. Thus its decline in parts of Europe may be explained both by agricultural intensification – reducing insect food and breeding territory – and by global warming – creating African droughts that make migration harder. Within Britain there are similar patterns: heaviest declines are in eastern regions, where agriculture is most intensive, while in western regions, which retain more traditional small-scale farming, populations continue to rise. The greatest fluctuations tend to occur at the highest latitudes, where weather conditions are most varied, unpredictable and extreme.

So, the Swallow may be holding its own in Britain, but there is little cause for complacency. How we manage our land and how we look after the broader environment in which the bird lives, will determine its future.

Making Swallows at home

Right: A Swallow returns to its nest inside of a building on St Agnes, Isles of Scilly, by entering through an air vent.

The good news for Swallows is that that they are generally popular and well-liked birds. Most householders and landowners are happy to host them and, where possible, will encourage them to breed.

If Swallows live in your neighbourhood, you can help provide them with a home. They prefer outbuildings with dark ledges and nooks and crannies for nesting: places that are cosy in cold weather and cool when it is hot. To invite them in, you must provide easy access; make sure a door or window remains open or that there is a small opening, at least 5cm (2in) high and 20cm (8in) wide. Inside, fix a platform where you would like the birds to nest – high in the building and out of the reach of cats. You can make a starter nest by attaching a sawdust-and-cement or papier-mâché cup to a wooden backing plate. Set a plastic bag below to catch droppings, and use polythene sheeting to block off any places where you would prefer the birds not to nest.

Occasionally a Swallow nest may tumble to the ground. You could replace it by fixing a shallow container (for example, a margarine tub or low plastic flower pot) at the old nest site, then placing the remains of the old nest inside and popping the nestlings back in. The parents will hear their young calling and should continue to feed them. If the parents do desert their chicks, the young will depend on human help for their survival. This is difficult and time-consuming and, if possible, best left to an expert (see page 126).

Below: A Swallow feeds its chicks at a nest built over a light bulb.

Enjoying Swifts and Swallows

There are many ways to engage with Swifts and Swallows. To make a practical contribution to their conservation, you could help provide homes and nest sites in some of the ways described in this chapter. Or, if you are a landowner, you can manage your land in a wildlife-friendly way, with wild verges, hedgerows, ponds and other features that provide plenty of insect food. If you enjoy collecting data, you can participate in surveys and censuses, such as the Breeding Bird Survey (see page 126). And you may like the challenge of recording the first Swifts and Swallows to arrive each year on migration, looking out for them around the coast or near your home. You can submit your migration records to BirdTrack (see page 126), the BTO's national project to monitor the movements of migratory birds throughout Britain and Ireland.

But you don't have to do any of these things. You could simply be one of those many people for whom these two magical birds provide endless pleasure – be it Swifts in a screaming summer evening fly-past, or Swallows twittering as they swoop and flutter around fields and farmhouse. And whether you believe it's Swifts or Swallows that most make a summer, surely no summer is complete without both birds in place.

Above and left: If we keep a close eye on the Swift (top) and Swallow (bottom), and help provide what they need, then we can continue to enjoy their company around our homes.

Glossary

Aerial plankton Insects, spiders and other tiny airborne creatures that are mostly invisible to the human eye but provide food for Swallows, Swifts and other birds.

Aspect ratio The ratio of the span of a wing to its width from front to back (wing chord). Long narrow wings have a higher aspect ratio than short, wide wings.

Cloaca The opening below a bird's tail for its reproductive and excretory tracts. Most mammals have a separate opening for each function.

Down A layer of soft insulating feathers grown by baby birds before they develop adult plumage. Adult birds retain a layer of down beneath their outer feathers.

Fledging The process through which baby birds develop the feathers and wing muscles required for flight and are able finally to leave the nest.

Gape The inside of a bird's open mouth. Also, the base of its bill where the two parts (mandible and maxilla) join. In young birds, a layer of bright skin around the gape (the gape flange) prompts parents to push food into the mouths of their brood.

Hirundine Any member of the Hirundinidae family of birds, which comprises the swallows and martins.

Invertebrates Insects, spiders and other small creatures often known as bugs. Invertebrate means 'without a backbone'; birds have backbones and so are vertebrates.

Nominate race The first-named race (subspecies) of any species. Its scientific name is generally the same as the species name. Thus in Barn Swallow, *Hirundo rustica rustica* is the nominate race of the species *Hirundo rustica*.

Passerine Any member of the Passeriformes order of birds, also known as perching birds or songbirds. This order comprises more than half of all bird species. Swallows are passerines, swifts are not.

Sahel A vast savannah region of north Africa lying between the Sahara Desert and the Equatorial tropics. Up to 1,000km (621 miles) wide, it stretches from Mauritania in the west to Sudan in the east.

Taxonomy The science of classifying all life forms, including birds.

Torpor A temporary state of lowered physiological activity, in which the metabolism and heart rate slow down and the body temperature falls.

Wing loading The ratio between the area of a bird's wings and its body mass, calculated by dividing mass by wing area. Birds with a low wing loading have a large wing area relative to their mass and are better able to glide and soar.

Further Reading and Resources

Chantler, Phil (Author) and Driessens, Gerald (Illustrator), *Swifts: A Guide to the Swifts and Treeswifts of the World* (Pica Press, 2000) Definitive illustrated reference guide to all the swifts of the world.

Derek Bromhall, *Devil birds: The Life of the Swift* (Hutchinson, 1980) Acclaimed study of a Swift colony in the tower of the University Museum at Oxford.

Clare, Horatio, *Single Swallow: Following an Epic Journey from South Africa to South Wales* (Vintage Books, 2010) Travel narrative based around the author's journey along the course of a Swallow migration route.

Glenday, John Summerton, R, et al. *Swifts* (Salty Press, 2010) Anthology of poetry and prose inspired by swifts, together with a brief life natural history of the Swift.

Lack, David, *Swifts in a Tower* (Unicorn, new edition 2018) New edition of the classic 1956 study, published in association with the RSPB for their *Oxford Swift City* project. Includes a new chapter that brings the study up to date.

Turner, Angela, *The Barn Swallow* (Christopher Helm, 2006) Comprehensive and fascinating monograph devoted to the natural history of this bird.

Turner, Angela (Author) and Rose, Chris (Illustrator), *A Handbook to the Swallows and Martins of the World* (Christopher Helm, 1989) Definitive illustrated reference guide to the swallows and martins of the world.

Conservation

RSPB (rspb.org.uk)
The RSPB is the UK's largest nature conservation charity and manages reserves around the UK for birds, other wildlife and their habitats. Check the website to find out about the RSPB's Swift Conservation Project.

Wildlife Trusts (wildlifetrusts.org)
UK conservation charity comprising 47 separate regional wildlife trusts across the UK. Offers information and advice on all aspects of British wildlife, and manages an extensive network of reserves.

British Trust for Ornithology (bto.org)
UK organisation devoted to the study of birds. The BTO operates a number of nationwide volunteer surveys, including BirdTrack (migration) and the Breeding Bird Survey, through which members of the public can contribute their own observations towards national monitoring schemes.

Swift Conservation (swift-conservation.org)
UK organisation dedicated to the conservation of Swifts. Their website is packed with information and advice about how you can help Swifts.

Action for Swifts (actionforswifts.blogspot.co.uk)
Forum for people across the UK concerned about Swifts. Includes the Swifts Local Network (SLN), through which many individuals and small regional groups can share ideas and experiences.

Acknowledgements

Many thanks to Julie Bailey and all at Bloomsbury Wildlife for bringing this book to fruition; especially to my editor Jenny Campbell for her patience and expertise, and to designer Rod Teasdale for his excellent layout. It was a pleasure, as ever, working with such a great team.

I am also grateful to the many naturalists whose studies over the years have helped illuminate the extraordinary lives of Swifts and Swallows, and to all those conservationists working hard to make the world a better place for these feathered globetrotters. Thanks especially to Angela Turner, whose excellent study

The Barn Swallow proved invaluable information during the writing of this book.

On a personal note, I would like to thank my own family: my parents, who encouraged my love of nature from the earliest days; and my wife Kathy and daughter Florence, with whom I have shared many memorable wildlife moments. A cheery wave also to my friends in Swaziland, southern Africa, who, in a former life, were bemused by my excitement every October when 'our' Swallows arrived in their country. Migrating birds bring people together.

Image credits

Index